KU-675-116

THE
FINANCIAL TIMES
GUIDE TO
USING THE
FINANCIAL
PAGES

ROMESH VAITILINGAM

with additional material by
Emma Tucker

FINANCIAL TIMES

PITMAN PUBLISHING

Pitman Publishing
128 Long Acre, London WC2E 9AN

A Division of Longman Group Limited

© Longman Group UK Limited, 1993

First published in Great Britain 1993
Reprinted 1993 (twice), 1994 (four times)

British Library Cataloguing in Publication Data
A CIP catalogue record for this book can be obtained from
the British Library

ISBN 0 273 60206 3 Paperback
ISBN 0 273 60205 5 Hardback

All rights reserved; no part of this publication may be reproduced,
stored in a retrieval system, or transmitted in any form or by
any means, electronic, mechanical, photocopying, recording, or
otherwise without either the prior written permission of the
Publishers or a licence permitting restricted copying in the
United Kingdom issued by the Copyright Licensing Agency Ltd,
90 Tottenham Court Road, London W1P 9HE. This book may
not be lent, resold, hired out or otherwise disposed of by way
of trade in any form of binding or cover other than that in
which it is published, without the prior consent of the Publishers.

Typeset by PanTek Arts, Maidstone, Kent
Printed and bound in Great Britain by
Biddles Ltd, Guildford and King's Lynn

All tables and figures reproduced by kind permission of the
Financial Times. The authors would like to thank those members
of staff at the *Financial Times* who have contributed their time and
assistance in the preparation of this book. They would particularly
like to thank Adrian Dicks and Gary Hayes.

CONTENTS

INTRODUCTION

Money and the financial markets, as reflected in the television or radio news or the financial pages of a newspaper like the *Financial Times*, may often seem to be a different world, something well beyond the experience of most people. But the global movement of capital, the constant shifting of what are often vast amounts of money, does have a connection with our daily lives. Everyone has some contact with the financial system: through having a bank account, through contributing to a pension fund, through buying an insurance or life assurance policy, or through taking out a mortgage or running up an overdraft. And despite its appearance as a foreign country accessible to only a favoured few, and dealing in a baffling language of numbers and jargon, its basic workings are fairly simple to grasp.

The markets are simply a huge clearing house where the different financial needs of individuals, companies and governments can be brought together and matched through appropriate pricing mechanisms. They might be actual places or they might be networks of screens and telephones. Either way, they address two fundamental needs: what is variously known as saving, lending or investing – the use of funds excess to spending requirements to secure a return; and borrowing – the demand for funds over and above those already owned, to put to work in various ways.

The players in the financial markets and in the wider economy can be classified into four broad groups:

- **Investors** who have money to spare to spend on assets and, indirectly, lend it to the issuers of those assets. This includes individual investors, though nowadays the bulk of investment is done by large investing institutions such as pension funds and insurance companies.
- **Companies** which want to borrow money in order to buy capital goods or increase the scale of their business.
- **Financial institutions** (banks, building societies, brokers, dealers, marketmakers, etc.) which act as intermediaries, bringing together the borrowers and lenders in various marketplaces.

- **Governments** which act as both borrowers and lenders, but which, in addition, regulate the markets and attempt to monitor and influence the state of the economy through fiscal and monetary policy.

The role and behaviour of each of these players are examined in the first four chapters of this book. The second part of the book looks at the different markets in which they operate: the stock markets, bond markets, international capital markets, foreign exchange and money markets, futures and options markets, and commodity markets. Each chapter takes the relevant charts and tables from the *Financial Times* and explains how they work, what their significance is, and how they might be read and employed by private individuals or business managers. Lastly, the final chapters broaden the picture, examining the UK, European and world economies, and the effects that key economic indicators have on the financial markets.

This book is intended for anyone who reads or needs to read the financial pages of a newspaper. It aims to provide a simple guide to understanding the statistics and the language of modern finance. Right from the first chapter, tables of figures with explanations are introduced to accustom the reader to the ease with which the numbers (as well as the reports and comments) can be interpreted and used with just a little background.

Much of the importance of the statistics is in the ratios between numbers rather than in the actual numbers themselves. It is the relationship between the figures, both across companies, industries, sectors and economies, and over time that is critical. It is these ratios that investors, companies and the finance types that 'make' the markets pore over to identify past patterns, future trends, and present opportunities and dangers.

The tables and charts of the financial pages are reference points, not fixed or up to date. Hence they are published every day as a snapshot of the state of the markets. But the markets themselves are dynamic, constantly in flux and, in some cases, trading twenty-four hours and across the globe. For readers needing immediate, real-time data, there are the more sophisticated sources of financial information of the computer age, screen-based data and telephone services.

Nevertheless, the FT's figures are a globally used reference point and the newspaper plays an important institutional role in the financial markets. It has pioneered such industry standards as the Footsie 100 index, used widely as an indicator of the state of the UK stock market, and as a benchmark for the performance of investors' asset portfolios. Furthermore, its pages fulfil the obligation of unit trusts to publish data on the value of their funds.

Although this is the FT guide to using the financial pages, the map it provides to understanding that newspaper's financial and economic reports, comments, tables and charts is equally applicable to other papers, and even to other media. The FT is merely the most detailed and widely used of the non-specialised media. Indeed, other papers frequently provide information on many of the leading indicators that the FT has developed, such as the Footsie and its derivative products.

Before turning to the markets and their statistical analysis, some basic and recurring mathematical concepts might be valuable:

- **Average:** a single number used to represent a set of numbers. It can be calculated variously as: a mode, the number that occurs most frequently in a set of numbers; a median, the number with 50 per cent of the rest lying below it and 50 per cent above, or if there is an even quantity of numbers, the average of the middle two; the arithmetic mean, the total sum of the numbers divided by the quantity of them; and the geometric mean, the figure that derives from multiplying the numbers together and taking their nth root, where n is the quantity of numbers.

- **Percentage:** the proportion that one number represents of another or the change in a number from one period to another. To calculate the proportion or percentage of y that x represents (whether x is another number or the difference between one number over two periods), x is divided by y. The result will be a fraction of 1, and to convert it into a percentage figure, it is simply multiplied by 100. Movements of a percentage figure might be mentioned in terms of points (one point is one per cent) or basis points (one basis point is one hundredth of one per cent). Percentage points or basis points are different from percentage changes.

- **Inverse and positive relationship:** the connection between two numbers. Numbers with an inverse relationship move in opposite directions; those with a positive relationship move together. This is the mathematical explanation of why, for example, bond prices and yields move in opposite ways; if x is equal to y divided by z, and y is constant, then as x rises, z falls or vice versa. But if x or z is constant, x and y or z and y will rise or fall together. The two pairs are in a positive relationship.

- **Index:** a number used to represent the changes in a set of values between a base year and the present. Index numbers distil many different ingredients into a single index, and measure changes in it by changes in its parts. This involves giving appropriate weighting to the components according to their importance in what is being measured. A weighted average is usually calculated as an arithmetic mean, either using the same weights throughout (a base-weighted index) or adjusting the weights as the relative importance of different components changes (a current-weighted index). Base-weighted indices may have the base shifted periodically.

With these simple tools and developments of them explained in the text, the reader should be well equipped to negotiate the figures of the FT's financial pages, analysed in what follows.

Part I

IDENTIFYING THE PLAYERS

1

INVESTORS

Most people have a weekly or monthly income – remuneration for the work they put in at their job. Once their basic needs (food, drink, clothing, accommodation) are taken care of, the choices for what they do with what is left over, if anything, are essentially two. They can spend it on more 'luxurious' items, such as holidays, music and books. This, together with the basic needs expenditure, is known as consumption. Alternatively, they can save it for future spending by them or their heirs, as a precaution against unanticipated future needs, or to generate future income.

Investors are people who have a surplus of money from their income that they want to save for any of these reasons. They can do this by keeping it in cash, or by putting it in a bank account or building society, the traditional meaning of savings. Alternatively, they can buy something that they expect at least to maintain its value, that might provide a flow of income, and that can be resold when needed. Any of these is an asset. How investors decide on the assets that they buy and own is the subject of this chapter.

BUYING ASSETS

Assets come in many shapes and forms: cash, bank and building society deposits, premium bonds, securities (that is, ordinary shares in a company or gilt-edged stocks, bonds issued by the government), life assurance policies, works of art and antiques, gold or foreign currencies, and houses and flats. Each type of asset has different characteristics, and the investor's preferences between those characteristics will determine which assets are bought.

The first characteristic of an asset that an investor might consider is its annual return: does ownership of it entitle the investor to receive any further income and, if so, how much? Obviously, for hard cash, the answer is no, but if that cash is placed in a building society account, the investor will earn monthly, quarterly or annual interest at a specified rate. Similarly, a premium bond does not pay its owner any interest (though it offers the regular chance of winning a prize), but a gilt-edged bond will pay a guaranteed fixed amount each year. And ownership of ordinary shares (equities) will generally mean that the investor gets a dividend, a slice of the profits made by the company over a six or twelve-month period.

Investors typically consider the return on an asset as an annual percentage of its value. This is the rate of return or yield, and is calculated by dividing the return by the asset's value. For example, if a building society adds £5 to every £100 deposited with it for a year, the return is that £5 and the rate of return is five per cent. In this case, of course, it is known as the interest rate. Similarly, the yield on fixed interest securities like gilts is the fixed amount each pays, known as the coupon, as a percentage of the current price quoted in the bond market.

The basic rate of return on a share, the dividend yield, is calculated in a similar way: the dividend paid by the company is divided by the price of the share as quoted on the stock market. Of course, unlike bonds or indeed bank deposits, the dividend payment is by no means guaranteed. The company may, for whatever reason, decide not to pay out a dividend. But with shares, there is another way of receiving a return and that is the second important characteristic of an asset, its potential for capital appreciation.

Capital appreciation or capital growth is an increase in the value of invested money. For example, money in building society and some bank accounts earns interest, but that is the only way in which it can gain in value. In fact, if inflation is high, higher than the rate of interest, money will lose value in terms of its purchasing power, that is, how many goods can be bought with it. Gold and houses, in contrast, do not earn interest, but they can appreciate in value, their prices can rise. When inflation strikes, gold has often been a good asset to protect or hedge against loss of purchasing power. Houses too generally maintain their real value at these times (though not in the United Kingdom in recent years!).

Ordinary shares possess both characteristics: they can earn a dividend as well as appreciate in value. A share bought at a price of 100 pence might receive a dividend of 5 pence for a year, and it might also increase in price to 110 pence. In this case, the profit or capital gain is 10 pence, the total return on the asset is 15 pence and the overall rate of return is 15 per cent. Of course, the share might also fall in price in which case the return might be negative. In this example, if the price dropped to 90 pence, the capital loss is 10 pence, and the share is said to have depreciated in value by 10 per cent. Because of the dividend, the overall loss is only 5 pence, but this still means that the overall rate of return is negative at minus 5 per cent.

Risk and return

The possibility of loss on an asset is the third characteristic an investor will look at. Different assets have different degrees of risk, and these usually relate to their potential for appreciation or depreciation. Bank deposits, for example, cannot appreciate or depreciate in price and, hence, are virtually risk-free: their level remains the same apart from the periodic addition of interest. Unless the bank goes under, a rather rare occurrence nowadays, the investor's money is safe. The interest rate may drop so that the annual return is lower, but the basic capital is protected from any loss except for the loss of value caused by inflation.

Gilt-edged securities, in contrast, can fall in value. However, since they are sold and therefore backed by the government, they do still guarantee to pay that fixed amount, the coupon. But ordinary shares carry the risks of both falling prices and falling yields. Not only might declining profits lead to share prices declining in the market, but they might also lead to a company deciding it cannot afford to pay as big a dividend as a proportion of the share price, or even to pay one at all. Thus, while equities offer attractive potential rewards and often a relatively safe haven from inflation, the uncertainty over the future movements of their prices makes them a risky proposition.

Clearly, some assets are riskier than others, and some offer potentially better returns, both in terms of yield and capital growth. These characteristics of risk and return that all assets possess are intimately related, and this relationship is the foundation of investment decision-making. Portfolio theory, the body of ideas that attempts to explain why investors select and organise their assets in portfolios in the way they do, has at its core the connection between risk and return, between safety and yield. And all investors should ask themselves the question: how much of my capital am I prepared to risk on an uncertain future, and how much should I ensure gets a safe, solid return?

Portfolio theory can provide a guide to making these kinds of decision, suggesting that the greater the riskiness of an asset, the greater the potential return. If an asset like a bank deposit earns a fairly certain yield, that yield will be lower than the uncertain return on an asset like an ordinary share. The owner of the riskier asset is compensated for taking on greater risk by the possibility of much higher rewards. The appropriate aphorism to encapsulate this concept might be 'nothing ventured, nothing gained'!

In practice, this risk/return relationship appears to be true: the yield on a government bond is usually more than the interest rate on a bank deposit while the return on a share can be far more than both. While the dividend yield on shares is usually low compared to gilt yields, the potential for capital gain can more than make up for it. At the same time, the risk of loss is higher than for either the bond or the bank deposit. Thus, there is a trade-off between risk and return, and the investor will choose assets on the basis of his or her attitude to risk. Risk-aversion means that the primary consideration is safety: the investor will prefer owning assets that cannot fall in price. Ideally, these assets should also avoid the possibility of falling in value, but, unfortunately the assets that best do that, gold and shares, run the risk of price falls. It is also desirable for the safer assets to offer a reasonable rate of return, but again a relatively poor yield may be the cost of safety. The investor can merely select the best return among the assets that carry the maximum level of risk he or she is prepared to take on.

Liquidity and time

Having weighed up the risk/return trade-off, the investor will probably want to consider how easy it will be to convert an asset into ready money in the event that it is needed. This is known as the liquidity of an asset, its fourth characteristic, and it too relates to the return on an asset. Generally, the more liquid an asset is, the lower its return. The easier it is for an investor to give up ownership of an asset without undue loss, the higher the price paid in terms of forgone return. Notes and coins, for example, the most liquid of assets, earn no interest and do not appreciate in value.

Liquidity is also used in a slightly different sense as a term to describe the nature of the markets in which assets are bought and sold. An asset that is in a liquid market can be bought or sold in a substantial quantity without the transaction itself affecting its price. The most liquid markets are those with a large amount of trading, a high turnover of assets. These generally include the currency and gilt markets, discussed in detail in chapters 9 and 10.

Asset liquidity and asset values are also affected by time, and this time value might be called an asset's fifth characteristic. For example, the longer money is tied up in a bank account, the more illiquid it is, and the higher the return it earns. Because of uncertainty about the future, especially about inflation, money today is worth more than money tomorrow. To bring their values into balance, and to encourage saving/investing rather than spending, the longer money is unavailable in the present, the more it needs to be rewarded. In addition, since the returns on other assets might change for the better over that period of time, the investor receives compensation for being unable to enjoy them. This is the second aphorism of portfolio theory: 'time is money'.

Another example in which time value affects asset value is the time to maturity of an asset with a finite life, such as a gilt. The nearer a gilt is to its redemption date (the time that the government will redeem it for its face value), the more likely it is to be priced at or close to its redemption value; the further out it is, the more uncertainty and time value come into play and the further the price can be from the gilt's redemption value. In the latter case, depending on investor expectations about the future, the price might be at a premium to (above) the redemption price or at a discount (below).

With other assets as well as gilts, uncertainty, expectations, and time all combine to influence their risk/return characteristics. The interaction of these factors can have dramatic effects on asset prices, and it is important for investors to understand them when evaluating an asset's prospects for yield and capital appreciation.

Portfolio diversification

In selecting an asset, an investor will look at not only its own various characteristics, but also those of other assets he or she owns or intends to purchase. The whole collection of assets an investor owns is known as a portfolio, and the risk/return relationship of any given asset can be tempered by adding assets with different risk/return characteristics to the total portfolio of assets. For example, a portfolio comprising only cash in a bank account offers a safe but unspectacular return, while a portfolio made up solely of shares might perform very well but may also fall dramatically in value.

A portfolio that contains a combination of stock and cash, say with money allocated 50/50 between the two, provides a risk/return trade-off somewhere in between. In the extreme case where share values fall to zero, the total portfolio still maintains half of its value, in contrast with both an all-stock portfolio which becomes worthless, and an all-cash portfolio which holds its value. At the same time, if shares double in price, the total portfolio only makes half the profits of the all-stock portfolio, but still significantly outperforms the all-cash portfolio.

With investment objectives that seek a certain degree of safety, but also some potential of higher rewards, it makes sense to own a balanced portfolio, a range of different assets with varying degrees of risk and potential returns. These might include shares, gilts, gold and cash plus some of the more exotic assets discussed in later chapters, such as options and Eurobonds. This is the principle of portfolio diversification, and the third aphorism of investment decision-making: 'Don't put all your eggs in one basket'.

Hedging and speculation

When weighing up which assets to buy or which to hold, investors will keep returning to the degree of risk involved. The more risk-averse ones will want as much protection of their assets' value as possible, and once they have taken the first step into the unknown of investing in assets more uncertain and riskier than a building society deposit, there are various means of achieving that.

The basic strategy is called hedging, and it is a version of the strategy of portfolio diversification: the investor holds two or more assets whose risk/return characteristics to some degree offset one another. One example might be simply to hold a low risk and low but solid return asset for every high risk and high potential reward asset. A more precise way to hedge is to use derivatives, the range of securities whose price depends on or derives from the price of an underlying security. A put option, for example, gives its owner the right but not the obligation to sell a share at a fixed price (the striking price) on or by a certain date. Owning one with the share itself means that the investor's potential capital loss is limited to the loss implied should the share fall to the striking price. If it falls further, the investor can use the option and sell the share at the striking price.

On the other side of the hedger's trading is the speculator, someone who is prepared to take on the extra risk that the hedger wants to avoid. Speculators are in the markets for the express purpose of making as large a profit as possible. They typically believe that they know the future prospects for asset prices better than the majority of investors, and hence are prepared to take bigger risks. The key characteristics of speculators are that they are prepared to leave themselves unprotected from possibly adverse market moves, and that they like to trade often and in substantial amounts. This behaviour is beneficial to other investors since it allows the more efficient management and transference of risk, and it gives the market greater liquidity.

With a put option, the speculator aims to make a profit from the premium paid by the hedger. He or she anticipates that the price of the underlying share will not fall to its striking price, and hence that the hedger will not need to exercise it. Of course, the risk taken on is substantial since, if the share price does fall below the striking price, the potential loss is unlimited: the speculator is obliged to buy the share at the striking price and can sell it only at whatever price it has fallen to.

The nature of the derivatives, or futures and options markets are discussed in more detail in chapters 11 and 12. For the moment, it is merely important to note that these derivatives can be used for the complementary aims of hedging and speculation across a wide range of markets, including future movements of interest rates, exchange rates, commodity prices and securities prices.

Both hedgers and speculators 'go long' in the assets they expect to increase in value, that is, quite simply, that they invest in them. But they can also 'go short': this means that they expect an asset to fall in value, and hence sell it on the expectation of buying it back in the future and realising a capital gain. It is quite possible for investors to short assets they do not own by borrowing them with the intention of returning them once the expected profits have been made. Of course, this is usually a highly speculative activity since the shorted assets may rise in value. It may be used by hedgers when the shorted asset offsets a long asset, for example, where selling a future (a contract to buy a certain asset at a fixed price on a fixed future date) protects against a fall in the price of the underlying asset over that period.

Investors, whether hedgers or speculators, who expect a rise in a particular asset price or in the market as a whole are known as bulls, while those who are pessimistic about future price prospects are known as bears. And it is quite possible to be bullish and bearish at the same time if contemplating contrasting assets or markets. For example, risk-averse investors wary of UK stock market prospects might view gilts as good buys, while ambitious speculators might short the pound or the franc and go long in gold or property.

COMPARING INVESTMENTS

It is important to clarify one potential source of confusion early on and that is the use of the words 'investor' and 'investment'. Popularly, and especially in financial markets, an investment is an asset purchased by an investor with a view to making money, either through its yield or its appreciation in price. But this kind of investment involves only a transfer of ownership. No new spending has taken place: in the language of economics, the 'investor' is actually saving! It might be better called financial investment.

Economists, on the other hand, define investment as spending by companies or the government on capital goods: new factories or machinery or housing or roads. This is capital investment. Generally, it is funded by borrowing from savers, perhaps through the issue of stocks or bonds. Thus, investment in this sense is the other side of the market from saving; it is borrowing rather than lending, spending rather than saving.

The financial pages of a newspaper may well use the words in both senses, though generally they will mean financial investment. Usually, though, the context will make it quite clear which is intended. In each case, the cost of the investment is determined in the markets for assets. The price of a stock or bond is on the one hand what an investor will have to pay to own it; on the other hand, it is what a company or government can expect to receive for the issue of a similar security.

Markets

Assets are bought and sold in markets, but what are these markets exactly? Essentially, they are institutions that allow buyers and sellers to trade assets with one another through the discovery of prices with which both parties are satisfied. They might be physical places where traders meet to bargain, but in an age of technology, they do not need to be: often, nowadays, they operate through computer screens and telephones. Open outcry is the term for an actual gathering of traders offering prices at which they are prepared to buy and sell. But a very similar process is happening when they list their desired prices over the telephone or on a screen.

In each case, what is taking place is a form of auction. For example, a trader might have ten lots of an asset to sell. If there are too many or too few buyers at his or her suggested price (more or less than ten), the trader will lower or raise the price until there are exactly ten buyers. In effect, investors wishing to buy an asset are looking for sellers offering it at a price they find acceptable; sellers are doing the reverse. If neither side find a counterparty willing to trade at that price, the buyers will raise the price they are prepared to pay, while the sellers will lower their acceptable price. Eventually, a compromise price is reached, and that becomes the current market price.

In the language of economics, this process is the balancing of demand and supply. The price of an asset moves to the level where demand and supply are equal. And since demand and supply continually shift with the changing patterns of investors' objectives and expectations, the price is continually moving to keep them in balance. In this environment of constant flux, it should, in principle, be possible for a seller to extract an excessive price from an unwary buyer if that buyer is kept unaware of the market price. Hence, another angle on the nature of a market is that it is a means for providing information. The more widely available that information, the better that market will operate.

Aggregating from the market for an individual asset produces a market in the recognised sense, an institution providing and generating prices for a range of assets with similar properties, and typically with an aggregate indication of which way prices are moving. In much financial reporting, this market is personified as having an opinion or sentiment. What this means is that the bulk of the traders in a market consider it to be moving in a particular direction: if buyers overwhelm sellers, it will be up, while if more traders are trying to leave the market than to come in, it will be down.

Financial markets can be classified in different ways. One basic distinction is between primary and secondary markets: in the former, new money flows from lenders to borrowers as companies and governments seek more funds; in the latter, investors buy and sell existing assets among themselves. The existence of the secondary market is generally considered to be essential for a good primary market. The more liquid the secondary market, the easier it should be to raise capital in the primary market by persuading investors to take on new assets. The secondary market allows them to sell it should they decide it is not an asset they want to hold.

Markets may also be classified by whether or not they are organised, that is, whether or not there is an overarching institution setting a framework of rules and ready to honour the contracts of a failed counterparty. For example, London's Stock Exchange is an organised market while the over-the-counter derivatives market is not. Similarly, markets might be physical places like the New York Stock Exchange, screen-based computer systems like London's Stock

Exchange Automated Quotation, or networks of telephone and electronic communication, such as those between the speculators and traders of foreign currencies. And, of course, markets can be classified by the assets that are traded on them: stocks, bonds, derivatives, currencies, commodities and so on. Although these are all distinct markets, and the analysis in later chapters examines them each separately, there are very strong connections between them, connections that grow stronger as increasing globalisation and improved technology allow better and better flows of information. Investors do not simply choose one category of asset – they can select a mix. This means they can constantly compare the potential returns (yields and price changes) on a variety of assets. Hence, the markets are all linked by the relative prices of assets traded on them, and by the most important price of all, the rate of interest.

Prices and interest rates

Interest rates are prices for the use of money. An investor holding cash rather than depositing it in an interest-bearing bank account is paying a price, the forgone interest. Once the money is deposited, it is the bank that pays the price for the funds it can now use, again the interest payable on that account. Lastly, when the bank lends the money to a company, the company is paying a price for being able to borrow – the interest the bank charges for loans which is normally higher than the rate it pays the investor so it can make a profit.

At any one time, there are different rates of interest payable on different forms of money. For example, money deposited long-term receives more interest than a short-term deposit. Similarly, money loaned to a risky enterprise earns more than that in a risk-free loan. Thus, an alternative view of the rate of interest is as the price of risk: the greater the risk, the higher the price.

All of these rates are intimately related: if one changes, they all do. This works by the same process as the changing prices of assets, that is, the rebalancing of demand and supply. If, for example, the rate of interest payable on short-term deposits were to rise, money in long-term deposits would flow into short-term deposits. The sellers or suppliers of long-term deposits would decline, and to attract them back, the price, the interest rate would need to rise in line with the short-term rate.

A rise in interest rates has a beneficial effect on investors with cash deposits in interest-bearing accounts. On the other side of the market though, the buyers of money or the borrowers face increased costs since the price has gone up. This would be the experience of companies borrowing to finance new investment, or of homeowners with monthly mortgage payments to make. But a change in interest rates also has effects on the prices of other assets, notably bond/gilt prices, equity prices and the prices of currencies.

The relationship between bond prices and interest rates is an inverse one: as one goes up, the other goes down. This is because a bond pays a fixed amount which, when calculated as a percentage of its market price, is the yield, equivalent to the rate of interest. If rates go up, the relative attractiveness of a deposit account over a bond increases. Since the coupon is fixed, for the yield on the bond to rise to offer an interest return once again comparable to that on the deposit account, the price of the bond must fall.

The relationship between bond prices and interest rates is simple and certain; that between equity prices and interest rates is more complicated and less predictable. As with bonds, the relative dividend yield of shares will be less attractive than the interest rate on a deposit account if interest rates rise. The yield will also be less attractive than that on the bond with its adjusted price. Furthermore, the yield may become even less desirable because the rate rise will raise the company's interest costs, reduce its profitability and perhaps lead it to cut the dividend. However, much of the return sought on shares is from their potential for capital growth and an interest rate rise need not affect that.

Interest rates tend to rise and fall in line with the level of economic activity. In a recession and the early stages of a recovery, they will generally be low and falling to encourage borrowing, while in the subsequent boom, they will rise as the demand for money exceeds the supply. Thus, a recession should be good for bond prices and a boom less positive. For shares, the rising interest rates of a boom might be bad, but the rising economy should be advantageous because of its opportunities for enhanced profitability. In the long-term, the prospects for the latter are far more of an influence on share prices than interest rates.

The last significant market influenced by interest rates is that for currencies. Exchange rates are in part determined by the relative rates across countries. If these change, by one country perhaps raising its rates, deposits in that country will become more attractive. To make the deposits, its currency will be bought and others sold, pushing up its price in terms of the other currencies. The higher value of a country's currency might also make its stocks and bonds more attractive relative to other international assets. On the other hand, a higher currency value makes exports more expensive, weakening the country's competitive position and potentially reducing exporters' profits. This may lead to equity price declines.

Each of these effects of changed interest rates could conceivably come before the change is actually implemented. This is because of the expectations of investors: if a rate rise is anticipated, bond owners will probably sell in the expectation of being able to buy the bonds back at the new lower price. This will cause prices to fall automatically because of surplus supply. Markets often discount the future in this way, building into the prices of the assets traded on them all past, present and prospective information on their future values. Expectations of company profits can influence the current price of a share just as much as actual announced profits, sometimes more so.

USING THE FINANCIAL PAGES

How do all these concepts work out in practice in the financial pages of a newspaper? And how does the investor check on the prices of assets owned or considered for purchase? The second part of this book covers the entire range of market information carried by the *Financial Times*, providing details on the background and operations of the various markets as well as a guide to how to read the daily charts and tables.

Saturday's FT is the issue that focuses most on the interests of the individual investor in its personal finance pages. The main table is titled 'Highest rates for your money', and it provides details on the best options available for depositing money in various kinds of accounts at major banks and building societies. The table lists the names of the financial institutions and accounts, telephone numbers, the notice periods for withdrawing funds from the account, the minimum deposits, and the interest rates and frequency at which they are paid.

In a sense, the table gives an indication of what is called the opportunity cost of an investment, the benefits lost by not employing the money in its most profitable alternative use. These rates of return represent the best alternative use of money invested elsewhere, and, of course, they are relatively risk-free investments as well. When making selections of assets, they serve as valuable benchmarks.

The concept of benchmarks is one that is repeated throughout this book: many of the figures provided by the FT fulfil this purpose of enabling both investors and borrowers to make comparisons. This is particularly the case with indices which provide investors with the guidelines for passive portfolio management. If the objective is to perform as well as, and no worse or better than the overall stock or bond market, the investor can simply buy the relevant index or mimic it by buying the equities or gilts whose values it measures. The converse of the passive approach is active management where the investor attempts to beat the market by following his or her personal philosophy of what moves asset prices.

Money markets

The money markets are the markets where highly liquid assets like money are traded. The term usually refers to the short-term markets in which financial institutions borrow from and lend to one another, as well as the foreign exchange markets. They are the short-term counterpart of the Stock Exchange's long-term investment market.

These markets are, for the most part, limited to a small number of institutional participants but they have the potential for enormous effects on the whole financial and economic system, and hence will be of interest to most investors and companies (see chapter 10). They directly involve the individual investor in a more simple way, through their provision of places to deposit money safely and with a reasonable rate of return, the interest rate.

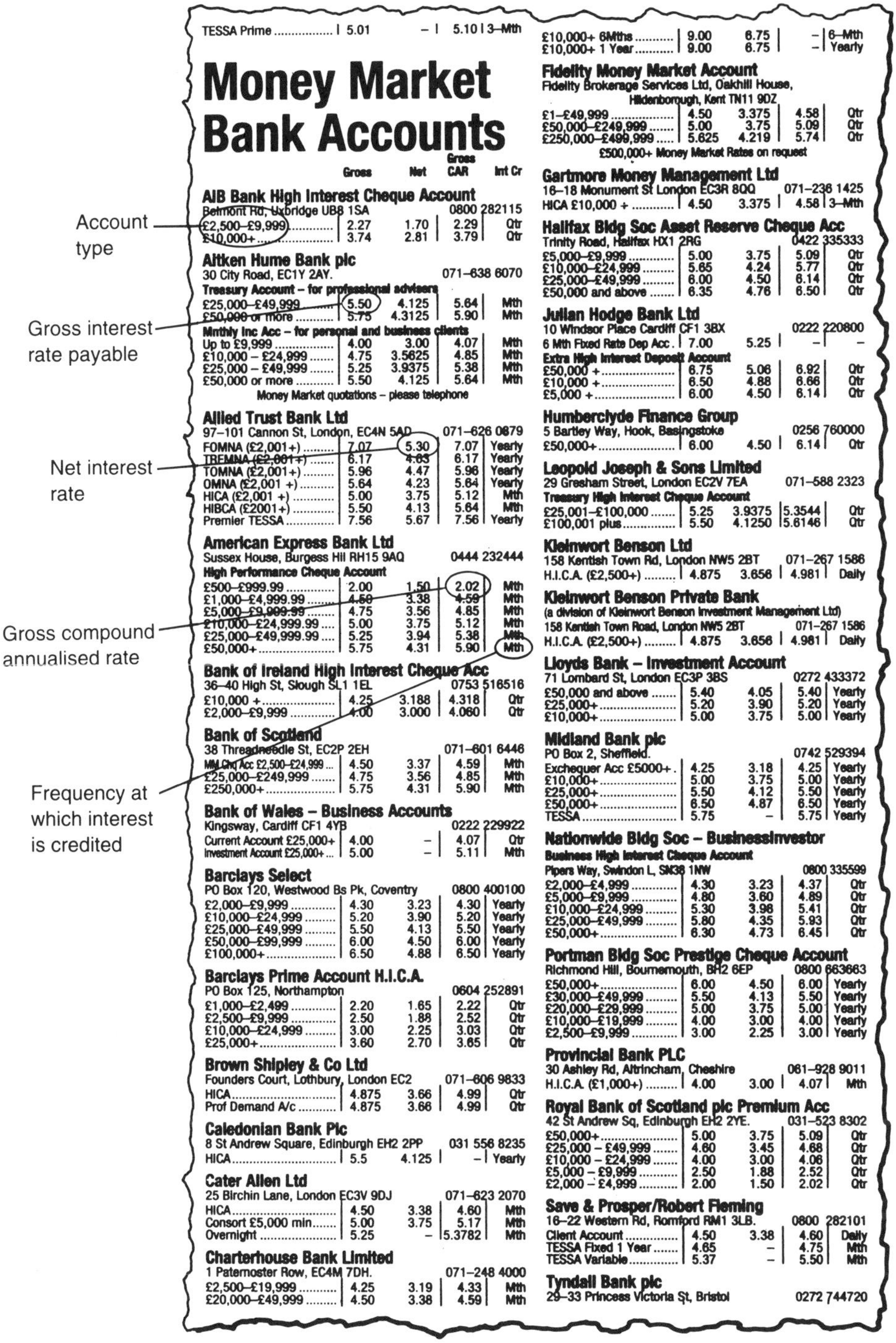

TESSA Prime .... | 5.01 | – | 5.10 | 3-Mth

Money Market Bank Accounts

	Gross	Net	Gross CAR	Int Cr

AIB Bank High Interest Cheque Account
Belmont Rd, Uxbridge UB8 1SA — 0800 282115
| £2,500–£9,999 | 2.27 | 1.70 | 2.29 | Qtr |
| £10,000+ | 3.74 | 2.81 | 3.79 | Qtr |

Aitken Hume Bank plc
30 City Road, EC1Y 2AY. — 071-638 6070
Treasury Account – for professional advisers
| £25,000–£49,999 | 5.50 | 4.125 | 5.64 | Mth |
| £50,000 or more | 5.75 | 4.3125 | 5.90 | Mth |
Mnthly Inc Acc – for personal and business clients
Up to £9,999	4.00	3.00	4.07	Mth
£10,000 – £24,999	4.75	3.5625	4.85	Mth
£25,000 – £49,999	5.25	3.9375	5.38	Mth
£50,000 or more	5.50	4.125	5.64	Mth
Money Market quotations – please telephone

Allied Trust Bank Ltd
97–101 Cannon St, London, EC4N 5AD — 071-626 0879
FOMNA (£2,001+)	7.07	5.30	7.07	Yearly
TREMNA (£2,001+)	6.17	4.63	6.17	Yearly
TOMNA (£2,001+)	5.96	4.47	5.96	Yearly
OMNA (£2,001 +)	5.64	4.23	5.64	Yearly
HICA (£2,001 +)	5.00	3.75	5.12	Mth
HIBCA (£2001+)	5.50	4.13	5.64	Mth
Premier TESSA	7.56	5.67	7.56	Yearly

American Express Bank Ltd
Sussex House, Burgess Hil RH15 9AQ — 0444 232444
High Performance Cheque Account
£500–£999.99	2.00	1.50	2.02	Mth
£1,000–£4,999.99	4.50	3.38	4.59	Mth
£5,000–£9,999.99	4.75	3.56	4.85	Mth
£10,000–£24,999.99	5.00	3.75	5.12	Mth
£25,000–£49,999.99	5.25	3.94	5.38	Mth
£50,000+	5.75	4.31	5.90	Mth

Bank of Ireland High Interest Cheque Acc
36–40 High St, Slough SL1 1EL — 0753 516516
| £10,000 + | 4.25 | 3.188 | 4.318 | Qtr |
| £2,000–£9,999 | 4.00 | 3.000 | 4.060 | Qtr |

Bank of Scotland
38 Threadneedle St, EC2P 2EH — 071-601 6446
Mkt Chq Acc £2,500–£24,999	4.50	3.37	4.59	Mth
£25,000–£249,999	4.75	3.56	4.85	Mth
£250,000+	5.75	4.31	5.90	Mth

Bank of Wales – Business Accounts
Kingsway, Cardiff CF1 4YB — 0222 229922
| Current Account £25,000+ | 4.00 | – | 4.07 | Qtr |
| Investment Account £25,000+ | 5.00 | – | 5.11 | Mth |

Barclays Select
PO Box 120, Westwood Bs Pk, Coventry — 0800 400100
£2,000–£9,999	4.30	3.23	4.30	Yearly
£10,000–£24,999	5.20	3.90	5.20	Yearly
£25,000–£49,999	5.50	4.13	5.50	Yearly
£50,000–£99,999	6.00	4.50	6.00	Yearly
£100,000+	6.50	4.88	6.50	Yearly

Barclays Prime Account H.I.C.A.
PO Box 125, Northampton — 0604 252891
£1,000–£2,499	2.20	1.65	2.22	Qtr
£2,500–£9,999	2.50	1.88	2.52	Qtr
£10,000–£24,999	3.00	2.25	3.03	Qtr
£25,000+	3.60	2.70	3.65	Qtr

Brown Shipley & Co Ltd
Founders Court, Lothbury, London EC2 — 071-606 9833
| HICA | 4.875 | 3.66 | 4.99 | Qtr |
| Prof Demand A/c | 4.875 | 3.66 | 4.99 | Qtr |

Caledonian Bank Plc
8 St Andrew Square, Edinburgh EH2 2PP — 031 556 8235
| HICA | 5.5 | 4.125 | – | Yearly |

Cater Allen Ltd
25 Birchin Lane, London EC3V 9DJ — 071-623 2070
HICA	4.50	3.38	4.60	Mth
Consort £5,000 min	5.00	3.75	5.17	Mth
Overnight	5.25	–	5.3782	Mth

Charterhouse Bank Limited
1 Paternoster Row, EC4M 7DH. — 071-248 4000
| £2,500–£19,999 | 4.25 | 3.19 | 4.33 | Mth |
| £20,000–£49,999 | 4.50 | 3.38 | 4.59 | Mth |

| £10,000+ 6Mths | 9.00 | 6.75 | – | 6-Mth |
| £10,000+ 1 Year | 9.00 | 6.75 | – | Yearly |

Fidelity Money Market Account
Fidelity Brokerage Services Ltd, Oakhill House, Hildenborough, Kent TN11 9DZ
£1–£49,999	4.50	3.375	4.58	Qtr
£50,000–£249,999	5.00	3.75	5.09	Qtr
£250,000–£499,999	5.625	4.219	5.74	Qtr
£500,000+ Money Market Rates on request

Gartmore Money Management Ltd
16–18 Monument St London EC3R 8QQ — 071-236 1425
| HICA £10,000 + | 4.50 | 3.375 | 4.58 | 3-Mth |

Halifax Bldg Soc Asset Reserve Cheque Acc
Trinity Road, Halifax HX1 2RG — 0422 335333
£5,000–£9,999	5.00	3.75	5.09	Qtr
£10,000–£24,999	5.65	4.24	5.77	Qtr
£25,000–£49,999	6.00	4.50	6.14	Qtr
£50,000 and above	6.35	4.76	6.50	Qtr

Julian Hodge Bank Ltd
10 Windsor Place Cardiff CF1 3BX — 0222 220800
| 6 Mth Fixed Rate Dep Acc. | 7.00 | 5.25 | – | – |
Extra High Interest Deposit Account
£50,000 +	6.75	5.06	6.92	Qtr
£10,000 +	6.50	4.88	6.66	Qtr
£5,000 +	6.00	4.50	6.14	Qtr

Humberclyde Finance Group
5 Bartley Way, Hook, Basingstoke — 0256 760000
| £50,000+ | 6.00 | 4.50 | 6.14 | Qtr |

Leopold Joseph & Sons Limited
29 Gresham Street, London EC2V 7EA — 071-588 2323
Treasury High Interest Cheque Account
| £25,001–£100,000 | 5.25 | 3.9375 | 5.3544 | Qtr |
| £100,001 plus | 5.50 | 4.1250 | 5.6146 | Qtr |

Kleinwort Benson Ltd
158 Kentish Town Rd, London NW5 2BT — 071-267 1586
| H.I.C.A. (£2,500+) | 4.875 | 3.656 | 4.981 | Daily |

Kleinwort Benson Private Bank
(a division of Kleinwort Benson Investment Management Ltd)
158 Kentish Town Road, London NW5 2BT — 071-267 1586
| H.I.C.A. (£2,500+) | 4.875 | 3.656 | 4.981 | Daily |

Lloyds Bank – Investment Account
71 Lombard St, London EC3P 3BS — 0272 433372
£50,000 and above	5.40	4.05	5.40	Yearly
£10,000+	5.20	3.90	5.20	Yearly
£10,000+	5.00	3.75	5.00	Yearly

Midland Bank plc
PO Box 2, Sheffield. — 0742 529394
Exchequer Acc £5000+	4.25	3.18	4.25	Yearly
£10,000+	5.00	3.75	5.00	Yearly
£25,000+	5.50	4.12	5.50	Yearly
£50,000+	6.50	4.87	6.50	Yearly
TESSA	5.75	–	5.75	Yearly

Nationwide Bldg Soc – Businessinvestor
Pipers Way, Swindon L, SN38 1NW — 0800 335599
Business High Interest Cheque Account
£2,000–£4,999	4.30	3.23	4.37	Qtr
£5,000–£9,999	4.80	3.60	4.89	Qtr
£10,000–£24,999	5.30	3.98	5.41	Qtr
£25,000–£49,999	5.80	4.35	5.93	Qtr
£50,000+	6.30	4.73	6.45	Qtr

Portman Bldg Soc Prestige Cheque Account
Richmond Hill, Bournemouth, BH2 6EP — 0800 663663
£50,000+	6.00	4.50	6.00	Yearly
£30,000–£49,999	5.50	4.13	5.50	Yearly
£20,000–£29,999	5.00	3.75	5.00	Yearly
£10,000–£19,999	4.00	3.00	4.00	Yearly
£2,500–£9,999	3.00	2.25	3.00	Yearly

Provincial Bank PLC
30 Ashley Rd, Altrincham, Cheshire — 061-928 9011
| H.I.C.A. (£1,000+) | 4.00 | 3.00 | 4.07 | Mth |

Royal Bank of Scotland plc Premium Acc
42 St Andrew Sq, Edinburgh EH2 2YE. — 031-523 8302
£50,000+	5.00	3.75	5.09	Qtr
£25,000 – £49,999	4.60	3.45	4.68	Qtr
£10,000 – £24,999	4.00	3.00	4.06	Qtr
£5,000 – £9,999	2.50	1.88	2.52	Qtr
£2,000 – £4,999	2.00	1.50	2.02	Qtr

Save & Prosper/Robert Fleming
16–22 Western Rd, Romford RM1 3LB. — 0800 282101
Client Account	4.50	3.38	4.60	Daily
TESSA Fixed 1 Year	4.65	–	4.75	Mth
TESSA Variable	5.37	–	5.50	Mth

Tyndall Bank plc
29–33 Princess Victoria St, Bristol — 0272 744720

Annotations (left margin):
- Account type
- Gross interest rate payable
- Net interest rate
- Gross compound annualised rate
- Frequency at which interest is credited

Fig. 1.1 Money market funds

The FT produces a daily table listing these money market bank accounts, of which Figure 1.1 is a sample extract. Tables and charts with annotations, commentary and explanation like this appear frequently throughout the rest of the book, as a guide to financial pages everywhere, and particularly the *Financial Times*. They are intended to show how easy the interpretation and use of the financial pages really are once the basic principles and jargon have been understood:

- **Account name and amounts:** the first column lists the name of the account and/or the minimum/maximum that needs to be deposited in it to earn the interest rates indicated.

- **Gross:** the second column shows the gross interest rate currently payable on money deposited in the account. Gross simply means the amount payable before deductions, in this case not allowing for deduction of income tax at the basic rate. As with all income, the interest received on an asset of this kind is liable to taxation and tax considerations will have an impact on all of the features of investment decision-making discussed above.

- **Net:** the third column indicates the interest rate payable on the account net of income tax at the basic rate. Net is the converse of gross, the amount payable after deductions. Some accounts are tax exempt (e.g. Tax Exempt Special Savings Accounts or TESSAs) under particular rules designed to shelter relatively modest savings. For these accounts, the gross and net rates are naturally the same.

- **Gross CAR:** the fourth column represents the gross compounded annualised rate. This applies to accounts where the interest is credited in periods more often than once a year. What happens here is that interest earned on the basic amount in the first period itself earns interest in succeeding periods, and so on. Hence the annualised rate is more than the sum of the interest paid in each period. It is instead said to be compounded.

- **Interest credited:** the final column supplies the detail on the frequency at which interest is credited to the account.

The early part of this chapter explained how the degree of risk affects the yield, with higher risk indicating higher potential return. Similarly, the time it takes to release money from an account, the notice period, affects its return. For example, savings accounts where the saver/investor is required to give thirty days' notice before withdrawing funds (or be penalised for early withdrawal) pay a higher rate of interest than those that allow immediate access. These tables indicate a third factor that affects return, namely the amount of money put into an asset. Generally, the more money an investor is prepared to tie up, the greater the return.

Latest value of the 'Footsie' (Financial Times – Stock Exchange 100) index, based on the closing price of 100 leading companies quoted on the Stock Exchange

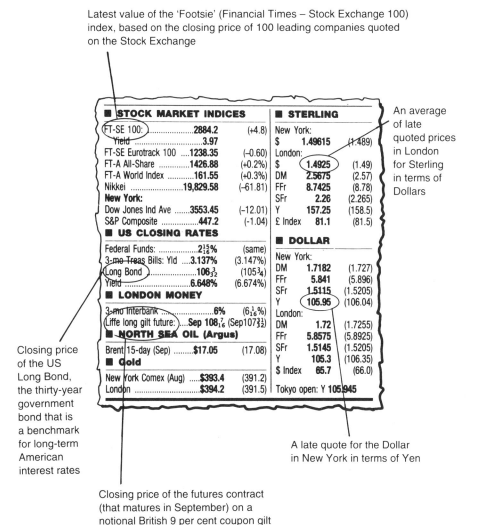

An average of late quoted prices in London for Sterling in terms of Dollars

Closing price of the US Long Bond, the thirty-year government bond that is a benchmark for long-term American interest rates

A late quote for the Dollar in New York in terms of Yen

Closing price of the futures contract (that matures in September) on a notional British 9 per cent coupon gilt

Fig. 1.2 Key market statistics

Major markets

The front page of the *Financial Times* carries a summary of values and changes in a number of key indicators across the broad range of markets (see Figure 1.2):

- **Stock market indices:** equity performance indicators for the London, Tokyo and New York exchanges, as well as broad indices for Europe and the world. These are explored in more detail in chapters 6 and 7.

- **US closing rates:** principal US interest rates and bond yields. These are explored in more detail in chapters 9 and 11.

- **London money:** the London interbank market rate and the price of a future on the long UK government bond. These are examined further in chapters 10 and 11.

- **North Sea oil and gold:** prices of these two key commodities in New York and London. These are examined further in chapter 12.

- **Sterling and dollar:** rates for these two currencies in New York and London in terms of each other and Deutsche marks, French and Swiss francs, and yen, as well as the value of sterling and dollar trade-weighted indices. These are the focus of chapter 10.

Stock markets

Major share price movements around the world are highlighted in a feature on the front of the FT's second section. This gives chief price changes on the previous day for equities not only in the United Kingdom, but also in Frankfurt, New York, Paris and Tokyo (see Figure 1.3):

- **Market, stock, closing price in the local currency and change on the previous trading day:** the prices shown are not necessarily those involving the greatest percentage change in the various markets since this often applies to relatively small companies with only a narrow market in their shares. The FT's table generally concentrates on the most interesting price movements among large companies.

Chief price changes yesterday

FRANKFURT (DM)			
Rises			
Horten	187	+	8
Volkswagen	359.7	+	11.7
Falls			
Colonia Knzn Pf	730	–	25
Preussag	422.5	–	7.5
Schmalbach Lub	340	–	7
Viag	425	–	11.5
NEW YORK ($)			
Rises			
Eastman Kodak	52⅜	+	1⅜
Ford	52	+	¾
General Motors	27⅛	+	2
Medco	34⅛	+	4⅜
Falls			
Chrysler	42⅝	–	2⅛
Merck	30¾	–	1⅜
PARIS (FFr)			
Rises			
Elf Aq'tain Cts	354.9	+	7.9
Taittinger	1875	+	75
Falls			
Bancaire Cie	524	–	13
Eaux Cie Genl	2130	–	60
Legris	174.9	–	9.9
Orsan	163.5	–	6.5
TOKYO (Yen)			
Rises			
Asahi Optical	460	+	18
Nippon Seisen	565	+	73
Sega Ent	10700	+	400
Seiyo Food Sys	1170	+	50
Falls			
Dowa Fire & Mr	673	–	20
Tokyo B'castng	1440	–	50

LONDON(Pence)			
Rises			
AcornComputer	110	+	5
Assoc Nursing	240	+	14
Banks (SC)	218	+	21
City of Lon PR	75	+	10
Cosalt	113	+	5
Cranswick	167	+	10
First Nat Fin	78	+	6
GBE Int	69	+	5
Goode Durrant	93	+	7
Lendu Hldgs	20	+	3½
Schroders NV	945	+	35
Swallowfield	106	+	8
Union Discount	169	+	9
Wellcome	696	+	31
Falls			
Andrews Sykes	100	–	17
Ashley (Laura)	94	–	5
Capita	151	–	12
Holt (Joseph)	2900	–	200
Prestwick	29	–	12
QS Hldgs	185	–	30
Radius	44	–	12
Reliance Sec	111	–	10
Wace	131	–	7
Wembley	11½	–	2

Fig. 1.3 Chief price changes

The information is a valuable checklist for the key moves in the major markets of the world. Much more detailed data, as well as reports on the markets and commentary on the main forces influencing them, are available throughout the rest of the newspaper. Explanations of how these work, and further background on the markets appear in chapters 5, 6 and 7. First, chapter 2 turns to the other side of the markets for capital, the companies who come to borrow and whose share prices are quoted on the stock markets.

2

COMPANIES

Companies are organisations established for some kind of commerce and with a legal identity separate from their owners. The owners are the shareholders who have rights to part of the company's profits, and who usually have limited liability. This means that the liability of the owners for company debts is limited to the amount paid for their shares. They can only lose what they invested.

Companies are often run by people other than the owners, although in theory at least the ordinary shareholders control the company. Management is expected to act in the best interests of the owners. Nonetheless, the ordinary shareholders are the last in the queue of claimants on a company: before they can receive anything, the demands of basic operating costs, interest payments and taxation must be met. This is especially evident when a business is wound up, and the owners become the final creditors to receive their stake.

Since this book is concerned with financial markets covered in the *Financial Times*, and in which, in principle, anyone can participate, the companies considered are typically public: this means that their shares are traded in a market, usually the Stock Exchange for UK companies and, for the most part, there are no dominant owners. The focus on companies in this chapter is on the features of corporate life over which the company has some direct control: its profitability, its dividend payments, its methods of raising new capital in the primary market, and its means of offence and survival in contests for corporate control. Chapter 5 focuses more on the secondary market, and the interplay of companies and investors in the context of the market for UK equities.

PRESENTING FIGURES

The primary source for data and analysis of a company is its annual report and accounts. These give all the information on its business and financial affairs, and their publication is one of a company's legal obligations to its shareholders. They describe the current trading conditions of the company, what it has sold (its turnover, sales or revenues) and what it has paid out in wages and salaries, rent, raw materials and other inputs to the production of the goods or services it sells (its costs). They also indicate the company's profits or losses, the state of its assets and liabilities at the start and end of the financial year, and its cash flow.

Detailed explanations of the various financial statements published by a company and the ratios that can be used to analyse and interpret them can be found in numerous publications. This book aims merely to outline some of the relevant figures and ratios. Readers seeking greater depth of analysis are referred to Ciaran Walsh's *Key Management Ratios: How to Analyse, Compare and Control the Figures that Drive Company Value (Financial Times*, Pitman Publishing, 1993).

There are essentially three financial statements in a company's annual report: the profit and loss account, the balance sheet, and the cash flow statement. From these three can be calculated all the significant ratios needed for companies to practise sound financial management of their business, and for investors to interpret corporate performance relative to the share price and the market more generally.

Profit and loss

A company's profit and loss account is a statement of the final outcome of all its transactions, all revenues and costs during a given period, usually a year. It shows whether the company made any money in the previous year, how it did it, and what it did with the profits, if any. It also allows comparison with previous years' performances and with other companies.

The total value of all goods sold by the company is known as its sales or turnover. Deducting from that figure the cost of achieving those sales either directly or indirectly (for example, either the raw materials in the sold products, or staff salaries paid for work on these and other products) gives the company's operating or trading profit. Deducting from that figure, in turn, the cost of interest payments made on loans from banks or in the form of corporate bonds, gives the company's pre-tax profit. This is the most widely quoted figure in financial reporting on company results and profitability.

The next deduction is tax: firstly, corporation tax is paid by the company on profits after all costs have been met except for dividends paid out to ordinary shareholders; and secondly, advance corporation tax, income tax paid on behalf of shareholders on their dividend income, is paid. Since 6 April 1993 the latter has been paid at the lower rate of 20%, and can be reclaimed or supplemented by the shareholders depending on their tax bracket. Companies can also partially offset tax payable on dividend distributions against mainstream corporation tax.

Money left once taxation demands have been met is known as after tax profit or equity earnings. This is now at the disposal of the company for distribution as dividends or ploughing back into the business as retained earnings. The allocation will depend on the conflicting aims of maintaining the level of dividends so that investor confidence in the share price remains solid, and having access to the least expensive source of funds for investment in further developing the business. The conflict corresponds to the dichotomy an investor faces between income and capital gain. The two do not preclude one another, but an appropriate balance needs to be struck.

The profit and loss account quantifies revenue and cost flows over a given period of time. In a sense, it links two versions of the second key financial statement, the balance sheet, one at the beginning of the year and the other at year end. The third document is the cash flow statement,which depends on a combination of the two balance sheets and the profit and loss account.

Balance sheets and cash flows

The balance sheet is a snapshot of a company's capital position at an instant in time. It details everything it owns (its assets) and everything it owes (its liabilities) at year end. The two sides of a balance sheet, by definition, balance. They are merely two different aspects of the same sum of money: where it came from and where it went. Essentially, liabilities are sources of funds while assets are the uses to which those funds are put.

A company's assets are made up of two items: fixed or long-term assets, such as land, buildings, and equipment; and current or short-term assets, such as stocks of goods available for sale, debtors or accounts receivable, and cash in the bank. Its liabilities are made up of three items, the first two being current or short-term liabilities, such as trade credit or accounts payable, tax, dividends, and overdrafts at the bank; and longer-term debt, such as term loans, mortgages and bonds.

The third form of liability is that of ordinary funds, and this in turn divides into three forms: revenue reserves or retained earnings – the company's trading profits that have not been distributed as dividends; capital reserves – surpluses from sources other than normal trading such as revaluation of fixed assets or gains due to advantageous currency fluctuations; and issued ordinary shares.

Ordinary shares have three different values: their nominal value, the face or par value at which they were issued and which may have no relation to the issue price or current trading price; their book value, the total of ordinary funds divided by the number of shares in issue; and their market value, the price quoted on a stock exchange. For the purpose of reading the financial pages, the last value is the one of primary significance.

The cash flow statement details the amount of money that flows in and out of a company in a given period of time. Cash flows into a company when a cheque is received and out when one is issued. This statement tracks the flow of the funds in those cheques: how much has flowed through the accounts, where the funds have gone to and where they have come from.

The balance sheet is a check of a company's financial health, and the profit and loss account an indicator of its current success or failure. Together they can be used to calculate a number of valuable ratios, and the cash flow statement can be used to understand what lies behind short-term movements in these ratios.

Investment ratios

Numerous ratios can be calculated from a company's financial statements, many of which are covered in detail in Ciaran Walsh's book. For the purposes of a reader of the FT's financial pages, some of the most useful are pre-tax profit margins, net asset values and the return on capital employed. Each of these allows valuable insights into corporate value and performance from the point of view of both investor and company manager.

The pre-tax profit margin is simply the pre-tax profit divided by the turnover for the period. Profit margins vary considerably between industrial sectors but can certainly be used to compare company performance within an industry. There are often rule-of-thumb industry standards.

Net asset value is the total assets of a company minus its liabilities, debentures and loan stocks. This is the amount that the ordinary shareholders will receive if the business is wound up, the sum left for the last claimants on a defunct company's assets. It is also known as shareholders' interests or shareholders' funds, and is effectively the total par value of the shares in issue plus all historic retained earnings.

Net asset value per share is calculated by dividing net assets by the number of shares in issue. This has varying degrees of significance depending on the nature of the business. For example, the net asset value of a company whose performance depends primarily on its employees will not be important since its tangible assets are few. In contrast, a business heavily built on assets, such as investment trusts or property companies, will find its share price considerably influenced by its net asset value per share. The share price might be at a premium or a discount to the net asset value per share.

Return on capital employed is a ratio that indicates the efficiency of a business by showing to what effect its assets are used. It is calculated as the pre-tax (and pre-interest payment) profit divided by the shareholders' funds and any long-term loans. The resulting figures enable comparison between one company and another within the same sector; for the investor, they can also be used to compare across different sectors.

Some other important ratios, including earnings per share, dividends per share and the debt/equity ratio, are explained below. Firstly, though, it is important to see how all these results and ratios feature in the pages of the *Financial Times*.

Company financial news

The 'Company News: UK' pages of the newspaper contain details of the financial results of all quoted British companies, and a handful of those without quotations. There may only be space for a sentence or two on the results of the smaller companies, but larger ones will be given a substantial news story as well as a separate comment in the Lex column on the results. The comment, clearly separated from the news, gives the FT's views on why the results are as they are, what the company's prospects might be, and whether its shares are rated appropriately by the market. These pages also report fully on rights and other share issues and large takeover bids. They include briefer items on many smaller acquisitions.

A typical news report on a company's results looks like this, with remarks on the underlying determinants of a company's performance, its plans and prospects, and the impact on the share price:

> Growing losses and closure costs at the Silo chain in the US pushed down annual pre-tax profits at Dixons, the UK's largest electrical retailer, to £33.5m. ... The losses, which overshadowed an encouraging performance by Dixons' UK chains, will increase pressure on the group to find a way of turning Silo around or make further closures. Dixons' share price fell 15p to 195p. (*Financial Times*, 8 July 1993)

In addition to the day-to-day reporting, the FT publishes an annual list of the top 500 UK companies, a ranking of companies quoted on the Stock Exchange as measured by market capitalisation. This analyses a range of key figures on the companies, including their turnover, profits, return on capital employed and employee numbers.

REWARDING SHAREHOLDERS

Saturday's FT contains a table of company results due. This includes all the companies expected to announce results in the following week, their sectors and announcement dates, and the interim and final dividends paid the previous year.

Results

Saturday's FT also lists recently announced preliminary results (actually the full year's results made to the Stock Exchange, to be fleshed out in the annual report a little later), and interim results (see Figure 2.1):

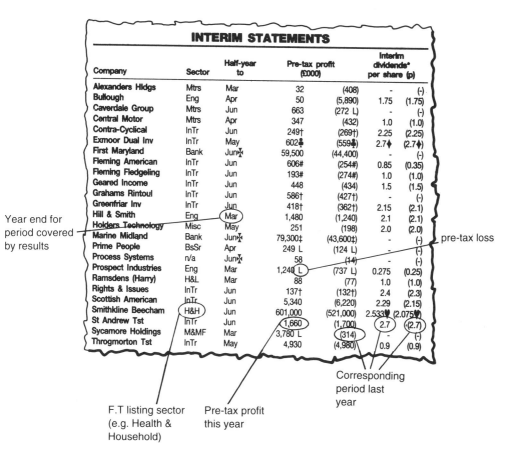

Year end for period covered by results

pre-tax loss

F.T listing sector (e.g. Health & Household)

Pre-tax profit this year

Corresponding period last year

Fig. 2.1 Interim statements

- **Name, sector and year to:** company details and the period covered by the results (half or full year) are given.

- **Pre-tax profits:** these are figures both for this year and the same period of last year (the figure in brackets) in thousands of pounds. A letter L indicates a loss.

- **Earnings per share:** this measures a company's total net return earned on ordinary share capital. It is calculated by first deducting tax, depreciation, interest and payments to preference shareholders (leaving after tax profit), and then dividing by the number of ordinary shares in issue. The figures given allow a comparison with the previous year.

- **Dividends per share:** is the total net dividend divided by the number of shares in issue. Again, the figures allow a comparison with the previous year.

Earnings per share is one of the most widely quoted statistics in discussion of a company's performance and share value. The growth and stability of this ratio are a good indicator of how much a company is increasing profits for its shareholders. But it is difficult to make comparisons across companies because of different methods of calculating earnings. The ability to offset advance corporation tax leads the FT to use three methods: one based on nil distribution of profits, one on net distribution and one on maximum distribution.

Dividends

In Monday's newspaper, 'The week ahead' page lists the dates of forthcoming company meetings that have been notified to the Stock Exchange. These board meetings are usually to consider the company's results and approve the level of the dividend, with an announcement on the figure coming either the same day or the following day. The page also lists the dividend and interest payments due to be made in the week ahead. A daily chart lists all dividends announced on the previous day (see Figure 2.2):

£15.1m in full.

However, Mr Hugo Bier- mann, Maddox chairman, was confident of converting £2m of into the p&l account once it was established that there were no problems with the business.

DIVIDENDS ANNOUNCED

	Current payment	Date of payment	Corres - ponding dividend	Total for year	Total last year
Bespak ....fin	6	Oct 6	5.5	10	9
Budgens ....fin	1	Sept 27	nil	1	nil
Dixons ....fin	4.6	Oct 1	4.4	6.2	6
EFM Japan Trust ......fin	0.4	-	-	0.4	-
Fleming Int High ....fin	2.5675	Sept 10	2.5675	3.5675	3.5675
Hadleigh Inds § ....fin	0.5	Oct 1	nil	0.5	1.25
Hollas ....fin	0.6	Oct 1	0.6	1.2	1.2
Joseph (Leopold) ....fin	13.5	Sept 3	12.75	16.6	15.85
Morris Ashby ....fin	3.7	Oct 1	3	5.4	4.7
St David's Tst ....int	3☆	Sept 30	3	-	14.5
Taunton Cider ....fin	3.6	-	-	6	-
Tops Estates ....fin	1.5225	Oct 29	1.45	2.1	2
Vardy (Reg) ....fin	2.9	Oct 1	2.7	4.2	4

Dividends shown pence per share net except where otherwise stated. §USM stock. ☆ Third interim; makes 9p to date.

Fig. 2.2 Dividends announced

- **Dividends announced:** this gives details of the companies that announced dividends the previous day, including: whether the payment is interim or final; the current payment; the date of the payment; the corresponding dividend the previous year; and the totals for the current and previous year.

Companies usually announce their dividends net of tax since they calculate them on the figure for after tax profit. The amount of the dividend paid as advance corporation tax, the twenty-two and a half per cent deduction for basic rate income tax, has already figured in the profit calculation. The gross dividend, the basis for estimating the gross yield (examined in chapter 5), is calculated by 'grossing up', that is, the net dividend multiplied by 100 and divided by 77.5.

Dividends are paid only out of earnings, but in order for companies to maintain some consistency in their payments, these need not necessarily fall into the same year as the dividends. Where there has been a loss, a company might choose to make dividend payments out of retained earnings, as in the following example:

> Dixons ended up with a post-tax loss. ... That led to a loss per share of 6.5p, compared with 6.5p earnings last year. A slightly increased final dividend of 4.6p, paid out of reserves, makes a total of 6.2p, up from 6p. (*Financial Times*, 8 July 1993)

RAISING FINANCE

From a company perspective, the financial markets exist to raise money through various financial instruments. The sources of capital are basically three: the permanent capital of shareholders (also known as equity capital, ordinary shares or, in the United States, common stock); ploughed back profits (equity funds or shareholders' reserves); and various forms of debt or loan capital.

Corporate finance, the subject of how companies arrange their capital structure, tends to focus on the relative benefits of financing via debt or equity. The relationship between the two elements in a company's capital structure is known as its gearing (or leverage in the United States), and is commonly calculated as total debt (current plus long-term liabilities) divided by ordinary funds (shareholder's equity plus retained earnings). The more highly geared or leveraged a company is, the higher are its borrowings relative to its share capital or turnover.

Gearing, in a general sense, is any situation where swings between profits and losses can be caused by quite small changes in underlying conditions. In the case of gearing with debt and equity, a small change in interest rates can have a dramatic effect: with an increase in the rate of interest, a highly geared company suffers much more from the increased payments necessary to service its debt. The small change can have a substantial effect on profits.

Equity

Equity finance is the capital that allows companies to take the risks inherent in business, embarking on risky new investment programmes. It is limited in a private company, and this is the main reason why such a company would want to 'go public'. In 'coming to the market', getting quoted on the Stock Exchange or the Unlisted Securities Market through a new issue, a company has access to significantly more money for investment in the business. The means by which this is done, and the FT's reporting of new issues, are discussed in chapter 5.

There are two common classes of equity capital: ordinary shares, which have no guaranteed amount of dividend payments, but which carry voting rights; and preference shares, which usually carry a fixed dividend and have preference over ordinary shareholders if the company is wound up, but which have no voting rights. There are also a number of variations, including cumulative preference shares and part paid shares. These are also discussed in more detail in chapter 5.

Companies already listed on the exchange and wishing to raise new equity capital would normally do so by a pre-emption rights issue. This means that existing shareholders have first option on the new shares or the right to sell that option. An increase in the number of ordinary shares in a company without a corresponding increase in its assets or profitability results in a fall in their value – what is known as a dilution of the equity.

To avoid immediate dilution of the shares in issue, a company might use an alternative financial instrument to raise capital, a convertible (also known as a convertible loan stock or a convertible bond). These are debt instruments that can be converted into ordinary or preference shares at a fixed date in the future, and at a fixed price. Their value to a company, besides avoiding dilution, is that, in exchange for their potential conversion value, they will carry a lower rate of interest than standard debt.

Another form of financial instrument that companies use to raise capital is the equity warrant. This is a security that gives the owner the right, though not the obligation, to subscribe cash for new shares at a fixed price on a fixed date. Warrants are themselves traded on stock markets and work in a way similar to options, which are discussed in detail in chapter 11. Since the subscription price on a new warrant will exceed the current market price of the underlying stock, the warrant is a speculative asset, gambling on a price rise. They are popular with companies since they can be issued without including them in the balance sheet.

Debt

The alternative to share capital as a source of finance is loan capital. Debt finance is attractive to companies since it allows the business to be developed without giving up a stake in the ownership, and the consequent loss of a share of the profits and a degree of control. It is also often more readily available than new equity capital other than that from retained profits, and it can be built into a company's capital structure as both short-term and long-term debt.

Like equity capital, corporate debt takes a number of different forms. Long-term loans are usually raised by issuing securities: the most common form in the United Kingdom is the debenture. Most debentures offer a fixed rate of interest payable ahead of dividends in the queue of claimants; and they are often secured on specific company assets. They usually trade on the Stock Exchange, involve less risk than equities, but pay a lower rate of interest than other kinds of debt.

Other forms of industrial or corporate loans include fixed and floating rate notes, and deep discount and zero-coupon bonds. These differ in how the interest or coupon is determined and paid. Fixed notes pay a specified amount whatever happens to interest rates generally, and hence their price in the secondary market varies inversely with interest rates in the same way as gilts. Bonds of this kind have been a central part of corporate finance in the United States for many years, but became more significant in the United Kingdom only when the temporary surplus in the government's budget between 1989–91 led to a shortage of gilts.

Floating rate notes are more prevalent in the Euromarkets, the markets in which players lend and borrow Eurocurrencies (currencies deposited and available for use outside their country of origin). These instruments pay a rate of interest determined by some standard rate such as the LIBOR, an agreed rate for short-term loans between banks. Deep discount and zero-coupon bonds in contrast pay little or no interest. Instead, the issuer offers them at a significant discount to their redemption value so that the investor makes most of the return from a capital gain rather than periodic interest payments. Each of these kinds of debt is discussed in more detail in chapter 9.

The most common form of short-term loan is the overdraft at the bank, where companies can borrow up to an agreed limit and only pay interest on the amount actually borrowed at any given point in time. Another form is the commercial bill, short-term counterparts of bonds, where the issuer promises to pay a fixed amount on a given date a short time in the future, usually three months. The bills are generally 'accepted' (guaranteed) by a financial institution, and sold at a discount ('discounted') to their face value to provide the buyer with an appropriate return and the issuer with immediate cash.

The most recent innovation in debt instruments is the junk bond, a form of finance developed and, for the most part, used almost solely in the United States. This is a bond that offers a higher rate of interest in return for a higher than usual risk of default by the issuer. In the 1980s, junk bonds were used as a means of generating substantial amounts of finance for the takeover of large companies by relatively small ones. They became a focal point of controversies over leveraged buyouts and other supposedly unwelcome or undesirable takeover bids.

CONTESTING CORPORATE CONTROL

One of the aspects of corporate life that features prominently in reporting on companies and the financial markets is the contest for corporate control. Mergers and acquisitions (M&A), bidders, targets, corporate control and corporate governance are issues that frequently make the headlines, and ones that often have an impact on the market far beyond the individual companies or sectors they involve. An extract from the *Financial Times* illustrates the excitement that surrounds them:

> Turnover in Hanson jumped to 21m after the market was enlivened by the news that the international conglomerate is to acquire Quantum Chemical, the US polyethylene and industrial chemicals group, in an agreed $3.2bn deal. Excited market watchers said the move may be the first signs of the return of big corporate deals after a four year absence. Hanson shares, which had eased to 222p just before the mid-afternoon announcement, closed 4 ahead at 226½p. (*Financial Times*, 1 July 1993)

In this example, the Hanson announcement not only offers encouragement to investors in Hanson shares: prices have 'firmed' (or gone up) after 'easing' (going down); it also suggests a possible resurgence of

M&A activity. The latter will certainly be beneficial to the financial institutions that stand to gain from the increased share trading that generally accompanies takeovers.

The primary argument in favour of acquisitions is that they are good for industrial efficiency: without the threat of their company being taken over and, in all likelihood, the loss of their jobs, managers would act more in their own interests than those of the owners. In particular, this might imply an inefficient use of company resources and a lack of concern about the share price, the value of which is often a sign of a company's vulnerability to takeover. Certainly, a bid is frequently beneficial to the shareholders of the target company in terms of immediate rises in the share price. On the other hand, it is argued that the threat of takeover means that management takes too short-term a view, bolstering the share price where possible and investing inadequately for the future, and, where a company has been taken over in a leveraged buyout, perhaps burdening it with too high a debt/equity ratio. The demands of making enough profits to meet interest payments might mean it is managed solely for the short-term.

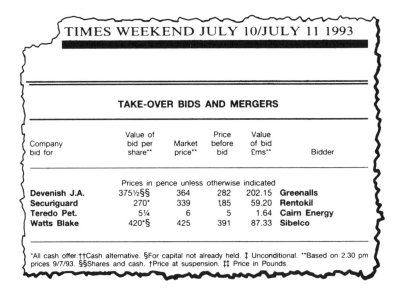

TIMES WEEKEND JULY 10/JULY 11 1993

TAKE-OVER BIDS AND MERGERS

Company bid for	Value of bid per share**	Market price**	Price before bid	Value of bid £ms**	Bidder
Prices in pence unless otherwise indicated					
Devenish J.A.	375½§§	364	282	202.15	**Greenalls**
Securiguard	270*	339	1,85	59.20	**Rentokil**
Teredo Pet.	5¼	6	5	1.64	**Cairn Energy**
Watts Blake	420*§	425	391	87.33	**Sibelco**

*All cash offer.††Cash alternative. §For capital not already held. ‡ Unconditional. **Based on 2.30 pm prices 9/7/93. §§Shares and cash. †Price at suspension. ‡‡ Price in Pounds.

Fig. 2.3 Takeover bids and mergers

Bids and mergers

Saturday's FT has a list of the takeover bids and mergers announced in the previous week and involving bidder and target companies primarily based in the United Kingdom (see Figure 2.3):

- **Bids:** these give details of current takeover bids for publicly quoted companies, naming the bidder and target, the value of the bid per share, the current market price, the price before the bid, and the total value of the bid in millions of pounds.

Bids might be made in the form of a cash offer for all the shares in issue (the value of the bid per share), a paper offer where shares in the bidder are exchanged for those of the target, or a combination of the two. The bids might be agreed to by the management of the target, or they might be defended or contested. The battles over corporate control have generated a new vocabulary of company life: white knights (alternative bidders who are preferred by the existing management of the target) and poison pill defences (tactics that mean a successful takeover triggers something deleterious to the target company's value) are just two of the most popular.

Cross-border deals

Monday's FT extends the coverage of M&A deals to international bids made in the previous week (see Figure 2.4):

- **Deals:** details of the bidder/investor, the target company, the industrial sector and the value of the bid in pounds are given.

- **Comment:** this is a phrase analysing the essential feature of the deal. Figure 2.4 includes the background on various deals, that is, some companies disposing of certain lines and others attempting to establish a broader foreign presence.

Throughout the 1980s, the market for corporate control was the source of considerable financial innovation as well as a significant degree of controversy, notably in the United States. A new kind of arbitrage also became prevalent at this time. Arbitrage is the technique of buying an asset at one price in a market, and almost simultaneously, selling it in another market for a profit.

Risk arbitrage dealt in the shares of companies targeted for takeover, buying before the announcement of a bid and selling when the usual price rise after announcement followed. At times it relied on inside information and the practice of insider trading, compounded with other financial scandals, undoubtedly earned financial institutions a dubious reputation. The next chapter presents the much more positive side of these institutions, their provision firstly of a marketplace for lenders and borrowers of money, and secondly of advice and assistance to these two sides of the market.

Stockbrokers, describes the decision to extend the number

a profit on BT have been virtually eliminated by the government-

tion of individuals owning shares.

CROSS BORDER M&A DEALS

BIDDER/INVESTOR	TARGET	SECTOR	VALUE	COMMENT
Blackland Oil (UK)	Kingsleigh Petroleum (China)	Energy	£26.7m	Payment by shares
Avonmore (Ireland)	Unit of Dairy Crest (UK)	Dairy products	£20.5m	Anticipating market changes
Yorkshire Food (UK)	Del Monte Dried Fruit (US)	Food	£17.8m	Buying 80% stake
France Telecom (France)	Sema Group Facilities Management	Facilities management	£8.8m	Sema sells 24.5% stake
Life Sciences International (UK)	ALKO Diagnostic Corp (US)	Scientific equipment	£4.3m	Cash buy
Nokia (Finland)/Mitsui & Co (Japan)	Joint venture	Mobile telecoms	£1.8m	Mobile marktng venture
Mid-States (UK)	Harts Autoparts (US)	Car parts	£1.2m	Deferred element
Thomson CSF (France)	Unit of Siemens (Germany)	Electronics	n/a	Consolidating market position
Bancorp Holdings (New Zealand)	International Pacific Securities (Australia)	Banking	n/a	Takeover spclst taken over
Sandoz (Switzerland)	Veneziani (Italy)	Construction	n/a	Buy through Italian arm

Fig. 2.4 Cross-border M&A deals

3

FINANCIAL INSTITUTIONS

The most basic financial institution is a market – a place, not necessarily physical, where buyers and sellers can come together to trade. There are essentially four kinds of markets in the financial system. The first type is the securities market where new capital is raised (the primary market) and where trading in existing shares and bonds takes place (the secondary market). Such markets include stock exchanges around the world, as well as the international capital markets. The other three kinds of markets are: the money markets where highly liquid financial instruments are traded; the foreign exchange markets where currencies are bought and sold; and the futures and options markets where these derivatives can be used to hedge or speculate in future interest rate, exchange rate, commodity price and security price movements.

All of these markets are organised in the sense that they operate on well-established custom and practice, and direct access to them is limited to professional participants. Investors and borrowers usually gain access to the markets through intermediaries. Beyond the organised markets are the over-the-counter (OTC) markets – places or, more often, computer screen-based or telephone networks where securities are traded outside the recognised exchange. The biggest of them all is the foreign exchange market, although the OTC derivatives market is also growing dramatically.

There are three basic functions that have to be performed in a financial market: distribution of assets into the portfolios of investors who want to own them; creation of new ones in order to provide funds for borrowers; and 'making' the markets, providing the means by which all of these assets can be easily traded. The first function relates more to investors, the second to companies, and the third is the central facilitating role to which all financial institutions contribute in one way or another.

One single financial institution might perform all three of these functions and do them across a broad range of markets. For example, some UK merchant banks and US investment banks are involved in portfolio management of clients' investments as well as corporate finance, arranging deals, helping clients raise money through flotations, rights issues and bond issues, and advising them on takeovers. Furthermore, they often act as marketmakers, trading on their own behalf, especially in the foreign exchange, Eurobond and derivatives markets.

The performance of a range of different roles, and the contrast between acting as a principal on one's own behalf or as an agent on behalf of a client, throw up a number of conflicts of interest. Such devices as Chinese walls, notional barriers intended to deter valuable market information being shared between parts of a company with conflicting interests, aim to prevent abuses. But this is still an area of considerable controversy. Apart from the benefits of specialisation, it is one of the reasons companies might focus on working different sectors and functions of the market.

MANAGING MONEY

Chapter 1 explained the principles of investment on the premise that an individual investor is the dominant player on the saving/lending/investing side of the capital markets, making and implementing his or her own investment decisions. In reality, individual investors acting alone form only a small part of the investment community. Nowadays the bulk of investment is done by large investing institutions such as pension funds and insurance companies, operating on behalf of the millions of people who put money into them. Furthermore, such individual investors as there are rely on the services of a range of market professionals, intermediaries who offer advice on and management of their asset portfolios.

Investing institutions and fund managers

Many people save in occupational pension schemes. These savings are administered by pension funds which have become the major players in equity and other markets, operating vast portfolios of assets on some of the basic principles outlined in chapter 1. Annually, the *Financial Times* publishes a survey of pension fund management. This lists leading pension fund managers, the value of the funds under their management, and the number of clients for whom they provide these services, with comparative figures for previous years. This is a valuable guide to the performance of these institutions, and their relative weight in the investment community.

Life assurance and general insurance companies are also key players in securities markets. In common with pension funds, they manage their funds on the principle of matching the nature of the assets they hold with that of their liabilities. Thus, pension funds and life assurance companies often have liabilities that will only fall due in the long-term. Hence, they typically have a preference for long-term assets, such as ordinary shares with good growth and capital gain potential. Insurance companies, whose liabilities might fall due much sooner, tend to prefer a portfolio containing some more liquid assets. In either case, the fund managers are bound to act prudently under their fiduciary obligations to the people who placed money in their care.

Unit trusts (known in the United States as mutual funds) are another form of managed investment. Investors buy units in a trust, and the trust manager invests the money in shares or any other assets laid down by the trust's investment objectives and its guidelines for decision-making. The advantage for investors is that relatively small amounts of money can be spread between a range of assets, securing the benefits of portfolio diversification: if invested well, the trust's capital grows and so does the price of its units. Unit trusts generally specialise in particular types of asset, such as equities of a certain industrial sector or a specific country or region.

Investment trusts are similar to unit trusts except that they have a limited size. Like unit trusts, they invest in equities and other assets, but whereas unit trusts are open-ended, with no limit on the amount of units that can be bought, investment trusts are closed-ended. In a sense, they are more like a regular company with a set number of shares in issue, and in fact their shares are usually listed on the stock markets. Shareholders receive their income on investment trusts from dividends as well as any capital gains. Both unit and investment trusts are examined in more detail in chapter 8.

Investing institutions will generally manage their asset portfolios themselves, but at times they will use the services of companies specifically set up to manage the portfolios of large institutional investors or wealthy individuals with substantial holdings. These are variously known as fund, asset, equity, capital or money management companies, and they will distinguish themselves both by the kinds of markets in which they operate, and by their investment philosophies. For example, certain companies may deal only in equity markets, others on such diverse principles as passive indexation, a preference for growth stocks, or the exploitation of market inefficiencies.

Pension funds and other investors, large and small, may also use the services of stockbrokers and other investment advisers. These brokers provide research to institutional and large individual investors for which they are paid by commission on business placed through them. They also provide market access for smaller retail clients, supplying a range of different services: relatively low-cost trading, advice on portfolio allocation, on particular transactions, and on tax issues. Stockbroking is often just one of the activities of a large diversified securities house or investment bank.

Clearing banks

The clearing banks' role in the management of money is very varied. Their key activity is as deposit-taking and loan-making institutions that make their money by borrowing (usually taking deposits, but also using wholesale funds from the money markets) at one rate of interest and lending at a higher one. Building societies operate in a similar way except that they specialise in lending for the purchase of property. But banks differ in that they also provide a range of other financial services, dealing directly with the public over matters from investment advice (both financial and capital) to foreign exchange needs for holidays or business trips abroad.

Banks also 'create' money through what is known as the money multiplier. What happens is that a bank receives a deposit, some of which is kept in liquid form as a safeguard in case the depositor needs it back, with the rest being lent on. The borrower will then spend the money on an item, the seller of which will deposit it in a bank. Again, part of the deposit will be kept liquid with the rest lent on, and so the cycle continues. If it were not for the fact that the banks do not lend all that they receive in deposits, the process would continue indefinitely with the amount of money in the economy, the money supply, ballooning.

In fact, the proportion of their deposits not lent determines how much a given deposit eventually becomes within the whole banking system. If, for example, all banks keep back 10 per cent of their deposits, an initial deposit can expand tenfold: of a £100 deposit, £90 is lent and deposited, of which £81 is lent and deposited, and so on. The eventual total of bank deposits is £1,000.

As a result of the money multiplier, banks are highly geared companies, with a substantial proportion of their capital made up of borrowed funds. Since high gearing implies that small changes can have major effects, it is critical that they lend soundly or a large credit failure by one of their borrowers could have devastating consequences. This is why the monetary authorities attempt to influence, at times by decree, the various ratios (such as cash, liquidity and reserve assets ratios) banks employ to manage their finances. The other reason they do so is to control the expansion of the money supply, one of the most important determinants of inflation and the overall level of economic activity. Alternative means by which this might be done are discussed in the next chapter.

FINANCING INDUSTRY

The provision of funds for industry is the role of the primary markets where new securities are issued on behalf of clients. The aim of the financial institutions that perform this service on behalf of client companies is to attract cash, in the form of either equity or debt finance, from individual and institutional investors, banks and, in some cases, the Euromarkets for new capital investment.

Merchant banks

When a company wants to raise new equity or debt finance, it will usually approach a merchant bank for advice and assistance, and a broker to sponsor the issue. The bank is responsible for advising on the terms of the issue and, in particular, designing its key features. This is one of the most fertile areas for innovation as banks create the new and more exotic financial instruments discussed in chapters 2 and 9. The bank will also arrange the mechanics of the issue, such as the various techniques for making new issues and rights issues discussed in chapter 5.

New issues of equity capital require the publication of a prospectus to satisfy the regulations of the Stock Exchange, which is naturally concerned to protect its reputation and the interests of its investors. The issues also require underwriting by the issuing house, the merchant bank. It must agree to subscribe for any shares not taken up by investors once the offer period has expired. The role of the sponsoring broker, which will be a member of the Stock Exchange, is to ensure that the Exchange's legal requirements are met, to pass on, if necessary, some of the risk of underwriting to sub-underwriters and to distribute the shares into the portfolios of willing investors.

As well as raising new capital, merchant banks will usually be involved on one side or the other of the market for corporate control, advising on strategies. Annually, the *Financial Times* publishes a survey of corporate finance. This ranks merchant bank corporate advisers by the value of their work in three areas: takeover bids, flotation of companies, and issues of shares by companies already with quotations. It is a valuable guide to how well the banks are performing against one another.

Securitisation

Of course, many companies might raise new capital through borrowing directly from a bank in the form of a loan. Nowadays, this has become less common owing to a process known as securitisation. This is the process that enables bank borrowing and lending to be replaced with the issue of some of the debt securities mentioned in chapter 2: commercial bills, bonds, and floating rate notes. It creates attractive new securities for investors, and it has significant benefits for the companies. In particular, bank charges are reduced, and the cost of raising funds may be even less expensive if the markets turn out to be more efficient judges of the creditworthiness of companies than banks. Of course, merchant banks will normally arrange the issue of these debt securities.

Securitisation also refers to the conversion of previously untradeable assets into securities that can be bought and sold. For example, an innovation of the 1980s was the mortgage-backed security. This is produced by converting the assets of a building society, the stream of payments due on its mortgages, into a tradeable security. Closer to the interests of the small investor is the certificate of deposit (CD), a very liquid, almost risk-free asset which pays a relatively low rate of return. It is analogous to an interest-bearing bank account, but it has the advantage that it can be traded; it is effectively a bank account that has been securitised.

MAKING MARKETS

Marketmaking is the central function of financial institutions in the secondary markets where existing securities are traded. The role of the marketmakers is to determine security prices and to ensure that buyers and sellers can trade without having a significant impact on prices. Efficient marketmaking avoids substantial price shifts or undue volatility in response to individual buy or sell orders, providing liquidity and allowing dealing to take place on a large scale. It also ensures that the costs of trading are not too high.

Marketmakers and broker-dealers

The companies or branches of companies that are marketmakers buy and sell securities on their own account, acting as a principal. With the right to trade in this way goes the obligation to make the market. Hence, it is conceivable that at the end of a day's trading a marketmaker will be left with unwanted stocks or an undesirable shortage of stocks. They will therefore always be seeking to find a price that 'balances their books'. Their activities are an important influence on stock price movements.

When quoting prices at which they will buy or sell securities, marketmakers list bid (buying) prices and offer (selling) prices. The difference between the two figures is known as the spread. Since marketmakers naturally aim to profit from their transactions, the bid price is invariably lower than the offer price. This is comparable to a bank that takes deposits (borrows or 'buys' money) at one rate of interest, and loans (sells) it at a higher price. Although the spread for the marketmaker or the rate differential for the bank may seem small, totalled over the huge amount of transactions they make, they are often able to make very considerable profits.

Stockbrokers or, as they are more commonly known nowadays, broker-dealers are companies that act both as an agent for the investor, and as a principal, trading on their own behalf. Such companies face especially difficult conflicts of interest. But for the existence of Chinese walls, their marketmaking arm might be inclined to encourage their broking arm to advise client investors to take on securities the former is keen to unload. Similarly, they may also be inclined to the practice of 'front running', buying promising securities or selling dubious ones ahead of clients, and potentially affecting the price adversely prior to the clients' trades.

Marketmakers and broker-dealers both thrive on activity: the more transactions they make or facilitate, the better their opportunities for profit or commission. Obviously, the benefit of the marketmakers' activity is to enhance market liquidity, but that of the brokers might not be so valuable. Again, there is a conflict of interest: the investor is aiming for return on assets; the broker is aiming partly for this (even if simply to ensure his or her services are retained), but also for commission on trades. The process of making trades frequently just to earn commission rather than for any long-term investment objective is known as churning.

Stock exchanges

The London Stock Exchange is the main securities market in the United Kingdom. This is the market for listed shares and gilts plus debentures, convertibles and warrants. For all of these securities, it is both a primary and secondary market. The second tier of the Stock

Exchange is known as the Unlisted Securities Market (USM). This market was established in 1980 to trade in shares not suitable for the main market. It enables smaller companies to 'come to the market' to raise capital without having to satisfy the more onerous listing and disclosure requirements of the Stock Exchange. The equities listed on both of these markets and the indices that measure their overall performance are the focus of chapters 5 and 6.

The most significant stock exchanges elsewhere in the world are in New York, Tokyo, Frankfurt and Paris. These are explored further in chapter 7. In terms of total market capitalisation, the sum of the 'market cap' (the share price multiplied by the number of shares in issue) of all the securities listed on them, the two that outrank the London Stock Exchange are the New York Stock Exchange and the Tokyo Stock Exchange. The indices that evaluate them (in the United States, the Dow Jones Industrial Average and the Standard and Poor's 500, and in Japan, the Nikkei) are some of the most important indicators of the state of the world's financial markets.

Until quite recently, trading on world stock exchanges was conducted in a physical setting, such as the City of London or Wall Street. The impact of technology has been that there are now fewer actual marketplaces. Instead, much trading is conducted through computer screen-based systems, such as London's Stock Exchange Automated Quotation (SEAQ) system and the National Association of Securities Dealers Automated Quotation system (NASDAQ) in the United States. These electronic trading systems are quote-driven, with marketmakers and dealers quoting bid and offer prices on screen for other traders to select from. This contrasts with the older order-driven system of trading where dealers listed their orders to buy and sell shares with the aim of finding a counterparty wanting to buy or sell that quantity at a price on which both parties could agree.

On top of technological advances, stock markets have also seen considerable deregulation in recent years – an easing of the restrictions on their operating methods. In the United Kingdom, the most notable event of this kind was the Big Bang of 1986. Prior to this deregulation, the two key institutions in the market were jobbers and brokers, each of whom operated in a single capacity. The jobbers were marketmakers who did not deal directly with customers, but only with brokers; the brokers placed their orders only through job-bers, and worked on behalf of customers but never dealt with them for their own account. The system protected investors from abuses of some of the conflicts of interest that arise from the principal/agent relationship, but it had a number of weaknesses.

The main problems of the pre-Big Bang Stock Exchange were that it operated as a cartel with fixed commissions on trades, it limited access to capital and new technology, and it constrained liquidity and the ability to make substantial trades without unduly influencing prices. The radical changes of Big Bang led to far more competition between financial institutions, a significant influx of outside capital as banks bought into the market, and the adoption of the screen-based trading system. Between them, these developments created a much more fluid market with information flowing more freely, liquidity enhanced, more and larger transactions made more feasible, and the costs of doing business, at least for the major players, notably reduced.

Money, currency and derivative markets

The money markets are markets where money and any other liquid assets such as Treasury bills and bills of exchange can be lent and bor-rowed for periods ranging from a few hours to a few months. Their primary function is to enable banks, building societies and companies to manage their cash and other short-term assets and liabilities, the short-term counterparts of the long-term capital markets. The main participants in these markets in the United Kingdom are: the banks, companies that issue short-term debt instruments, money market bro-kers and the discount houses, which act as the marketmakers for most of these assets. Discount houses are discussed in the next chapter.

The foreign exchange markets deal in currencies, for the most part the leading currencies of the developed world: the dollar, the yen, the pound, the Swiss franc and the currencies of the European Monetary System (EMS). The main players are the marketmakers, primarily banks, who buy and sell currencies on their own account and deal with customers and other banks, and brokers who try to find trading counterparties for their clients. This is an over-the-counter market with business transactions conducted almost exclusively through a telephone network. Both the money and currency markets are explored in more detail in chapter 10, while the EMS and its exchange rate mechanism form part of the subject of chapter 14.

The derivatives markets deal in futures and options, and increasingly in more exotic financial instruments such as interest rate and currency swaps. Futures and options originated in the commodities markets, the markets for raw materials and primary products, as a means of protecting against seriously adverse price swings. They are still used today in such markets as the London Metal Exchange and the London Commodity Exchange, but contracts and markets have also now evolved for a range of other securities, debt instruments and indices. In the United Kingdom, the focal point for this activity is the London International Financial Futures and Options Exchange, the LIFFE. There is also a growing market in over-the-counter derivatives, custom-built contracts between very large investors and borrowers usually created by the investment banks. The markets for futures and options other than those traded over-the-counter are discussed in chapter 11, while the commodities markets feature in chapter 12.

MOVING PRICES

Chapter 1 examined how changes in interest rates might affect the prices of equities, bonds and currencies, but what other factors move the prices of individual assets and of whole markets? Obviously, supply and demand are the basic influences for an individual asset, but what are the underlying determinants of these economic forces, and what causes substantial broad market moves? These are questions surrounded in controversy, especially related to the stock market, and it is important to differentiate between various kinds of price movement.

In the stock market, there are essentially three kinds of moves: the long-term trend of the overall market as reflected in various indices; short-term moves around the trend; and the movements of individual shares and sectors. For the most part, individual sectors broadly follow overall market trends, though some may be growth industries, some may be mature or declining industries, or some may simply be the beneficiary or victim of a particular event with ramifications peculiar to that industry (for example, the oil industry and the Gulf War, or the pharmaceutical industry and government plans to alter radically the health-care system). In those cases, sector values can diverge from the market trend.

The price movements of individual stocks are influenced by a range of factors specific to the business. Most of these are explored in chapters 5, 6 and 7, but the more common include company profits, the growth of those profits, dividends and takeover bids. These are the fundamentals of corporate life and fundamental analysis aims to uncover the truths about a company behind the figures to determine whether its shares are over- or underpriced. The way changes in company fundamentals actually cause price movements is not always obvious because of the market's capacity to discount future events. These are news events, the core of the forces that move individual stock prices, but expectations of future news events can be just as powerful.

The fact that prices move on account of expectations of the future, as well as being determined by historic and current knowledge of a company's performance, suggests that they incorporate all known information about the value of shares. This is the foundation of one of the most powerful theories of asset valuation, the efficient market hypothesis. The predictions of this theory are that no one can forecast future price moves consistently and that, over the long-term, without inside information, no one can beat the market. The corollary is that stock prices follow what is called a random walk: at any point in an equity's price history, it is impossible to predict whether its next move will be up or down. Hence, investment strategies based on technical analysis, the study of past price trends or chartism, will not perform dependably.

Market movements

As well as causing individual equity price movements, news about particular companies can also have an impact on the whole market. This is especially the case with blue chip companies, the most highly regarded companies in the market and usually ones with substantial assets, a strong record of growth, and a well-known name. The following extract illustrates their importance:

> ... the FT-SE 100 moved into overdrive when the Hanson acquisition news was announced. ... Traders adopted a much more bullish view of UK equities following the Hanson deal, which it was said transformed the mood of the market. 'Hanson set the tone and moving into the third quarter we expect more support from the institutions,' said a senior marketmaker at a leading UK house. (*Financial Times*, 1 July 1993)

There is much dispute about what causes broad market moves like this. In this case, it is almost certainly a short-term move and these tend to be affected by such intangibles as sentiment, investor psychology and how the market is 'feeling'! Medium-term moves seem to be influenced by supply and demand factors, such as the weight of money moving into or out of stocks.

It is probable that long-term moves depend on fundamental economic and political factors. The market often follows the broad patterns of economic activity, and certainly news about inflation, productivity, growth and the government's fiscal and monetary stance can have major effects on the level of the market. Hence the importance of understanding what the economic indicators mean and how they relate to the markets. These are the subject of the last chapters of this book.

On occasion, stock prices can plummet in a way that appears to bear no relation to fundamentals, supply and demand or even, at least in its early stages, to market sentiment. Such an occasion was Black Monday and the stock market crash of 1987, when prices fell by record amounts in markets throughout the world. Much analysis of this event has been conducted and there is still no agreement on its root causes. Certainly, fundamental economic forces do not appear to have been critical, since most economies continued to grow reasonably well in its aftermath, and the downturn did not come until the very end of the decade. Part of this was due to the prudent economic policies of key governments, which avoided some of the disastrous policy mistakes made after the last major market meltdown, the crash of 1929. The central role of governments in financial markets and economic policy more broadly is the subject of the next chapter.

4

GOVERNMENTS

Lenders/investors and borrowers/companies are the two sides of the interactions that meet in the financial markets, with financial institutions the third party, facilitating these transactions. The government is the fourth player in this picture. It typically acts as both borrower and lender but, in addition, it will frequently intervene, directly, through legislation or by persuasion, to regulate the markets.

Overarching all of these roles, is the government's position as primary economic agent, attempting to monitor and influence the state of the economy. The principal means by which it does this are: fiscal policy, the budgetary balance between public spending and taxation; and monetary policy, essentially control of the money supply and manipulation of interest rates. How these impinge on the financial markets is the subject of this chapter. Further details on the economy feature in the closing chapters of the book.

BALANCING THE BUDGET

Governments spend money on a range of different goods, services, salaries, subsidies, and other payments. These include defence, education, health, public transport, public infrastructure, public housing, the pay of public sector employees, social security, and interest on government borrowings. To help pay for the services this spending provides and, to some extent, to redistribute incomes from the wealthier to the poorer, the government raises money, primarily through taxation. Some taxes are direct, levied on personal and corporate income;

some are indirect, levied on sales, value-added, imports, and certain products such as petrol, cigarettes and alcohol.

The difference between public spending and taxation is known as the budget balance, the budget being the collective term for the government's annual decisions on how its tax and spending plans will be designed and implemented. It might be a balanced budget where revenues equal expenditure, a budget surplus where revenues exceed expenditure, or, most typically for the UK government, a budget deficit, where expenditure exceeds revenues. Net income is known as the public sector debt repayment (PSDR) since the surplus allows repayment of debts from previous years. This was the UK government's position for a brief period a short while ago. More commonly, there is a net outflow, the public sector borrowing requirement or PSBR. The cumulative total of all PSBRs and PSDRs is known as the national debt.

Throughout the 1980s, the UK government had one other source of revenue, namely the receipts from the sale to the public of nationalised industries – the process of privatisation. The influx of cash from 'selling the family silver' had a very positive effect on government finances, and, naturally enough, through the issue of a significant amount of new equities, aroused considerable interest in the financial markets. Many new investors were tempted to participate in the stock market, particularly with its 'stag' opportunities, buying the privatised stocks in the primary market and selling them shortly afterwards at a premium in the secondary market. These matters are examined further in the next chapter.

Fiscal policy

Fiscal policy is used by the government in a variety of ways: to provide services, such as education, health, defence, and infrastructure, that might not be so well provided by the free market; to meet social goals of alleviating poverty and assisting the disadvantaged; to influence the behaviour of individuals and companies, encouraging desirable activities like investment and discouraging undesirable ones like smoking; and to manage the overall level of demand for goods and services in the economy, and hence the degree of economic activity and the rate of inflation. The government goal that may affect financial markets most significantly is that of influencing behaviour. For example, different tax treatment of different categories of assets will influence investment decision-making. Similarly, the tax treatment of corporate earnings will affect a company's dividend policy and its choice between raising capital through debt or equity. More broadly, government spending policy, perhaps in public procurement, might mean increased turnover and profitability for companies in the relevant industries. This might have a positive effect on their share prices. On the other hand, excessive borrowing might drive up the costs of funds for all borrowers, perhaps resulting in a crowding out of private capital investment.

Achievement of the government ambition of demand management is generally attempted through countercyclical policy: the government aims to smooth out the more extreme patterns of the business cycle, damping demand in a boom and boosting it in a recession. This can be done in a boom either through raising taxes or cutting spending; in a recession, it may try lowering taxes or increasing spending. To some extent, there are built-in stabilisers, and this is what is meant by the cyclical effects of the business cycle. For example, in a recession, people are earning and spending less which means that the government's tax revenues fall. Of course, if the budget is already in deficit at that point, the deficit will expand even further. The government's problem then is to decide between raising taxes and cutting spending to ease the deficit or the reverse to help pull the economy out of recession. At such a point, it may turn to monetary policy.

CONTROLLING THE MONEY SUPPLY

In order to finance their frequent budget deficits, and in common with any other individual or organisation that wants to live beyond their means, the government has to borrow in the financial markets. This it does by issuing securities with a range of different maturities, from the short, medium, long and irredeemable gilt-edged stocks traded on the Stock Exchange to three-month Treasury bills issued weekly in the money markets.

The government's agent for the sale of its debt instruments is the Bank of England, often known simply as the Bank. The stocks are first created by the Treasury and then the Bank arranges their sales, purchases and redemptions. New issues replace the ones that have matured in order to meet the government's continuing financing needs and the market's demand for a balance of differently dated stocks. Most are redeemable at some specified date, although a few, such as War Loan and Consols, are irredeemable.

Longer-term government debt takes the form of gilts. These are examined in detail in chapter 9. For the present, it is merely important to distinguish gilts from fixed-interest stocks generally. Not all gilts are fixed-interest, nor are all fixed-interest stocks gilts. For example, some of the corporate debt instruments discussed in chapter 2 are fixed interest while some gilts are index-linked with their interest payments determined by the prevailing rate of inflation.

For a period in the late 1980s, the government's budget surplus meant that there were no new issues of gilts, whether fixed interest or index-linked. However, as the budget returned to deficit, the Bank of England resumed issuing new ones early in 1991. The means by which this is done, the public offering of stocks where a minimum price is set and tenders invited, is most easily illustrated through the way the government's shortest-term debt securities are issued, the Treasury bills.

Treasury bills and open market operations

Treasury bills are bills of exchange, short-term debt instruments issued by the Bank of England on behalf of the UK government. They have a three-month maturity but carry no interest, the total yield being the difference between the purchase and redemption prices. The bills are issued by tender each week to the discount houses in units of between £5,000 and £100,000, and every Monday the *Financial Times* contains a table with details of the tender (see Figure 4.1):

• **Bills on offer, total of applications and total allocated:** the value of the bills on offer is £100 million and the value of the total applications to buy those bills is a measure of market enthusiasm for them.

| 480 | Nil | 10/8 | 79pm | 49pm | Utd. Newsapapers .... | 62pm | +13 |
| 148 | Nil | 13/8 | 20pm | 11pm | Wimpey (G) .... | 11½pm | -2½ |

For notes on symbols refer to The Guide to The London Share Service.

BANK OF ENGLAND TREASURY BILL TENDER

	Jul 9	Jul 2		Jul 9	Jul 2
Bills on offer	£100m	£100m	Top accepted rate of discount	5.1541%	5.1541%
Total of applications	£405m	£394m	Average rate of discount	5.1496%	5.1541%
Total allocated	£100m	£100m	Average yield	5.2166%	5.2212%
Minimum accepted bid	£98.715	£98.715	Amount on offer at next tender	£100m	£100m
Allotment at minimum level	68%	95%	Minimum accepted bid 182 days	£97.360	£97.360

Fig. 4.1 Bank Treasury bill tender

In this example, the later tender was more oversubscribed than the earlier one. Since there is almost invariably oversubscription, naturally the total allocated is the same as that offered.

- **Minimum accepted bid and allotment at minimum level:** the former is the lowest bid price accepted, in these cases £98,715 for every bill with a face value of £100,000. The bid is lower than the redemption price so that the purchaser can make money on the difference. The allotment is simply the proportion of the bills sold at the minimum price; the rest would have been sold for higher prices (lower discounts).

- **Rates of discount and yield:** the top accepted discount rate is the other side of the minimum accepted bid, with the average rate calculating in the discount on the bills sold for higher prices. The discount rates do not correspond exactly to the actual discount since they are presented as annual rates even though the bills mature in three months. Loosely speaking, these are the rates a buyer would earn for purchasing four consecutive bills. The discount rate is calculated as the difference between the purchase and redemption prices as a percentage of the latter. In contrast, the yield is the difference as a percentage of the former. Thus, it corresponds to any other current yield, that is, annual return divided by current market price.

The discount houses have a special relationship with the Bank of England that is central to the implementation of the government's monetary policy. First of all, they act as marketmakers in the money markets and, as such, they are obliged to cover the amount of bills on offer in a Treasury bill tender as well as having a bid price for other bills of exchange and certificates of deposit. These then are their assets; their liabilities are deposits by banks of what is known as call money. This is money borrowed at interest rates lower than the discount houses earn on bills (again, as marketmakers, they are obliged to take the deposits), but which can be withdrawn at very short notice.

Discount houses can take on these obligations because the Bank stands behind them as the 'lender of last resort'. If they run short of funds, either because banks have withdrawn money or because they have been obliged to purchase other money market instruments, perhaps the weekly Treasury bill tender, they can go to the Bank. Every day the Bank estimates the market's fund shortage and usually meets it by buying bills from the discount houses. In doing this they are injecting funds into the whole financial system; if instead they sell bills, they are withdrawing funds – effectively mopping up surplus money. This is known as open market operations and is one of the means by which the government controls the money supply.

Interest rates and monetary control

The extension of this control is how the Bank of England manipulates the level of interest rates. Since it deals actively in the bill markets through open market operations, it is in a position to create a shortage of cash when it wishes to. In that case, the discount houses are obliged to borrow, and as the lender of last resort, the level at which the Bank provides funds is an indication of the level of short-term rates of which it approves. These rates can then be used to influence rates across the whole economy.

As the previous three chapters make clear, the rate of interest, that is, the price of money, is one of the most powerful forces in the financial markets. Under the relatively free market approach of recent UK governments, interest rates have been allowed, for the most part, to be determined by market forces with the Bank's guidance. But, with this system, the Bank has to be careful to give only very subtle indications of where it wants rates to go: if it alerts the market to its intentions, the force of expectations will have immediate ramifications throughout the economy as traders discount the future.

An alternative method of controlling the money supply is using direct controls on bank lending, aiming to limit money multiplier effects. This might be achieved by changing banks' reserve asset ratios, that is, the proportions they keep liquid from any given deposit, by imposing limits on total bank lending or consumer credit, or simply by persuading bankers to restrict their lending. A further technique, which has been popular in the United Kingdom since the late 1970s, is setting targets for monetary growth. The current target in the United Kingdom is the monetary base: this consists of cash in circulation plus banks' deposits at the Bank of England. To date, this appears to have been reasonably effective in restraining inflation, the primary goal of monetary policy.

The last way in which the Bank of England acts in the financial markets is with foreign exchange where it may intervene to try to raise or lower the value of sterling. This again can be done through short-term interest rates: usually raising them attracts investors into buying sterling, while lowering encourages selling. The Bank might also work on the currency by using its official reserves of foreign currencies to buy pounds and, through the weight of its intervention, push up its value or at least hold it steady. But, nowadays, with the vast speculative volume of transactions in the foreign exchange markets, a successful intervention may need international cooperation. A government acting alone is no longer able to manage the financial markets or its national economy.

Part II

INTERPRETING THE MARKETS

5

STOCKS AND SHARES
The UK equity markets

An equity is a stake in a company, a risk-sharing ownership of a part of a company's capital. The buyer of a share receives the rights to a probable flow of income in the form of dividends (which vary with the profitability of the company) and a potential capital gain.

The UK equity markets trade stocks across a wide spectrum of companies, ranging from established blue-chip equities to higher risk stocks.

The *Financial Times*' coverage of UK equities, the shares in British companies that have a stock market quotation, consists of four main interlocking components:

- A daily report of the most interesting trading features in the stock market.
- The share prices of individual companies and various financial ratios based on those prices.
- Detailed reports and comment in the news pages of the paper on events in company life.
- A number of stock market indices which chart the overall progress of equity share prices.

UK company news was explored in chapter 2 while indices are the subject of the next chapter. This chapter focuses on FT reporting on the market for UK equities, as reflected in its stock market reports and the London share service.

FT coverage of the UK equities market begins with reports on the London Stock Exchange on the back page of the second section. This is headed with an overview of the movements in the stock market indices of the previous day and possible reasons for them, as well as highlights of individual sectors that have moved significantly or individual shares that have been particularly prominent in trading. It also examines the main share price movements of the day in individual stocks, and suggests reasons for them. Particularly important movements are explored in separate stories further down the page.

THE LONDON SHARE SERVICE

This is the most complete record of UK stock market statistics readily available to the public and covers around 3,000 shares. That is practically all of those actively traded in the London stock market, together with gilt-edged stocks, already mentioned in chapter 4 and discussed in more detail in chapter 9.

The London share service is divided into various geographical and industrial classifications, derived from the groupings used in the FT-Actuaries All-Share Index discussed in detail in the next chapter. Categorisation in this way allows easy comparison of companies within the same industrial sector.

The share service covers not only companies that have a full stock market listing, but also those quoted on the Unlisted Securities Market (USM). The USM has less onerous listing requirements than the main market and is designed to encourage smaller, fast-growing businesses to seek a quotation. Generally, there is less trading in USM stock, and hence shares may be less easy to buy and sell. In addition, the service incorporates many non-UK companies whose shares are traded in London, and a number of UK companies traded under Stock Exchange Rule 535(2).

The standard version of the share service is published on Tuesday to Saturday, just before the back page of the second section of the newspaper. Figure 5.1 is a sample industrial category from the daily London share service, annotated with brief explanations of price, price change and 1993 high and low, market capitalisation, yield and price/earnings ratio.

Market price

Name and notes

Market capitalisation

Gross dividend yield

Price/earnings ratio

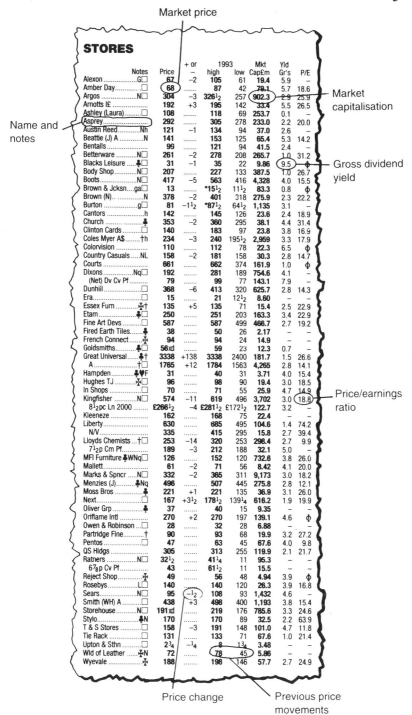

Price change

Previous price movements

Fig. 5.1 Daily London share service – Stores

READING THE FIGURES

- **Name and notes:** the first column lists the company name or its abbreviation, plus various symbols representing particular features of its shares. For example, a square indicates the most actively traded shares, including those UK stocks where transactions and prices are published continuously through the Stock Exchange Automated Quotation (SEAQ) system. A Maltese cross indicates shares traded on the USM. A heart symbol indicates a stock not officially listed in the UK, for example many shares of overseas mining companies.

- **Market price:** the second column shows the average (or mid-price) of the best buying and selling prices (in pence) quoted by market-makers at the 4.30pm close of the market on the previous trading day. Most prices are obtained from the Stock Exchange throughout the day via a direct computer link with the last transmission of data taking place at 4:45pm. If trading in a share has been suspended, perhaps because the company in question is involved in takeover negotiations, the figure shown is the price at suspension and this is indicated by a symbol. The letters 'xd' following a price mean ex-dividend, and indicate that a dividend has been announced recently but that buyers of the shares will not be entitled to receive it.

- **Price change (plus or minus):** the third column gives the change in the closing price compared with the end of the previous trading day.

- **Previous price movements:** the fourth and fifth columns show the highest and lowest prices recorded for the stock during the current year.

- **Market capitalisation:** the sixth column is an indication of the stock market valuation of the company in millions of pounds sterling. It is calculated by multiplying the number of shares by their market price. In order to calculate the number of shares in issue from the figures listed here, the market capitalisation figure can be divided by the market price. If there are other classes of share capital in issue, their value would need to be added in order to calculate the company's total market capitalisation.

- **Gross dividend yield:** the seventh column shows the percentage return on the share before income tax is deducted at the rate of 20 per cent. It is calculated by dividing the gross dividend by the current share price.

- **Price/earnings (p/e) ratio:** the final column is the market price of the share divided by the company's earnings (profits) per share in its latest twelve-month trading period. Yields and p/e ratios move in opposite directions: if the share price rises, since the gross dividend remains the same, the dividend yield falls; at the same time, since the earnings per share is constant, the p/e ratio increases.

USING THE INFORMATION

The first indicator to look at in a share is its price. This is a reflection of the discounted value of future dividend payments plus a premium for the risk that the company may not pay dividends in the future and/or go under. On its own, though, it conveys minimal information since it needs to be seen in the context of its history and possible future.

The figures for high and low provide some of the historical perspective on the share price. If, for example, the present price is a long way below its high point for the year, and performing against the market trend, the indications are that the market is expecting trouble. The reverse is true in the case of a share that is pushing up strongly to new points when the market or its sector is not. The difference between the high and low also gives an indication of the price volatility of the stock.

The prices quoted are mid-prices between the bid or buying price and the offer or selling price at which marketmakers will trade. The difference between bid and offer is known as the spread, and it represents marketmakers' profit on any given transaction, a reward for taking the risk of making the market. The implication of this spread is that investors will only be able to buy at a higher price and sell at a lower price than that printed in the newspaper. Of course, since the share service is in effect merely a historical record of prices the previous day, actual prices subsequently may be very different.

Market capitalisation is a measure of the size of a company. Since the total value of a company's shares will rise and fall according to its financial results, it is a good guide to performance over time. It also has other advantages over alternative yardsticks of size: it gives a proper weighting to banks and commodity groups which get distorted in lists based on turnover; and it takes account of loss-making companies which disappear from lists based on profits.

Dividends depend on profits which in turn depend on the quality of a company's management and the state of the economy. The dividend yield, though, since it is partly determined by the current share price, is a reflection of the way that the market values a share. If the company is thought to have a high growth rate and a secure business, then its current dividend yield will probably be relatively low, since the scope for increasing dividends in the future ought to be above average. Sales will be expanding, earnings growing, and often investment in new products and new capital goods will be substantial.

If, by contrast, the company is involved in a mature or dying industry or is exposed to high levels of business or political risk, its dividend yield will normally be high. Thus, the yield on a share can be a valuable indicator when an investor is deciding between income and capital growth from an investment. For example, a growth stock, perhaps in high-technology industries, suggests a preference for capital appreciation, while a share in a company in a mature industry like textiles would indicate a desire for income.

Of course, as seen in chapter 2, the dividend is, to some degree, an arbitrary figure, decided at the whim of the company. Hence the figure for yield is not always a good indicator of the value of a share. Price/earnings ratios are generally better since they are independent of possibly arbitrary corporate decisions.

Price/earnings ratios are the most commonly used tool of stock market analysis. In general, the higher a company's ratio, the more highly rated it is by the market: investors expect the relative expense of the company's shares to be compensated for by higher than average earnings over the next few years. But high ratios can also mean that the market is expecting a poorly performing company to be on the receiving end of a takeover bid, with the predator being prepared to pay a premium for control.

High price/earnings ratios are usually associated with low yields, and certainly they move in opposite directions. Thus, a high ratio suggests a growth stock, and is, like a low yield, an indicator of an investment where capital growth might be more important than income.

Investors can use price/earnings ratios to gauge whether one company's share price is too high or too low compared with competitors with similar products and earnings performance, compared with the market as a whole, or compared with past ratios. But, since the methods of calculating the ratios can give significantly different results, the investor's prime concern should be to use ratios that are consistent (that is, from the same source) when making comparisons.

It is also important to be aware of the difference between the historic ratios in the FT and what the market's expectations are for the future, expressed more through forecasts of prospective price/earnings ratios. In addition, there is a distinction between nil and net ratios: the former ignores the distribution of dividends. Reports on companies might also distinguish historic and prospective yields.

Evaluating weekly performance

Monday's edition of the *Financial Times* brings some important changes to the share information service, concentrating on changes that do not take place daily. Figure 5.2 shows an example. The special weekly columns provide information on the following:

- **Price change:** the weekly percentage change in the price of the stock.

- **Net dividend:** the after-tax dividends paid in the company's last full financial year. A double dagger sign shows that the interim dividend has been cut in the current financial year, while a single dagger indicates an increased interim dividend.

- **Dividend cover:** the ratio of profits to dividends, calculated by dividing the earnings per share by the gross dividend per share. This indicates how many times a company's dividend to ordinary shareholders could be paid out of its net profits. Another way of looking at dividend cover is as a percentage of profits: this is the way it is done in the United States where it is known as the payout ratio.

	Notes	Price	W'k% ch'nge	Div net	Div cov.	Dividends paid	Last xd	City line
Alexon	G□	73	......	3.0	–	Jan	16.11	1565
Amber Day	□	68	4.6	3.1	1.2	Jul Dec	24.5	1582
Argos	N□	304	–1.6	7.0	1.7	Nov May	29.3	1411
Arnotts I£		187	–1.1	Q10%	0.9	Jun Dec	11.5	1357
Ashley (Laura)	□	108	–1.8	0.1	–	Jul	7.6	1664
Asprey	✠	293	1.7	5.1	φ	Jan Aug	14.12	1671
Austin Reed	Nh	122	–1.6	2.5	0.6	Jul Dec	10.5	3798
Beattie (J) A	N	141	–1.4	6.0	1.7	Nov Jul	10.5	1784
Bentalls		99	......	1.9	–	Jun Nov	10.5	1808
Betterware	N□	269	5.9	2.0	4.2	Jul Jan	7.6	4536
Blacks Leisure	♣□	34	......	2.25	φ	Feb Oct	14.12	1846
Body Shop	N□	197	2.6	1.7	4.6	Jul Jan	7.6	1864
Boots	N□	425	–2.1	13.4	2.0	Feb Mar	29.3	1876
Brown & Jcksn	ga□	12¾	–3.8	0.08	φ	Jul	24.5	1984
Brown (N)	N	380	–1.6	7.0	2.4	Jan Jul	7.6	1985
Burton	g□	83½	–2.9	2.0	0.3	Feb Jul	21.6	2020
Cantors	h	142	......	2.67	2.1	Apr Nov	15.3	2056
Church	♣	355	......	12.5	0.9	May Oct	29.3	2136
Clinton Cards	□	140	–2.1	4.25	2.0	Nov May	19.4	4978
Coles Myer A$	†h	236	9.3	Q17.3c	1.7	Dec Jun	1.6	2183
Colorvision	‡a	111	13.3	5.4	1.1	Mar Sep	1.2	2192
Country Casuals	NL	161	–2.4	3.5	2.8	Dec Jul	24.5	2566
Courts		661	0.5	5.5	φ	Apr Oct	1.2	2257
Dixons	Nq□	200	–5.7	6.2	–	Mar Oct	18.1	2355
(Net) Dv Cv Pf		80	–1.8	5.0	–	Jan Jul	7.3	2356
Dunhill	□	383	–.5	8.15	2.8	Jan Jul	21.6	2386
Era	□	15	–6.3	–	–	–	11'89	2491
Essex Furn	✠†	118	......	2.75	2.1	Apr Nov	29.3	5313
Etam	♣□	250	......	6.9	1.6	Jan Jul	24.5	2499
Fine Art Devs	□	584	1.2	12.75	2.4	Jan Jul	24.5	2563
Fired Earth Tiles	♣	38	......	–	–	–	3'92	2207
French Connect	✠	90	1.1	–	–	–	5'92	2633
Goldsmiths	♣□	56xd	–3.4	0.3	–	Aug	5.7	3676

Fig. 5.2 Monday's London share service – Stores

- **Dividend paid:** the months in which the dividends are actually paid, usually either twice or four times a year.

- **Ex-dividend date:** the last date on which a share went ex-dividend, expressed as a day and month unless a dividend has not been paid for some time in which case the date may be a month and year. On and after this date, the rights to the last announced dividend remain with the seller of the stock.

- **Cityline:** the FT Cityline code by which real-time share prices are available over the telephone by calling 0336 43 or 0891 43 plus the four digit code for any given share. This telephone information service is designed primarily for investors wanting to keep track of their own investments, or the activity of the UK and world stock markets at any point during the day or night.

The key information from this listing is the figure for dividend cover. This indicates how safe the dividend is from future cuts. The higher the figure, the better able the company will be to maintain its dividend if profits fall. Even at a time of losses, a company may decide to pay dividends out of its reserves, though this clearly could not continue indefinitely.

A relatively high dividend cover might also reflect a commitment to investment and growth, implying a substantial retention of earnings to be ploughed back into the business. On the other hand, if the dividend cover is too high, the shareholders may complain that the company should increase its payout.

Fig. 5.3 London Stock Exchange: dealings

Other share dealings

On Saturday, the FT expands its share price coverage to cover dealings in securities which are not included in the standard FT share information service (see Figure 5.3). It covers many fixed interest securities issued by companies, as well as dealings in some smaller company shares and those traded under Stock Exchange rules on securities incorporated in the United Kingdom and Ireland but not listed on any exchange, and securities where the principal market is outside the British Isles. The actual selection is variable according to whether a stock has been traded during the five days ending each Thursday. If it has not been traded it will generally not be included. Information is provided on:

- **Name and stock type:** chapter 2 detailed some of the different forms of corporate finance available, and these securities provide a number of examples. Marks and Spencer's 10 per cent cumulative preference shares with a par value of £1, for instance, are shares that pay a fixed dividend, 10p. The payment can be suspended in the event of losses, but when the company returns to profit, all dividends in arrears are guaranteed to be paid ahead of dividends on ordinary shares.

- **Prices:** these are reproduced from Thursday's Stock Exchange official list. They show the prices at which business was done in the 24 hours up to 4.30pm on the previous Thursday. For shares where no business was recorded during that period, the latest recorded business in the previous four days is listed with the relevant date.

Trading volume

The back page of the FT's second section includes a useful reference table with the trading volume and basic price information for a selection of the largest capitalised and most active stocks (see Figure 5.4). The information includes:

- **Volume, price and change:** the daily trading volume for these stocks (including all of the constituents of the FT-SE 100 index which are discussed in detail in the next chapter) plus the day's closing price and change on the previous trading day. Trading volume figures count both the buying and the selling of a particular share, so that the number of shares actually changing hands is really half of the total.

TRADING VOLUME IN MAJOR STOCKS

	Volume 000's	Closing Price	Day's change		Volume 000's	Closing Price	Day's change		Volume 000's	Closing Price	Day's change		Volume 000's	Closing Price	Day's change
ASDA Group†	2,200	61¾	-½	De La Rue†	2,100	641	-1	MB Caradon†	347	279	-1	Siebe†	659	480	-3
Abbey National†	22,000	409	-5	Dixons	1,300	192		MEPC	225	440	+6	Slough Ests	1,200	225	+7
Albert Fisher	940	63		Eastern Elect.	1,600	490	-6	MFI	1,700	126		Smith (W.H.) A	2,200	438	+3
Allied–Lyons†	2,600	540	+3	East Midland Elect.	1,500	465	-9	Manweb	297	535	-9	Smith & Nephew†	2,700	143½	+1
Anglian Water†	769	491	+1	Eng China Clays	679	414	-9	Marks & Spencer†	3,700	332	-2	SmKl Beecham†	1,100	424	
Argos	277	304	-3	Enterprise Oil†	1,500	449	+2	Midlands Elect.	761	511	-3	SmKl Beecham Uts.†	1,200	376	+2
Argyll Group†	7,200	307	-3	Eurotunnel Units	289	406	+3	Morrison (Wm.)	1,100	134	-6	Smiths Inds.	1,000	364	-3
Arjo Wiggins†	2,100	168		FKI	1,500	139	+1	NFC†	620	244		Southern Elect.	693	491	-8
Ass. Brit. Foods†	59	.467	-3	Fisons	1,300	177	+1	NatWest Bank†	4,400	497	+5	South Wales Elect.	371	552	-7
Ass. Brit. Ports	123	409	+5	Foreign & Col. I.T.	646	231		National Power†	4,800	349	-9	South West Water	470	520	+1
BAA†	3,800	727	+10	Forte†	3,700	220	-1½	Next	2,300	167	+3½	South West. Elect.	661	501	-7
BAT Inds.†	9,400	418	+2	Gen. Accident†	922	624	+2	North West Water†	502	478		Southern Water	302	488	-2
BET	3,500	117	+1½	General Elect.†	3,600	320	+4½	Northern Elect.	567	530	-9	Standard Chartd.†	974	827	+23
BICC	328	401		Glaxo†	3,500	553	-3	Northern Foods†	2,700	253	-2	Storehouse	1,800	191	
BOC†	2,100	646	-8	Glynwed Int.	3,600	296		Norweb	38	516	-7	Sun Alliance†	437	372	-1
BP†	3,600	298½	-½	Granada†	1,500	407	-3	Pearson†	1,900	442	-18	T&N	1,400	186	-1
BPB Inds.	865	217	+2	Grand Met.†	7,600	409	-6	P & O†	1,700	618	-2	TI Group†	340	332	-8
BT†	4,500	410½		GUS A†	438	1765	+12	Pilkington	2,000	132	+2	TSB†	1,500	195	-1
BTR†	2,500	363	+2	GRE†	3,800	202		PowerGen†	4,100	371	-10	Tarmac	789	131	-½
Bank of Scotland†	5,200	158	+3½	GKN	914	455	+3	Prudential†	5,500	342	+3	Tate & Lyle†	1,300	385	-5
Barclays†	4,100	485	+4	Guinness†	2,500	454	-13	RMC†	265	754	+4	Taylor Woodrow	1,100	106	+6
Bass†	2,200	464	+4	HSBC (75p shs)†	1,000	656	-3	RTZ†	2,700	670	-10	Tesco†	7,700	201½	-5½
Blue Circle†	1,000	244	+2	Hammerson 'A'	18	307	+2	Racal	869	217		Thames Water†	1,200	489	-1
Booker	2,000	398	-8	Hanson†	4,900	237		Rank Org.†	1,600	767	+8	Thorn EMI†	560	905	-1
Boots†	2,300	417	-5	Hanson Warrants	571	25		Reckitt & Colman†	1,300	551	-20	Tomkins†	3,900	221	+2
Bowater†	1,200	450	-3	Harrisons Crosfield	597	182		Redland†	179	468	-1	Trafalgar House	693	101	
Brit. Aerospace†	2,500	420	-7	Hillsdown	549	142		Reed Intl.†	1,700	653	-12	Unigate	314	347	-3
British Airways†	2,800	304		IMI	289	273	+1	Rentokil†	1,300	203	+5	Unilever†	7,400	953	-24
British Gas†	4,300	290½	-½	ICI†	1,400	642	-3	Reuters†	1,900	1394	-6	United Biscuits†	2,300	370	+3
British Land	842	341	+4	Inchcape†	2,400	543	+1	Rolls Royce	979	141	-3	Utd. Newspapers	693	516	-5
British Steel†	10,000	100	+3½	Johnson Matthey	247	456	+1	Rothmans†	434	669	+7	Vodafone†	602	440	+1
Bunzl	402	128		Kingfisher†	3,800	574	-11	Ryl Bk Scotland†	2,400	290	+3	Warburg (SG)†	523	740	+6
Burmah Castrol†	613	713		Kwik Save	482	684	-8	Royal Insurance†	1,700	321	+2	Wellcome†	1,600	654	+2
Burton	7,700	81	-1½	Ladbroke†	3,000	188	+2	Saatchi	100	162	-1	Welsh Water	557	553	-7
Cable & Wire.†	2,300	770	+7	Land Securities†	1,100	598	+12	Sainsbury†	2,300	431	-5	Wessex Water	64	580	
Cadbury Schweppes†	3,400	439	-9	Laporte	3,200	609	-2	Scottish & New.†	874	464	+2	Whitbread 'A'†	3,000	479	
Calor Group	333	238		Legal & General†	380	503	+3	Scot. Hydro-Elect.†	500	336	-3½	Williams Hldgs.†	1,200	320	+2

Fig. 5.4 Trading volume in major stocks

Trading volume is an indication of the liquidity of a stock. The higher the figure, the easier it will be to buy or sell significant quantities of a stock without having a major impact on its price.

Rises and falls, highs and lows

The newspaper also carries two other lists for quick reference on share price movements. First, there is a list of rises and falls for broad share categories (see Figure 5.5):

- **Rises and falls:** the daily version of this table shows how many securities rose, fell and stayed at the same price level during the

RISES AND FALLS YESTERDAY

	On Friday			On the week		
	Rises	Falls	Same	Rises	Falls	Same
British Funds...............................	21	48	10	117	192	86
Other Fixed Interest.....................	0	3	12	15	14	46
Commercial, Industrial.................	270	301	842	1,213	1,446	4,398
Financial & Property....................	145	128	529	654	681	2,664
Oil & Gas....................................	29	12	42	97	85	233
Plantations.................................	1	0	7	4	1	35
Mines...	61	20	55	137	223	324
Others..	47	47	55	168	267	297
Totals	574	559	1,552	2,405	2,909	8,083

Fig. 5.5 Rises and falls yesterday

previous trading session. It is broken down into eight different categories of security and shows how movements in the main share price indices were reflected in trading across various broad market subdivisions. Saturday's version, reproduced here, also lists rises and falls on the week as a whole.

The second list covers individual stocks that have recorded new highs and lows for the year (see Figure 5.6):

NEW HIGHS AND LOWS FOR 1993

NEW HIGHS (136).
BRITISH FUNDS (35) OTHER FIXED INTEREST (10) CANADIANS (1) Toronto-Dom., BANKS (6) ANZ, Bk. Leumi, Bk. Scotland, Natl. Australia, NatWest, Standard Chrtd., BREWERS (1) Bulmer (HP), BLDG MATLS (1) Heywood Williams, BUSINESS SERVS (1) Porvair, ELECTRICALS (2) Ericsson, Motorola, ELECTRICITY (1) Midlands, ELECTRONICS (3) Elect'comps., Electron Hse., Scantronic, ENG GEN (3) Dyson (J & J), Do A, Kvaerner, FOOD MANUF (1) Avonmore, HOTELS & LEIS (2) Friendly Htls., Prism, INSCE BROKERS (1) Lowndes Lambert, INSCE COMPOSITE (1) GRE, INSCE LIFE (1) Legal & Genral, INV

- **Highs and lows:** this table shows which shares have on the previous trading day reached new high or low points for the year. If space is limited, only the number of shares in each sector is listed and not their names.

This list helps to highlight companies that are moving against the trend of their sector. Warnings signs would

NEW LOWS (29).
BRITISH FUNDS (1) Treas. 8½pc '94, AMERICANS (1) Woolworth, BANKS (1) Espirito Santo, BUSINESS SERVS (2) Holmes Prctn., RCO, CHEMS (2) BOC, Caird, CONTG & CONSTRCN (1) EBC, ENG GEN (1) Barry Wehmiller, FOOD MANUF (4) BSN, Cranswick,

Fig. 5.6 New highs and lows for 1993

start to flash if a company featured repeatedly in the 'new lows' section when the sector as a whole was not moving in this direction. The list can be used in conjunction with the listing of rises and falls to compare individual share price movements with overall market sector moves.

Highlights

Saturday's newspaper features a table of highlights of the week in share price movements. This summarises the chief price changes of the week in the shares of fairly large companies, and adds a brief suggestion of the reasons for the moves (see Figure 5.7):

HIGHLIGHTS OF THE WEEK					
	Price y'day	Change on week	1993 High	1993 Low	
FT-SE 100 Index	2827.7	-5.3	2957.3	2737.6	UK political uncertainty
FT-SE Mid 250 Index	3202.9	-14.6	3241.7	2876.3	Profit-taking in second liners
Anglia TV	331	+17	357	194	Favourite in firm sector
Argyll	291	-17	407	287	Downgrades after cautious agm
BOC	660	+20	770	635	Hoare Govett upgrades
BT	416½	+8	445½	376	Positive sentiment from BT3
Britannic Assurance	435	-33	498	359½	Commission disclosure worries.
British Aerospace	404	-15	429	165	Taiwan funding worries.
Bullough	111	-9	120	91	Fall in figures.
Burton	71	-10½	87½	64½	Kleinwort Benson downgrades
Campari Intl.	138	+25	292	110	Recovery buying in tight market
GEC	336	+17½	343	264	Brokers rec. big buy order.
Norweb	535	+25	544	439	Switching into defensive utilities
Stakis	56	+5	57	34½	Hoare Govett positive/analysts visit
VSEL	903	+55	915	513	Squeeze, solid buying.

Fig. 5.7 Highlights of the week

- **Price, change and high and low:** an overview of the week's movements and how they compare with prices in the rest of the year to date.

- **Explanation:** in this example, the upward and downward moves are put down to a number of different factors, including economic news, positive or negative company news, shifts in market sentiment, and public evaluations by financial institutions.

ISSUING NEW SECURITIES

The *Financial Times* provides detailed information on the secondary market for company securities. But the exchanges also have a vital role as a primary market, providing new long-term capital for investment through the offering of new issues. These might be for companies entering their shares on the market for the first time or for companies already listed but requiring further capital. In each case, the FT offers extensive coverage.

There are three daily published tables for new securities: equities (ordinary shares issued by newly floated companies); fixed interest stocks (corporate bonds, such as convertible preference shares that yield a fixed rate of interest now and can be converted into ordinary shares at a later date); and rights offers (trading in the rights to issues of new shares in existing companies to which current shareholders are given the first right of refusal). In addition, Saturday's FT carries one list of forthcoming rights issues, and another of new companies coming to the market through what are known as offers for sale, placings and introductions (see Figure 5.8).

OFFERS FOR SALE, PLACINGS & INTRODUCTIONS

Britton Group is to raise £19.7m via a placing & intermediaries offer.
CrestaCare is to raise £33.3m via a placing at 40p.
Quadramatic is to join the main market via a placing & intermediaries offer which will raise £20m.
Second HGSC Index Inv Tst is to raise £25.1m via a placing & open offer.
Select Appointments is to raise £9m via an open offer of 9m cumulative redeemable preference shares.
Stratagem is to raise £7.9m via a placing & offer.
Select Appointments is to raise £9m via an open offer of 9m cumulative redeemable preference shares.
Stratagem is to raise £7.9m via a placing & offer.

Fig. 5.8 Offers for sale, placings and introductions

Launching companies

Companies can raise money by selling some of their shares to investors before getting them quoted on the stock market. Shares may be being sold by original owners/existing shareholders or by the company to raise new capital: so sometimes the money goes into the business, sometimes to the existing shareholder.

There are three ways of floating shares on the market:

- **Offers for sale:** these are shares offered to the public through advertising and the issue of prospectuses and application forms. The most notable form in the 1980s has been the privatisation issues, especially British Gas and British Telecom. These are the kinds of new issue likely to be of most interest to the small, private investor.

- **Placings:** private sales of shares to a range of investors through a broker. The broker will typically go first to its clients, and subsequently shares may be available to a wider public through the stock market. This is a popular way for smaller companies to come to market, often through the Unlisted Securities Market (USM), and companies may combine a placing with an open offer for sale.

- **Introductions:** these take place when there is already a number of shareholders, and the company is simply seeking permission for the shares to trade on the market. Such issues do not raise new capital, but might allow a company to move up from the USM to the main market, or a foreign company to trade in London as well as in its home market.

Offers for sale are the most prominent form of new issue. They can come in two forms. In the first, the company offers the public a fixed number of shares at a fixed price. The price is set by the sponsors of the issue, usually a merchant bank, based on forecasts of likely future profits. The sponsor will have two conflicting objectives in mind: a low enough price to ensure that the shares trade well in the secondary or aftermarket; and a high enough price for the client raising the money.

Since fixed price offers for sale often underprice the issue, they provide a good opportunity for stags. These are investors who buy in anticipation of an immediate price rise, and a quick profit right away. Prices often rise well above the sale price when dealings start, and the potential premiums encourage speculators seeking to benefit from the mistakes made by the issuers.

The alternative, and the way to avoid excessive stagging, is the tender offer. In this case, no price is set in advance but, instead, the price is determined by what investors are prepared to pay. Investors are invited to bid for shares and, if the issue is fully subscribed, the price will generally be set at a little below one at which all available shares can be sold. For example:

> The SG Warburg machinery clicking into place for the worldwide sale of the UK government's remaining 22 per cent stake in British Telecommunications, is highly computerised. ... Today, SG Warburg, coordinator for the third and last stage of the government's sale, launches the US-style 'bookbuilding' operation to collect investors' bids for the shares and help establish the selling price. (*Financial Times*, 8 July 1993)

With either the fixed price or tender offer, the shares might be oversubscribed, and a decision needs to be made on the appropriate allocation of shares. This might be done by ballot, by scaling down certain over-large applications, or by giving preferential treatment to certain investors, usually small, private ones. Alternatively, an issue might be undersubscribed, and this is why new issues are underwritten by big investors who guarantee to buy any unwanted shares. If underwriting is needed, shares will overhang the market as underwriters wait to sell when the price is rising. A result of this is that the share price will tend to stay flat until the majority of the shares are in firm hands, the portfolios of investors who want to hold them.

The timetable for a new issue is usually fairly standard: an early announcement is made without information on the intended share price, prospective yield and price/earnings ratio. This is followed by the publication of the full prospectus, incorporating price and yield details and with a cut-off date for applications and a date on which decisions on the allotment will be made. The Stock Exchange then decides on a date on which official dealings begin.

Because of the size of the issues and the desire to appeal to first-time investors in the markets, the privatisation issues follow a rather longer schedule. In the case of BT3, the third British Telecom offer, for example, the government and SG Warburg, the global coordinator of the issue, were keen to ensure that such a significant launch should not have a deleterious effect on the whole market, and that downward pressure on the issue price should be resisted with 'stabilising' buying by the underwriters. The FT has a special table listing information on shares in newly floated companies (see Figure 5.9):

- **Issue price:** the price at which the security was issued.

LONDON RECENT ISSUES

EQUITIES

Issue Price	Am'nt Paid up	Latest Renunc Date	1993 High	1993 Low	Stock	Closing Price	+or -	Net Div	Times Cov'd	Gross Yield	P/E Ratio
100	F.P.	–	107	78	Anagen	79	–	–	–	–	–
339	F.P.	–	356	356	Baring Chrysalis C	356		–	–	–	–
$10	F.P.	–	679	679	Baring Emrg Mkts	679		–	–	–	–
†150	P.P.	–	173	150	British Telecom (P/Paid)	172	+$\frac{1}{2}$	N15.6	1.4	4.5	20.4
120	F.P.	–	148	131	Business Post	143	–3	L2.9	2.5	2.5	20.0
148	F.P.	–	171	148	Carpetright	166	+1	W3.89	1.7	2.9	24.4
100	F.P.	–	117	99	Celsis Intl.	101		–	–	–	–
225	F.P.	–	210	184	Court Cavendish	197	+1	W3.6	2.8	2.3	†3.3
–	F.P.	–	16$\frac{1}{2}$	7	Creston Warrants	7		–	–	–	–
170	F.P.	–	200	191	Devro Intl	194	+1	W5.5	1.9	3.5	18.4
–	F.P.	–	100	97	Eaglet Inv Trust	97		–	–	–	–
–	F.P.	–	37	33	Do Warrants	34	+1	–	–	–	–
110	F.P.	–	120	113	Enviromed	115		–	–	–	49.4
–	F.P.	–	18$\frac{1}{2}$	11	Eurotunnel Wts 1993	18$\frac{1}{2}$	+1$\frac{1}{2}$	–	–	–	–
250	F.P.	–	290	276	Field Group	288	–1	NW6.4	2.0	2.8	22.8
210	F.P.	–	261	233	Fine Decor	261		u7.5	1.7	3.6	20.0
–	F.P.	–	149	149	Finsbury Smllr. Co's. C	149		–	–	–	–
–	F.P.	–	101	94	Govett Emrg Mkts	101	+2	–	–	–	–
–	F.P.	–	52	44	Do Warrants	46		–	–	–	–
100	F.P.	–	103	100	Johnson Fry Utilities	103		M7.2	–	8.7	–
–	F.P.	–	102$\frac{1}{2}$	101	Do Zero Pf	102		–	–	–	–
–	F.P.	–	265	250	Kerry Grp A	265		Q30.1%	7.9	1.2	14.5
100	F.P.	–	96	94	Kleinwort Emrg Mkts	96	+1	–	–	–	–
–	F.P.	–	61	55	Do Warrants	57	–1	–	–	–	–
108	F.P.	–	137	126	Metrotect Inds	127		W3.24	2.2	3.2	17.6
100	P.P.	–	141	100	Northern Ireland Elect	138		W10.02	2.3	4.9	8.6

FIXED INTEREST STOCKS

Issue Price £	Amount Paid up	Latest Renunc Date	1993 High	1993 Low	Stock	Closing Price £	+ or -
-	F.P.	-	169$\frac{1}{2}$p	167p	Finsbury Smaller Co's. C Pf.	169p	–$\frac{1}{2}$
-	F.P.	-	125	117$\frac{1}{2}$	Hemmingway Props. 7$\frac{1}{2}$pc Ln. 2027	117$\frac{1}{2}$	
-	F.P.	-	122p	120p	Sterling Publsg Cnv Pf	122p	

Fig. 5.9 Recent issues

- **Amount paid up:** the amount of the issue price that had to be paid up immediately by the investor. Most issues are fully paid but some, including many government privatisations, have only required the investor to pay in stages. These part-paid shares are highly geared since if, after issue, a premium or discount emerges on the full issue price, it will be a significantly higher percentage of the part-paid investment. A small movement in the full price will be a relatively big movement in the part-paid price.

- **High and low:** figures representing the highs and lows for the year.

- **Name:** the name of the security and its nominal value in the case of fixed interest securities.

- **Price and change:** the closing price the previous night, and the change on the day.

- **Dividend, cover, yield and p/e ratio:** for new equity issues, details of the net dividend, cover, gross yield and p/e ratio are provided. In the case of newly floated companies, these figures are based on the figures given in the launch prospectus until the company issues audited financial reports.

- **Fixed interest:** corporate bonds, generally issued by an existing company seeking extra funding.

New equity issues remain in the table for around six weeks after the company comes to market depending on the volume of new issues, and most then choose to be transferred to the London share service.

Raising extra funds

Rights issues are the way in which companies raise additional equity finance for expansion or re-finance if they are over-borrowed. They are issues of new shares in a company already on the market to which existing shareholders are given the right of first refusal. Shares are issued in proportion to existing holdings and at a discount to the current share price to give shareholders an incentive to take them up. The discount has the effect of depressing the price of existing shares and so shareholders will naturally want the rights to them. If they do not actually want to buy the shares, they can sell their rights.

Details of forthcoming rights issues are listed in a table in Saturday's FT (see Figure 5.10):

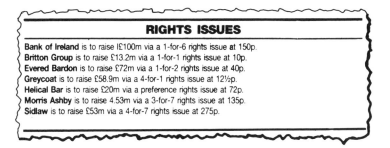

RIGHTS ISSUES

Bank of Ireland is to raise I£100m via a 1-for-6 rights issue at 150p.
Britton Group is to raise £13.2m via a 1-for-1 rights issue at 10p.
Evered Bardon is to raise £72m via a 1-for-2 rights issue at 40p.
Greycoat is to raise £58.9m via a 4-for-1 rights issue at 12½p.
Helical Bar is to raise £20m via a preference rights issue at 72p.
Morris Ashby is to raise 4.53m via a 3-for-7 rights issue at 135p.
Sidlaw is to raise £53m via a 4-for-7 rights issue at 275p.

Fig. 5.10 Rights issues

- **Rights issues:** the table lists the companies, the amount they are seeking to raise and the number of shares they are planning to issue at what price. A 1-for-6 issue means that a shareholder is entitled to buy one new share for every six currently held; a 4-for-1 issue indicates an offer of four new shares for every one held.

The Stock Exchange sets a cut-off date after which the shares go ex-rights ('xr' in the share service tables). After this date the buyer does not get rights, and clearly at this point the share price has to adjust. Shares with the rights are known as cum-rights.

Nil paid rights (that is, rights for which the subscription price has not yet been paid) can be bought and sold. Their value is the ex-rights price less the subscription price for the new shares. These too are highly geared investments. The FT lists them in a table of rights offers (see Figure 5.11):

- **Issue price and amount paid up:** as for the new issues, these are the price at which new shares are issued and the proportion of price already paid, if any.

RIGHTS OFFERS

Issue Price p	Amount Paid up	Latest Renunc Date	1993 High	1993 Low	Stock	Closing ·Price p	+ or –
123	Nil	27/8	38pm	33pm	ACT	35pm	$-\frac{1}{2}$
60	Nil	6/8	3pm	2pm	Alexon	2pm	$-\frac{1}{2}$
140	Nil	25/8	94pm	82pm	Bank of Ireland	85pm	–5
135	Nil	3/9	19pm	17pm	Birkby	17pm	
152	Nil	23/8	18pm	$5\frac{1}{2}$pm	Cranswick	$5\frac{1}{2}$pm	$-1\frac{1}{2}$
345	Nil	1/9	52pm	33pm	Frogmore	50pm	–2
150	Nil	13/8	39pm	14pm	Gt Portland Ests	39pm	
30	Nil	18/8	9pm	4pm	Moran Hldgs	8pm	
5	Nil	9/8	$1\frac{1}{2}$pm	1pm	Premier Land	$1\frac{1}{4}$pm	
210	Nil	1/9	53pm	45pm	Smith New Court	48pm	–1
$8\frac{1}{2}$	Nil	13/8	5pm	1pm	Sutcliffe Speakman	$4\frac{3}{4}$pm	

pm Price at a premium. † Price offered to public.
For other notes please refer to the Guide to the London Share Service.

Fig. 5.11 Rights offers

- **Latest renunciation date:** the last date by which holders of rights can dispose of their allotments to purchasers who will not have to pay stamp duty. Before this date, all dealings are for cash rather than the account.

- **Closing price (as a premium), change and high and low:** the price quoted for rights to buy new shares, plus the change on the previous day and the highest and lowest points for the year. The price is actually a premium for the right to subscribe. Percentage swings in price can be large because of gearing.

- Rights issues normally remain in the table until they are fully paid.

The price of new issues is pitched well below the market price to ensure maximum take-up of the issue although, as with new issues, the shares will be underwritten, usually by a merchant bank. A standard issue might aim to raise up to 30 per cent more equity capital with shares at about a 20 per cent discount to market price. Rarely, a company might do a deep-discount rights issue that does not need to be underwritten.

Reports of new issues look like these examples:

> Postel, the UK's largest pension fund, yesterday announced plans for a £120m rescue package for Greycoat, which will give it up to 87.7 per cent of the troubled property company. ... In a complex deal, Postel is underwriting a £58.9m rights issue of ordinary shares at 12.5p and a £6.25m preference rights issue. Greycoat is also placing £4.5m of shares with Postel and issuing it with warrants. (*Financial Times*, 7 July 1993)

> The Rank Organisation ... reported a near fivefold increase in first-half profits. The pre-tax figure rose from a restated £19.8m to £95.7m. Rank said it would pay the full-year dividend at the interim stage with an enhanced share alternative ... of receiving new shares to the value of 46.5p. ... If all shareholders take up the offer, Rank will save £96m on dividends and £27.8m of advance corporation tax. (*Financial Times*, 16 July 1993)

The price at which the shares are pitched does not matter since the company already belongs to the shareholders. The only benefit they get is on the yield if the dividend per share remains the same amount. Because the equity is diluted, the price drops: naturally, if the dividend is static, the yield goes up.

Other techniques by which new issues in existing companies can be arranged include vendor placings, placings and bought deals and convertible loan stock sold through the Euromarkets.

There is also the scrip issue or capitalisation issue where a company turns part of its accumulated reserves into new shares. This is essentially an accounting transaction to convert the part of shareholders' funds that is not revealed by stock market capitalisation into stock. It keeps the number of shares in issue in line with the growth of the business, and keeps their prices down. It can also be a tax-efficient way of handing part of the company's added worth back to shareholders.

The Stock Exchange sets a date when shares go 'xc' (ex-capitalisation), after which the price will go down. The only real effect is if the dividend remains the same, in which case the yield has gone up. It also makes it difficult to compare share prices over time unless calculations have made the appropriate adjustment. The term 'xa' means a share is ex-all, not entitled to scrip issues, rights issues or dividends.

ACCOUNT DEALING

The Stock Exchange year is divided into twenty-four share trading or accounting periods. These determine the payment dates for stocks bought and sold. Each trading period normally lasts two weeks, though it can stretch to three when public holidays intervene. Within that period, transactions are recorded but no money changes hands.

The first dealing day of an account is usually a Monday and the last the Friday of the following week. The account day, sometimes known as the settlement day, is the Monday six business days after the last dealing day. On account day, all transactions have to be settled: buyers have to pay for what they have bought during the period, while sellers receive their cash.

At settlement, share certificates pass on to the new owner and changes are made to the register of shareholders. Some account dealings dates are shown in Figure 5.12.

Account Dealing Dates

*First Dealings:		
Jul 5	Jul 19	Aug 2
Option Declarations:		
Jul 15	Jul 29	Aug 12
Last Dealings:		
Jul 16	Jul 30	Aug 13
Account Day:		
Jul 26	Aug 9	Aug 23

*New time dealings may take place from 8.30am two business days earlier.

Fig. 5.12 Account dealing dates

- **Dates:** the details of the current and two following account periods plus the day for the declaration of traditional options (see chapter 11).

The account dealing system allows scope for speculative be-haviour with the minimum capital outlay, since for shares bought and sold within an account period, only differences have to be settled. In the course of an account dealing period, optimistic (or bullish) speculators may buy stocks intending to sell them at a higher price before settlement day. Similarly, pessimis-tic speculators (bears) may 'short' sell a stock that they do not own in the hope of obtaining it for a lower price before settlement.

The result of this system is that market movements can be affected by the account dealing periods: the market often will move up at the beginning of a period as bullish speculators start buying, and down at the end as profits are taken.

'New time' dealings can take place on the two business days leading up to the start of the account. This means that a purchase can count as being made in the following period. Such transactions incur a premium in the dealing price to take account of the intervening weekend.

6

INDICES AND AGGREGATES
Market indicators

The fundamental data of the equities markets are the prices of shares and the various ratios that can be calculated from them. But while this information is highly valuable for understanding both the performance of individual companies and investors' evaluation of their prospects, it does not indicate the state of the market as a whole, nor a given company's relative performance. This question of share price measurement for the stock market as a whole led to the development of figures for baskets of shares, or indices. An index is purely a number to compare the value of companies now with their value at the starting date.

All indices are an attempt to create order and direction out of diversity. Stock market indices are designed to pull together the disparate movements of different share prices, each responding to a myriad of individual pressures, to find out whether the market, or a subsection of it, is moving up or down, in a bullish or bearish direction. There are numerous ways of composing equity indices, each with advantages and disadvantages, and the one selected will depend on just what it is that is being tracked. Indices are important benchmarks for measuring the performance of the fund managers who put money into the stock market on behalf of investors. Most will try to out-perform the various benchmarks, though some will passively aim merely to 'track' the rise and fall of the indices. In its simplest form, this could be attempted by buying the stocks that constitute the index.

FINANCIAL TIMES EQUITY INDICES

Perhaps the FT's greatest contribution to investment statistics has been its pioneering of stock market indices. The oldest and most familiar of these is the FT Ordinary Share Index, also known as the FT 30 share index, or simply the FT index. Started in 1935 with a base 100, it is compiled from the share prices of thirty leading British companies, chosen to be representative of British industry and is calculated as a geometric mean. It is biased towards major industrial and retailing companies, the traditional blue chips, but now includes financial and oil stocks which have become more important (see Figure 6.1).

- **Ordinary share:** the movements of the FT index over the past five trading days, together with its level a year ago, and the values and dates of its highs and lows for this year. The basis of 100 dates from the index's inception on 1 July 1935.

- **Yields and ratios:** Ordinary dividend yield, earnings yield percentage full, and price/ earnings ratios on a net and nil basis.

- **Gold mines:** the movements of the FT Gold Mines Index based on the past five days' London trading of twenty-four South African mines.

- **Ordinary share hourly changes:** the hourly movements of the FT Index through the previous trading day plus the day's high and low point of the index.

- **Volume:** the figures for SEAQ Bargains are the number of transactions of equities and gilts on the Stock Exchange's SEAQ trading system by 4.30pm on the five most recent trading days, as well as a year earlier. The figures for equity turnover are the value of the volume of equities traded. Equity bargains is the number of transactions, while shares traded is the actual number of shares to have changed hands. As with trading volume on individual shares, all volume figures should be divided by two since each share is recorded twice as being both bought and sold.

Hopes of strong sales in the   LVMH, the French luxury
month of August helped motor   goods group which has a 24.6

FINANCIAL TIMES EQUITY INDICES

	July 26	July 23	July 22	July 21	July 20	Year ago	* High	* Low
Ordinary share	2254.2	2234.6	2226.3	2220.1	2221.3	1767.0	2299.5	2124.7
Ord. div. yield	4.09	4.13	4.14	4.15	4.16	5.25	4.52	4.07
Earning yld % full	4.87	4.92	4.93	4.95	4.95	7.60	6.38	4.82
P/E ratio net	26.28	26.04	25.95	25.87	25.85	16.76	26.57	19.40
P/E ratio nil	24.28	24.06	23.97	23.90	23.88	15.42	24.60	18.14
Gold Mines	214.9	218.4	210.6	218.1	221.4	90.5	239.3	60.0

*for 1993. Ordinary share Index since compilation: high 2299.5 10/3/93 - low 49.4 26/6/40
Gold Mines index since compilation high: 734.7 15/2/83- low 43.5 26/10/71
Basis Ordinary share 1/7/35; Gold Mines 12/9/55.

Ordinary Share hourly changes

Open	9.00	10.00	11.00	12.00	13.00	14.00	15.00	16.00	High	Low
2238.3	2241.0	2251.3	2250.0	2252.0	2252.4	2251.0	2250.9	2253.1	2254.7	2237.6

Volume		July 26	July 23	July 22	July 21	July 20	Year ago
SEAQ Bargains		25,503	24,894	24,427	25,990	28,067	18,956
Equity Turnover(£m)†	-		1220.4	1286.9	1327.1	1455.9	1273.1
Equity Bargains†	-		28,933	30,573	31,458	32,793	21,333
Shares traded (ml)†	-		474.8	538.8	500.5	515.3	525.6

† Excluding intra-market business and overseas turnover.

London report and latest Share Index
Tel. 0891 123001. Calls charged at 36p/minute cheap rate. 48p at all other times.

Fig. 6.1 *Financial Times* equity indices

Although in terms of public attention the FT-30 has now been super-
seded by the Footsie, it is still a sensitive short-term indicator of the
mood of the market. But it is not suitable for measuring the performance of a typical investment portfolio over time because of its mathematical structure.

FT-SE ACTUARIES SHARE INDICES

More widely based indices have been developed by the *Financial
Times*, the Stock Exchange, the Institute of Actuaries and the Faculty
of Actuaries and are now administered by a series of self-governing
committees set up in 1992 by the FT, the Stock Exchange and the
English and Scottish actuaries professional bodies. These indices are
based on market capitalisation rather than crude price movements.
For most purposes, the Footsie has replaced the FT-30.

The FT-Actuaries All-Share Index (Figure 6.2) is the professional investor's yardstick for the level of the whole UK equity market. There are thirty-five component indices relating to different industrial sectors of the market.

READING THE FIGURES

- **FT-SE 100:** the Footsie index was started with a base of 1,000, in January 1984 to fill a gap in the market. At that time, the FT-30 index was calculated only hourly, and there was demand for a constantly updated – or real time – index in view of both the competition from overseas and the needs of the new traded options and financial futures markets. The index, amended quarterly, includes the 100 largest UK companies in terms of market capitalisation.

- **FT-SE Mid 250:** an index of the next 250 companies in market capitalisation, those directly beneath the FT-SE 100. These are companies capitalised at between £150 million and £1 billion. It is calculated on two formats, one that includes and one that excludes investment trusts.

- **FT-SE-A 350:** the combination of the FT-SE 100 and the FT-SE Mid 250.

- **FT-SE SmallCap:** the 500 to 600 companies capitalised at between £20 million and £150 million, including the smallest 450 in the All-Share index. Like the Mid 250, this index is again calculated on two formats.

- **Industrial group:** aggregate performance measures for key industrial sectors, excluding oil companies, providing investors with a valuable yardstick for assessing the performance of a stock relative to its sector. The Group comprises Capital Goods, the Consumer Group and Other Groups, each of which is further broken down into various sub-sectors.

- **The '500' Share index:** all except financial and property companies, and now comprises a little over 600 companies.

- **Financial group:** financial and property companies and is divided into sub-sectors such as Banks, Insurance and Property.

- **FT-A All-Share index:** the full 800-plus companies. Introduced on a daily basis in 1962, it is far more representative than the FT index.

FT-SE Actuaries Share Indices — THE UK SERIES

FT-SE 100	FT-SE MID 250	FT-A ALL-SHARE
2844.2 +16.5	3215.2 +12.3	1409.55 +7.16

		Day's				Year	Dividend	Earnings	P/E	Xd adj	Total
	Jul 26	change %	Jul 23	Jul 22	Jul 21	ago	yield %	yield %	Ratio	ytd	Return
T-SE 100	2844.2	+0.6	2827.7	2820.1	2814.1	2348.0	4.02	5.93	20.99	54.69	1023.68
T-SE Mid 250	3215.2	+0.4	3202.9	3200.5	3195.4	2296.8	3.76	6.05	20.48	59.74	1150.58
T-SE Mid 250 ex Inv Trusts	3227.0	+0.3	3216.1	3214.7	3209.4	2310.0	3.87	6.47	19.32	61.30	1150.65
T-SE-A 350	1423.0	+0.5	1415.4	1412.2	1409.4	1139.2	3.96	5.96	20.87	27.15	1049.95
T-SE SmallCap	1633.45	+0.1	1631.84	1631.92	1630.51	–	3.48	4.27	32.80	25.35	1222.69
T-SE SmallCap ex Inv Trusts	1632.28	......	1631.86	1632.41	1631.07	–	3.69	4.71	30.68	26.76	1223.00
T-A ALL-SHARE	1409.55	+0.5	1402.39	1399.44	1396.75	1124.19	3.93	5.85	21.35	26.59	1058.68
1 CAPITAL GOODS(214)	1009.74	+0.3	1007.01	1003.07	1000.02	727.17	3.94	4.19	31.72	21.04	1185.21
2 Building Materials(28)	1063.31	+0.9	1054.17	1046.64	1050.03	768.95	4.40	3.66	38.48	21.26	1228.54
3 Contracting, Construction(29)	928.17	+0.1	927.43	923.99	923.17	639.65	3.54	1.41	80.00†	14.25	1281.54
4 Electricals(15)	2971.42	+0.5	2956.99	2948.60	2974.13	2233.13	4.54	4.96	25.84	66.90	1197.62
5 Electronics(38)	2804.68	+0.6	2787.32	2776.86	2747.88	1884.15	3.08	5.96	20.69	61.50	1227.24
6 Engineering-Aerospace(7)	416.42	+0.4	414.64	410.41	408.10	300.41	3.55	‡	‡	6.61	1437.86
7 Engineering-General(48)	583.25	+0.2	582.00	580.42	580.93	450.15	3.72	6.13	20.21	11.06	1165.07
8 Metals & Metal Forming(10)	439.32	+0.1	438.68	436.49	426.39	281.03	2.49	‡	‡	6.06	1386.25
9 Motors(20)	422.50	−0.2	423.25	422.51	421.81	310.86	5.15	4.42	31.71	9.86	1156.95
10 Other Industrials(19)	2097.88	−0.2	2101.57	2097.48	2091.97	1554.29	4.30	5.40	22.19	50.05	1081.11
21 CONSUMER GROUP(235)	1593.51	+0.8	1581.05	1574.88	1570.86	1509.07	3.61	7.04	17.30	28.44	924.49
22 Brewers and Distillers(30)	1825.20	−0.1	1827.53	1825.61	1841.68	1921.55	4.03	8.51	14.21	41.62	893.50
25 Food Manufacturing(22)	1260.76	+1.1	1247.56	1246.08	1241.08	1158.36	4.03	7.79	15.47	27.47	972.30
26 Food Retailing(17)	2788.05	+1.8	2738.35	2713.78	2721.63	2701.32	3.35	9.28	13.37	47.61	872.53
27 Health & Household(30)	3265.52	+1.1	3229.28	3203.07	3148.04	3741.99	3.77	6.71	17.42	43.19	775.93
29 Hotels and Leisure(20)	1326.35	+0.3	1321.79	1329.25	1332.18	1069.49	4.49	6.37	19.65	36.08	1061.62
30 Media(33)	1979.79	+0.9	1962.74	1962.15	1959.97	1406.57	2.62	5.11	23.69	26.36	1099.18
31 Packaging and Paper(24)	834.56	+0.9	827.48	817.65	816.29	712.10	3.53	5.76	21.36	13.84	1085.63
34 Stores(39)	1162.55	+0.7	1154.77	1150.17	1150.34	959.53	3.09	5.96	21.53	18.39	1017.02
35 Textiles(20)	782.99	−0.3	785.49	783.37	784.25	609.46	3.90	6.15	20.36	14.90	1066.20
40 OTHER GROUPS(141)	1498.08	+0.3	1494.32	1489.48	1487.96	1174.70	4.29	7.32	16.56	27.79	1061.19
41 Business Services(27)	1573.68	−0.4	1580.63	1580.70	1570.73	1194.73	2.92	7.47	15.29	21.29	1047.68
42 Chemicals(23)	1502.86	+0.2	1499.95	1494.12	1489.80	1293.14	4.37	0.30	‡	35.15	1079.69
43 Conglomerates(11)	1411.22	+0.1	1409.46	1417.33	1431.82	1163.13	5.43	7.71	14.63	29.85	1039.77
44 Transport(15)	2966.06	+0.5	2951.95	2930.95	2893.60	2177.49	3.89	5.13	24.66	53.82	1093.06
45 Electricity(16)	1804.24	+0.7	1791.61	1780.98	1787.29	1298.67	4.36	12.35	10.05	52.22	1186.89
46 Telephone Networks(4)	1773.14	+0.5	1764.38	1754.67	1759.85	1341.91	3.82	5.90	20.88	8.19	1055.92
47 Water(13)	3225.16	+0.1	3222.02	3233.02	3229.62	2717.36	5.50	13.66	8.04	106.71	1026.30
48 Miscellaneous(32)	2337.69	−0.3	2344.40	2331.98	2308.44	1917.10	4.41	7.32	16.28	49.93	963.62
49 INDUSTRIAL GROUP(590)	1428.98	+0.5	1421.85	1416.62	1413.59	1206.74	3.91	6.55	18.77	26.68	1015.26
51 Oil & Gas(18)	2449.29	+0.4	2439.50	2414.32	2400.01	1825.87	4.47	5.71	22.19	48.05	1114.81
59 "500" SHARE INDEX(608)	1519.55	+0.5	1512.14	1505.48	1501.64	1266.62	3.97	6.45	19.09	28.54	1025.34
61 FINANCIAL GROUP(90)	1062.79	+0.6	1056.65	1067.05	1068.21	671.44	4.01	3.51	42.42	21.70	1243.37
62 Banks(9)	1447.92	+1.1	1431.49	1434.22	1438.46	898.79	3.73	4.27	32.23	28.48	1241.27
65 Insurance (Life)(6)	1901.32	−1.3	1926.87	2052.13	2080.96	1381.68	4.70	5.05	24.90	47.49	1105.91
66 Insurance (Composite)(7)	693.41	......	693.28	706.79	700.37	418.66	4.49	‡	‡	15.60	1132.18
67 Insurance Brokers(10)	907.57	+1.2	896.69	893.17	889.43	742.44	3.99	5.53	25.65	16.62	1196.60

Fig. 6.2 FT-SE Actuaries share indices

Its mathematical structure makes it a reliable yardstick against which to measure portfolio performance, and hence it represents an essential tool for professional investment managers.

- **For each index:** the UK Series lists yesterday's closing value, the percentage change on the previous day, the three previous days' closing values and the value of the index one year ago. The further performance indicators of earnings yield, dividend yield and price earnings ratio are also provided.

- **Ex-dividend adjustment year to date:** when a share goes ex-dividend, all else being equal, its price will drop by the amount of the dividend per share. This is the ex-dividend adjustment. The figure in the indices is the cumulative total of the aggregate of the ex-dividend adjustments multiplied by the relevant number of shares in issue. It allows the investor to assess the flow of income on a portfolio.

- **Total return:** calculated at the close of each trading day, total return figures reflect both the price and dividend performance of stocks.

USING THE INFORMATION

The Footsie is calculated from the price movements of 100 of Britain's largest companies. Since it incorporates fewer companies than the All-Share index, it can be calculated more rapidly and frequently. It was introduced mainly as a basis for dealing in equity index options and futures (see chapter 12). It rapidly became a key indicator of the stock market's mood, not least because it is quoted widely throughout the day. In many respects, the market thinks in terms of the Footsie figures with particular points being seen as psychological watersheds. For example:

> The last trading session of the half-year saw UK equities stage a strong late move to regain the 2,900 level on the FT-SE 100 index ... . (*Financial Times*, 1 July 1993)

The Footsie was the first real-time index in the UK and was the first index to be specifically designed for derivative trading in Europe.

The FT-All-Share accurately reflects the whole market. With over 800 constituents, it has a very broad coverage, encompassing 98 per cent of the market's aggregate capitalisation with each company weighted according to its market value so that a move in the price of a large company has more effect than that of a small one. It can be used as a measure of the market's performance over long periods. It serves as a reliable yardstick against which to assess portfolio performance. As a weighted arithmetic index it is designed to behave as an actual portfolio would behave.

The breakdown into industry groups allows investors to track the performance of particular sectors. This is of great assistance to specialist sector analysts, as well as allowing more general investors to improve their understanding of the structure of the market as a whole. Industrial classification is highly important since it is normally accepted by the stock market and institutional research departments as the basis for the analysis of companies. Correctly classifying all companies traded on the London market is the responsibility of the FT-SE Actuaries Industry Classification, made up of market practitioners, investment managers and actuaries.

FT-SE Actuaries Share Indices				Quarterly Valuation		
	Market capitalisation as at Jun 30 1993 (£m.)	% of all share index	Market capitalisation as at Mar 31 1993 (£m.)	% of all share index	Market capitalisation as at Dec 31 1992* (£m.)	% of all share index
-SE 100 †	463,000.00	72.78	455,000.00	73.6	447,000.00	75.2
-SE Mid 250 †	135,000.00	21.13	127,000.00	20.6	116,000.00	19.5
-SE Mid 250 ex Inv Trusts	121,000.00	19.06	-	-	-	-
-SE-A 350 †	598,000.00	93.91	582,000.00	94.2	563,000.00	94.7
-SE SmallCap †	39,000.00	6.09	36,000.00	5.8	31,200.00	5.3
-SE SmallCap ex Inv Trusts †	32,000.00	5.08	30,000.00	4.9	26,200.00	4.4
-A ALL-SHARE	636,790.95	100.0	617,987.70	100.0	594,374.08	100.0
CAPITAL GOODS GROUP 213	92,244.73	14.49	85,886.68	13.90	77,916.77	13.11
Building Materials 27	15,222.08	2.39	13,655.14	2.21	12,399.66	2.09
Contracting, Construction 29	5,121.98	0.81	4,390.98	0.71	3,777.91	0.64
Electricals 15	3,014.39	0.47	2,724.00	0.44	2.506.58	0.42
Electronics 37	15,842.18	2.49	14,927.09	2.42	13,133.66	2.21
Engineering-Aerospace 7	4,585.42	0.72	3,795.55	0.61	3,251.35	0.55
Engineering-General 51	11,802.66	1.85	10,946.33	1.77	10,146.33	1.71
Metals and Metal Forming 10	3,793.29	0.60	3.642.64	0.59	3,038.28	0.51
Motors 19	5,798.77	0.91	5,413.87	0.88	5,023.82	0.85
Other Industrial 18	27,063.96	4.25	26,391.07	4.27	24,639.19	4.15
CONSUMER GROUP 236	214,219.48	33.64	208,810.58	33.79	219,568.43	36.94
Brewers and Distillers 30	35,955.50	5.65	37,228.61	6.02	39,445.11	6.64
Food Manufacturing 22	23,760.59	3.73	25,596.71	4.14	23,910.38	4.02

Fig. 6.3 FT-SE Actuaries share indices – quarterly valuation

Institutional investors attempt to beat the index most relevant to their portfolio. Increasingly, investors want a set of indices that cover the capital structure of the UK market so that they can accurately assess the performance of large, medium and small companies within the framework of the whole market. There has also been a growing interest in the performance of medium-sized companies. The newer indices increase the visibility of many medium and small companies.

The FT-SE Actuaries 350 provides a real-time measure covering around 90 per cent of the UK equity market by value. The SmallCap is higher risk but likely to boom in a recovery. It is good for the visibility and marketability of smaller companies.

Evaluating quarterly performance

The quarterly valuation (see Figure 6.3) surveys the market capitalisation of the FT-SE Actuaries Share Indices over the preceding three quarters.

- **Market capitalisation:** represents comparative figures for the past three quarters of the market capitalisation of the various sectors and indices that make up the All-Share index.

- **Percentage of All-Share index:** the proportion of the All-Share index that each sector and index took up at the end of the past three quarters.

The All-Share index

A snapshot of recent price and trading activity in the equities market is provided by the FT-A graphs (see Figure 6.4).

- **FT-A All-Share index:** this index provides investors with an instant overview of movements in the UK equity market over several months. It moves more sluggishly than the 30-Share index because it has a large number of comparatively inactive constituents which lag behind the market leaders.

- **Equity shares traded:** the volume of shares traded over the comparative period, excluding intra-market and overseas turnover.

- **Performance against the market:** indices useful for weighing up the performance of a share in comparison with the market or sector of which it is a part.

Hourly movements and industry baskets

An hourly breakdown of the previous day's trading in the UK equities market is also recorded in the share indices (see Figure 6.5).

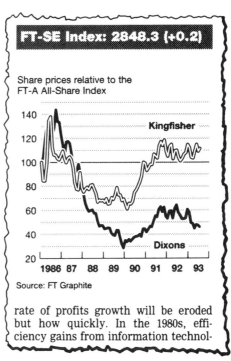

Fig. 6.4 (a) FT-A All Share index and equity shares traded

Fig. 6.4 (b) FT-SE index (comparison)

FT-SE   Actuaries Share Indices   THE UK SERIES

Hourly movements

	Open	9.00	10.00	11.00	12.00	13.00	14.00	15.00	16.10	High/day	Low/day
FT-SE 100	2831.2	2837.4	2845.5	2843.2	2843.7	2843.0	2840.6	2841.6	2844.4	2846.0	2831.2
FT-SE Mid 250	3204.4	3206.1	3213.0	3213.6	3213.8	3214.1	3213.1	3212.3	3214.6	3215.2	3204.4
FT-SE-A 350	1416.9	1419.5	1423.3	1422.5	1422.7	1422.5	1421.4	1421.7	1423.1	1423.6	1416.9

Time of FT-SE 100 high: 10.24am low: 8.30am

FT-SE Actuaries 350 Industry Baskets

Hourly	Open	9.00	10.00	11.00	12.00	13.00	14.00	15.00	16.10	Close	Previous close	change
Constrcn	1808.7	1810.7	1811.5	1813.2	1813.9	1813.9	1815.1	1817.2	1812.6	1812.6	1810.3	+2.3
Health & H	974.5	976.2	976.8	976.8	977.6	977.0	977.0	979.5	983.6	982.7	971.4	+11.3
Water	1322.9	1324.0	1333.7	1334.0	1332.2	1332.0	1331.5	1331.0	1331.0	1330.4	1329.1	+1.3
Banks	1748.8	1754.9	1762.2	1760.0	1760.0	1759.5	1758.1	1758.2	1759.5	1759.9	1739.9	+20.0

Fig. 6.5 FT-SE Actuaries share indices

- **Hourly movements:** displays the values of the key indices at hourly intervals throughout the previous day's trading.

- **FT-SE Actuaries 350 industry baskets:** the real-time industry sector indices calculated on the 350; these provide an instant view of industry performance across the market.

Hourly movements for the FT-SE A 350 industry baskets are further broken down into industrial sectors, enabling investors to react quickly to industry-wide news and events.

Highs, lows and base dates

Saturday's edition of the *Financial Times* carries an expanded table of the FT-Actuaries All-Share index (see Figure 6.6):

- **Highs and lows:** the highs and lows for each index both for the current year and for the whole period since the FT-Actuaries series was started in 1962. The latter are loosely termed 'all-time' highs and lows.

	Jul 23	Day's change	Jul 22
FT-SE 100	2827.7	+0.3	2820.1
FT-SE Mid 250	3202.9	+0.1	3200.5
FT-SE Mid 250 ex Inv Trusts	3216.1	......	3214.7
FT-SE-A 350	1415.4	+0.2	1412.2
FT-SE SmallCap	1631.84	......	1631.92
FT-SE SmallCap ex Inv Trusts	1631.86	......	1632.41
FT-A ALL-SHARE	1402.39	+0.2	1399.44
1 CAPITAL GOODS(214)	,1007.01	+0.4	1003.07
2 Building Materials(28)	1054.17	+0.7	1046.64

1993 High	Low	Since Compilation High	Low
2957.3 8/3	2737.6 19/1	2957.3 8/3/93	986.9 23/7/84
3241.7 1/7	2876.3 13/1	3241.7 1/7/93	1379.4 21/1/86
3257.6 1/7	2874.6 1/1	3257.6 1/7/93	1378.3 21/1/86
1457.1 8/3	1348.7 19/1	1457.1 8/3/93	664.5 14/1/86
1649.82 29/6	1377.88 4/1	1649.82 29/6/93	1363.79 31/12/92
1653.43 29/6	1380.06 4/1	1653.43 29/6/93	1363.79 31/12/92
1438.22 8/3	1330.19 19/1	1438.22 8/3/93	61.92 13/12/74
1013.55 28/6	869.89 13/1	1038.07 16/7/87	50.71 13/12/74
1110.81 25/5	882.69 12/1	1381.08 16/7/87	44.27 11/12/74

Equity section or group	Base date	Base value
FT-SE SmallCap	31/12/92	1363.79
FT-SE SmallCap exInv Trust	31/12/92	1363.79
FT-SE Mid 250	31/12/85	1412.60
FT-SE-A 350	31/12/85	682.94
FT-SE 100	31/12/83	1000.00
Business Services	31/12/90	999.65
Electricity	31/12/90	999.65
Media	31/12/90	1228.68
Engineering - Aerospace	29/12/89	486.00

Equity section or group	Base date	Base value
Other Financial	31/12/70	128.06
Food Manufacturing	29/12/67	114.13
Food Retailing	29/12/67	114.13
Insurance Brokers	29/12/67	96.67
All Other	10/4/62	100.00
British Government	31/12/75	100.00
Do. Index-linked	30/4/82	100.00
Debs & Loans	31/12/77	100.00

Fig. 6.6 Saturday's FT-SE Actuaries All-Share indices

- **Equity section or group, base date and value:** Saturday's FT also has details of the starting date and base value for each sector. Over time, as the structure of British industry has shifted, it has been necessary to amalgamate sectors and create new ones. For example, Radio and TV, Teas and Diamonds have gone, while Health and Household Goods and Insurance Brokers have been formed. When a new group is created, its initial value is set at the level of its immediate predecessor.

Leaders and laggards

Leaders and laggards, a table of notable performances, either good or bad, lists percentage changes in value in the current year for various indices (see Figure 6.7).

FT-A INDICES LEADERS AND LAGGARDS

Percentage changes since December 31 1992 based on Friday 23 July 1993

Gold Mines Index	+ 241.78	Oil & Gas	+	8.27
Property	+ 45.59	Transport	+	6.28
Engineering-Aerospace	+ 39.81	Packaging, Paper & Printing	+	5.46
Merchant Banks	+ 36.00	Other Industrials	+	5.09
Metals & Metal Forming	+ 35.83	Chemicals	+	4.71
Contracting, Construction	+ 25.45	Textiles	+	4.49
Financial Group	+ 20.20	Telephone Networks	+	4.44
FT-SE SmallCap ex Inv Tst	+ 19.66	Business Services	+	3.51
FT-SE SmallCap	+ 19.65	Other Groups	+	3.39
Banks	+ 19.41	FT-A All-Share	+	2.83
Building Materials	+ 18.57	Hotels & Leisure	+	2.19
Electronics	+ 18.39	FT-SE-A 350	+	1.93
Electricals	+ 15.55	Conglomerates	+	1.19
Insurance Brokers	+ 15.21	"500" Share Index	-	0.34
Capital Goods	+ 14.98	FT-SE 100	-	0.66
Investment Trusts	+ 14.35	Stores	-	1.03
Engineering-General	+ 13.37	Industrial Group	-	1.32
Electricity	+ 13.29	Water	-	1.64
Motors	+ 12.34	Food Manufacturing	-	6.16
Ft-SE Mid 250 ex Inv Tst	+ 11.88	Consumer Group	-	10.24
FT-SE Mid 250	+ 11.87	Brewers & Distillers	-	12.97
Insurance (Composite)	+ 9.83	Food Retailing	-	16.02
Insurance (Life)	+ 8.83	Health & Household	-	24.41

Fig. 6.7 Leaders and laggards

- **Index:** the percentage changes in the year in various detailed markets, subsections of the FT-Actuaries indices.

Based on the preceding Friday's closing prices, FT and sector indices are ranked in order of percentage increase in value in the current year to date.

Eurotrack indices

A summary of current performance in the European equities markets is provided by the European Series indices (see Figure 6.8), tracking a sample of major continental companies.

FT-SE	Actuaries Share Indices

July 26   THE EUROPEAN SERIES

Hourly changes	Open	10.30	11.00	12.00	13.00	14.00	15.00	Close
FT-SE Eurotrack 100	1236.02	1236.88	1237.16	1238.19	1238.64	1238.83	1239.12	1240.21
FT-SE Eurotrack 200	1291.97	1294.04	1293.60	1295.96	1295.26	1293.92	1294.62	1294.91

	Jul 23	Jul 22	Jul 21	Jul 20	Jul 19
FT-SE Eurotrack 100	1224.42	1217.14	1212.75	1224.85	1235.43
FT-SE Eurotrack 200	1279.96	1275.93	1266.97	1275.46	1283.54

Base value 1000 (26/10/90) High/day: 100 - 1240.21; 200 - 1295.96 Low/day: 100 - 1236.02 200 - 1291.97.

Fig. 6.8 Eurotrack indices

- **FT-SE Eurotrack 100:** yesterday's hourly changes and high for the day, and the previous five trading days' closing values of an index monitoring 100 major companies in continental Europe. This index was launched on 26 October 1990 with a base value of 1,000. In 1991, LIFFE issued options on the index. It is based on the prices of constituent companies' London dealings only, not those of the home markets, and is intended to reflect the role of the London market as the leading international market in European shares.

- **FT-SE Eurotrack 200:** an index of 100 UK and 100 continental European stocks, with all its constituents traded in a single financial centre, London. Launched on 25 February 1991, the index combines the stocks in the UK Footsie with those in the Eurotrack 100.

By bringing together the United Kingdom and continental Europe, the Eurotrack 200 provides the investment community with an instant overview of securities trading throughout Europe. Continuous real-time prices from the Stock Exchange's SEAQ and SEAQ International allow the Eurotrack 200 to operate without interruption throughout the trading day and provide a means of measuring the performance of European financial markets. This leads to international equities, the subject of the next chapter.

7

INTERNATIONAL EQUITIES
The world stock markets

The abolition of exchange control restrictions and the widespread deregulation of financial markets have made possible the globalisation of trading in equities. This has led to an upsurge in the buying and selling of shares across national boundaries. In the United Kingdom the removal of exchange controls in 1979 led to a massive upsurge in foreign investment. During the 1980s, an increasing proportion of Japan's enormous capital surplus was for the first time being directed towards the world's equity markets. In the United States fund managers had long taken an excessively parochial view but had made cautious moves towards greater foreign equity investment. This pace has quickened in recent years.

London remains a pivotal point in the global equity market, but it is just one market, albeit in a favourable time zone. For many years, New York had been attracting more equity business, and for a while Japan outstripped the United States in terms of market capitalisation before Tokyo's major shakeout in 1990.

WORLD STOCK MARKETS

The International Companies and Finance pages of the *Financial Times* contain the bulk of global corporate news: financial results, whether quarterly, half-yearly or annual; essential developments in bids and deals; new or revised funding arrangements; changes to the shareholding structure; joint ventures; or new products or production processes. In fact they contain anything that is valuable for an accurate and timely assessment of trends and prospects for shareholders and potential investors alike.

The reports attempt to cover all companies in the FT-Actuaries World Indices, plus many more that are heavily traded and might have a historical relationship with Britain or with UK companies, such as those in the old Commonwealth or the Americas.

World stock price listings cover over 2,000 shares, a little over a third being from the two New York exchanges (the NYSE and the American), and the national screen-based trading market (NASDAQ), with a further 470 listings for Japan. Figure 7.1 provides examples.

WORLD STOCK MARKETS

AUSTRIA

July 28	Sch	+ or −
Austrian Airlines	1,830	−40
Bank Austria	1,035	....
Creditanstalt Pf	661	−7
EA General	3,430	−35
EVN	1,008	+16
Lenzing	895	−16
OeMv	838	....
Perlmooser Zement	990	−35
Radex Heraklith	442	−1
Steyr Daimler	193	+2
Veitscher Magnesit	341	+6
Verbund (Br) A	590	−9
Vienna Int Airport	481	+1
Wienerberger	3,430	−100

BELGIUM/LUXEMBOURG

July 28	Frs.	+ or −
AG Group	2,530	−20
Ackermans	3,220	+10
Almanij	7,860	+20
Arbed	3,625	+15
BBL	3,650	−50
Bank Intl a Lux	13,450	....
Banq Gen Lux Pts	18,375	....
Banque Nat Belg	34,800	+175
Bekaert	16,925	+50
CBR Ciment	11,000	+50
CMB	1,920	....
Cobepa	5,230	+30
Cockerill Priv	125	+7
Colruyt	6,340	+10
Delhaize Frs Lion	1,280	−2
Electrabel	6,130	−20
Electrabel AFV1	6,000	−120
Electrafina ACT	2,650	−25
GBL	3,390	−10
GBL AFV 1	3,325	−25
GIB Group	1,248	−2
Generale Banque	8,200	+10

FRANCE (continued)

July 28	Frs.	+ or −
BIC	1,223xd	+10
BSN	858	−11
BNP Cert Inv	527	−1
Bancaire Cie	524	−13
Bongrain	2,410	−25
Bouygues	683	−6
CGIP	1,154	−6
Canal+	1,258	−18
Cap Gemini S	186.40	+.40
CarnaudMetalbox	216	+.50
Carrefour	2,905	+5
Casino	152.90	+1.90
Chargeurs	1,033	−16
Club Mediterranee	382	−2.40
Cogifi	340.50	....
Coparex Int	551	....
C C F	232	−5.50
Cr Fonc France	1,059	+23
Cred Lyon (Cl)	664	−6
Credit Local Fr	404.10	−6.40
Credit Nationale	1,253	+8
Damart	4,000	+50
Docks de France	556	+5
Dollfus Mieg Cie	271	−3
EBF	630	−10
Eaux Cie Genl	2,130	−60
Ecco	488.50	+3.50
Elf Aquitaine	415.90	+6.90
Elf Aquitaine Certs	354.90	+7.90
Elf Sanofi	933	+16
Eridania B–Say	765	+5
Eridania B–Say Cl	601	+16
Essilor Int	475.20	+.20
Etex	1,900	....
Eurafrance	1,830	+10
Euro RSCG	564xd	+3
Euro Disney	58.20	−1.30
Finextel	133.50	+1
Fonc Lyonnaise	703xd	−17
Fromageries Bel	4,460	−40
GTM–Entrepdse	460	+5
Gal. Lafayette	1,680	−10

Fig. 7.1 World stock markets

Monday's variation of the world stock market figures gives highs and lows over the year for all stocks plus their closing prices on the previous Friday.

The information given here is limited to stock prices and price movements. One problem for international investors is the unreliability of indicators such as price/earnings ratios for the purposes of international comparison. Different countries employ different accounting conventions, and therefore often differ in their treatment of the earnings component of such ratios.

Nowadays it is much easier to deal foreign shares, and, because of market interactions, it is important to understand these markets. For example:

> The stock market successfully resisted another bout of downside pressure yesterday ... with the upturn fuelled by a general advance by international stock markets. (*Financial Times*, 8 July 1993)

The New York Stock Exchange

The New York Stock Exchange (NYSE) is the main US exchange. It lists America's largest corporations and is known colloquially as the Big Board.

The complete listing of all shares, including prices, volumes traded, yields and price/earnings ratios quoted in the New York Stock Exchange, together with extensive coverage from the Amex and the NASDAQ, is provided in the International Edition of the *Financial Times*. UK editions of the FT carry composite indices and summarise trading activity in the NYSE in the international indices examined below.

With many major stocks traded in both London and New York, and increasing interaction between the two markets, the performance of share prices on Wall Street can have a significant impact on prices in London. This internationalisation of major equity markets was graphically illustrated during the October 1987 crash, the impact of which spread rapidly from Wall Street to the London Stock Exchange.

INTERNATIONAL EQUITY INDICES

The international equity indices are a useful tool in the world of international investment, acting as valuable barometers of local market performance for investors faced with limited background knowledge of foreign stocks. In such circumstances the active management of an international portfolio may be too costly and risky an exercise, and many fund managers may aim merely to match the performance of equity indices. The more passive management of indexed funds relies largely on the computerised tracking of price movements, and international equity indices hence become the key benchmarks for performance measurement.

North American equity indices

The United States provides the largest range of indices (see Figure 7.2).

- **Dow Jones and Standard & Poor's (S&P):** the closing figures for the day alongside the closing for the previous three trading days; the highest and lowest trading level for the year with dates; and the highest and lowest trading level since compilation began, also with dates.

- **NYSE composite index:** the most broadly based of the US indices, covering all common shares on the exchange, plus indications for the Amex and NASDAQ.

- **Dividend yields and price/earnings ratios:** yields for the Dow and S&P are calculated on the basis of the last declared dividend worked out at an annual rate. The S&P industrials' p/e ratio is measured by dividing the last four quarterly earnings figures into the latest share price.

- **NYSE:** figures on the previous day's most actively traded stocks, the number of issues traded and aggregate rises and falls as well as trading activity on the Amex and NASDAQ.

INDICES

NEW YORK

DOW JONES

	July 26	July 23	July 22	July 21	1993 HIGH	1993 LOW	Since compilation HIGH	Since compilation LOW
Industrials	3567.70	3546.74	3525.22	3555.40	3567.70 (26/7)	3241.95 (20/1)	3567.70 (26/7/93)	41.22 (2/7/32)
Home Bonds	107.49	107.48	107.82	107.66	107.82 (22/7)	103.49 (11/1)	501.97 (27/4/93)	54.99 (1/10/81)
Transport	1594.80	1592.45	1575.99	1573.21	1683.08 (16/4)	1453.84 (4/1)	1683.08 (16/4/93)	12.32 (8/7/32)
Utilities	248.88	247.10	246.84	246.84	248.88 (26/7)	217.14 (8/1)	248.88 (26/7/93)	10.50 (8/4/32)

DJ Indl. Day's High 3584.74 (3569.37) Low 3541.43 (3508.17) (Theoretical▲)
Day's High 3571.05 (3548.42) Low 3546.74 (3524.38) (Actual▲)

STANDARD AND POOR'S

	July 26	July 23	July 22	July 21	1993 HIGH	1993 LOW	Since compilation HIGH	Since compilation LOW
Composite ‡	449.09	447.10	444.51	447.18	456.33 (10/3)	429.05 (8/1)	456.33 (10/3/93)	4.40 (1/6/32)
Industrials♥	509.49	507.33	504.36	507.61	524.99 (10/3)	496.48 (26/4)	524.99 (10/3/93)	3.62 (21/6/32)
Financial	45.79	45.50	45.13	45.54	46.67 (13/4)	39.89 (8/1)	46.67 (13/4/93)	8.64 (1/10/74)
NYSE Composite	248.68	247.46	246.26	247.60	251.36 (10/3)	236.21 (8/1)	251.36 (10/3/93)	4.46 (25/4/42)
Amex Mkt. Value	433.76	432.05	431.36	433.31	440.95 (4/6)	395.84 (8/1)	440.95 (4/6/93)	29.31 (9/12/72)
NASDAQ Composite	704.55	700.24	695.52	700.08	712.49 (14/7)	645.87 (26/4)	712.49 (14/7/93)	54.87 (31/10/72)

	Jul 23	Jul 16	Jul 9	year ago (approx.)
Dow Industrial Div. Yield	2.93	2.95	2.93	3.17

	Jul 21	Jul 14	July 7	year ago (approx.)
S & P Industrial div. yield	2.55	2.52	2.56	2.68
S & P Indl. P/E ratio	25.09	25.37	24.89	28.50

NEW YORK ACTIVE STOCKS

Monday	Stocks traded	Closing price	Change on day
Chase Man	4,524,200	$32\frac{1}{8}$	$+ \frac{1}{2}$
Shanghai Pet	4,483,700	$20\frac{1}{4}$	... .
IBM	3,916,300	$42\frac{1}{8}$	$- \frac{1}{8}$
RJR Nabisco	3,581,500	$5\frac{1}{2}$	... .
Telefonos	3,002,700	$50\frac{1}{8}$	$+ \frac{3}{4}$
Am Express	2,741,300	$33\frac{5}{8}$	$+ 1$
Citicorp	2,253,700	$32\frac{1}{2}$	$+ \frac{3}{4}$
Merck	2,236,300	$32\frac{1}{4}$	$- \frac{1}{2}$
Brown Ferris	1,757,500	$24\frac{5}{8}$	$- 1\frac{3}{8}$
Sunshine Min	1,719,200	3	$+ \frac{1}{4}$

TRADING ACTIVITY

† Volume	July 26	July 23	July 22
New York SE	222.579	218.065	248.085
Amex	15.936	14.730	17.608
NASDAQ	(u)	237.579	256.823
NYSE			
Issues Traded	2,588	2,580	2,579
Rises	1,225	1,023	769
Falls	758	873	1,207
Unchanged	605	684	603
New Highs	84	50	69
New Lows	33	39	43

Millions

CANADA

TORONTO

	July 26	July 23	July 22	July 21	1993 HIGH	1993 LOW
Metals & Minerals	2883.27	2854.62	2838.87	2847.75	3020.48 (2/7)	2743.31 (21/1)
Composite	3869.50	3830.20	3838.50	3867.38	3997.72 (2/7)	3275.80 (21/1)
MONTREAL Portfolio	1840.59	1820.96	1820.96	1838.01	1939.10 (25/6)	1720.97 (21/1)

Fig. 7.2 Indices

- **Three Canadian indices:** there are two for Toronto, the most widely used of which is the Toronto Composite (a broadly based index similar to the S&P 500), and a much smaller one for the market in Montreal.

The Dow Jones Industrial Index (DJIA), the main US index, takes share prices of thirty 'typical' industrial companies and measures their movements. It is calculated by adding the New York closing prices and adjusting them by a 'current average divisor', an adjustable figure formulated to preserve the continuity of the Dow over time amid changes in its component parts. Other specialist indices are provided for groups of shares like transport, utilities and bonds.

The Dow often reaches new 'highs' but since it is not adjusted for inflation it can only reliably indicate direction of movement. Begun in 1928, the Dow – not an index but an 'average' – is the most widely followed in the US, providing a guide to the daily mood of the industrial share markets as the FT 30-Share index does for the United Kingdom. The Standard & Poor's series is a more comprehensive guide to the American market. Like the FT-Actuaries series, individual companies are weighted according to their market capitalisation.

OTHER INTERNATIONAL INDICES

Figure 7.3 shows indices for other international markets.

- **Indices:** for most markets, a single national index is recorded daily with the base date indicated. The base figure for almost all indices is 100 and the few exceptions are listed at the bottom of the page.

All these indices are benchmarks commonly used by local investors. They are designed to provide an accurate reflection of the daily movement of individual markets. More than one national index is published in the case where a single index does not give the full picture or where two or more are commonly used. For example, one national index may comprise the market's major companies while a second may reflect a wider market. In Australia, the Metals and Minerals index is given

	July	July	July	July	1993	
	26	23	22	21	HIGH	LOW
AUSTRALIA						
All Ordinaries (1/1/80)	1795.7	1806.8	1802.6	1818.5	1818.50 (21/7)	1495.00 (13/1)
All Mining (1/1/80)	822.7	826.4	826.8	843.5	856.70 (12/7)	584.70 (13/1)
AUSTRIA						
Credit Aktien (30/12/84)	385.61	376.94	371.46	367.20	385.61 (26/7)	300.26 (14/1)
Traded Index (2/1/91)	962.42	936.90	923.25	912.57	962.42 (26/7)	712.06 (15/1)
BELGIUM						
BEL20 (1/1/91)	1307.18	1307.02	1301.65	(c)	1331.53 (15/7)	1125.46 (4/1)
DENMARK						
Copenhagen SE (3/1/83)	310.39	310.02	310.97	311.69	314.85 (30/6)	261.90 (4/1)
FINLAND						
HEX General (28/12/90)	1226.4	1225.2	1240.7	1259.4	1259.40 (21/7)	843.10 (22/1)
FRANCE						
CAC General (31/12/81)	547.68	541.66	536.92	540.08	547.68 (26/7)	471.24 (13/1)
CAC 40 (31/12/87)	2006.22	1995.04	1965.72	1947.53	2035.91 (30/3)	1772.21 (29/1)
GERMANY						
FAZ Aktien (31/12/58)	716.22	709.18	707.24	705.83	716.22 (26/7)	598.92 (14/1)
Commerzbank (1/12/53)	2035.8	2017.1	2011.6	2008.8	2035.80 (26/7)	1694.30 (14/1)
DAX (30/12/87)	1854.52	1830.83	1823.52	1823.81	1854.52 (26/7)	1516.50 (13/1)
HONG KONG						
Hang Seng Bank (31/7/64)	6858.08	6750.33	6760.02	6839.98	7447.24 (27/5)	5437.80 (4/1)
IRELAND						
ISEQ Overall (4/1/88)	1624.33	1619.47	1628.70	1627.68	1639.76 (15/7)	1191.19 (11/1)
ITALY						
Banca Com. Ital. (1972)	549.33	550.17	552.57	558.37	561.74 (20/7)	446.33 (6/1)
MIB General (4/1/93)	1211.0	1213.0	1218.0	1231.0	1238.00 (20/7)	992.00 (11/1)
JAPAN						
Nikkei (16/5/49)	19822.08	19734.57	20115.81	20080.91	21076.00 (3/6)	16287.45 (25/1)
Tokyo SE (Topix) (4/1/68)	1615.55	1609.33	1634.29	1636.32	1676.13 (3/6)	1250.06 (25/1)
2nd Section (4/1/68)	2201.51	2207.87	2222.07	2225.25	2384.97 (7/6)	1651.72 (26/1)
MALAYSIA						
KLSE Composite (4/4/86)	758.35	757.65	759.76	761.60	761.60 (21/7)	614.28 (13/1)
NETHERLANDS						
CBS Tll.Rtn.Gen.(End 1983)	355.4	352.1	351.3	348.1	355.40 (26/7)	295.70 (4/1)
CBS All Shr (End 1983)	233.2	231.1	230.5	228.4	233.20 (26/7)	198.60 (13/1)
NORWAY						
Oslo SE (Ind) (2/1/83)	853.33	847.44	847.48	848.43	856.66 (14/7)	669.93 (27/1)
PHILIPPINES						
Manila Comp (2/1/85)	1704.10	1715.78†	1706.95	1681.86	1715.78 (23/7)	1270.68 (4/1)
SINGAPORE						
SES All-Singapore (2/4/75)	454.63	450.21	448.42	451.19	468.48 (31/5)	394.10 (13/1)
SOUTH AFRICA						
JSE Gold (28/9/78)	1853.0♥	1863.0	1812.0	1861.0	2092.00 (7/7)	775.00 (5/1)
JSE Industrial (28/9/78)	4515.0♥	4527.0	4548.0	4568.0	4719.00 (6/7)	4333.00 (19/4)
SOUTH KOREA**						
Korea Comp Ex. (4/1/80)	745.07	741.81	746.56	751.94	777.25 (9/6)	605.93 (6/3)
SPAIN						
Madrid SE (30/12/85)	261.64	260.40	258.99	258.21	264.92 (22/6)	215.60 (4/1)
SWEDEN						
Affarsvarlden Gen. (1/2/37)	1171.2	1154.5	1145.7	1142.4	1171.20 (26/7)	879.10 (28/1)
SWITZERLAND						
Swiss Bank Ind. (31/12/58)	1032.2	1020.2	1020.2	1002.4	1046.60 (13/7)	904.80 (11/1)
SBC General (1/4/87)	818.8	808.4	807.4	793.9	827.90 (13/7)	678.70 (11/1)
TAIWAN**						
Weighted Price (30/6/66)	4083.87	4027.58	3932.15	3906.97	5013.28 (7/4)	3088.43 (9/1)
THAILAND						
Bangkok SET (30/4/75)	890.54	894.07	897.44	894.55	998.44 (25/1)	818.84 (1/6)
WORLD						
M.S. Capital Intl.(1/1/70) $	568.8*	565.8	566.6	566.6	576.30 (3/6)	488.60 (13/1)
Euro Top-100 (26/6/90)	1045.58	1036.19†	1031.47	1023.32	1045.58 (26/7)	862.73 (13/1)

**Saturday July 24: Taiwan Weighted Price; 4030.42, Korea Comp Ex; 741.83.
♥ Subject to official recalculation.   † Correction.   *Calculated at 15.00 GMT.

Fig. 7.3 Indices

alongside the All-Share Ordinary Index because of the heavy weighting of resource stocks in the Australian market.

For France there are two indices: the CAC General Index records the opening prices on the Paris 'comptoir' or cash market, while the CAC 40 is a real-time index of the largest stocks. In Germany, three indices are commonly used: the Frankfurter Allgemeine Zeitung, the Commerzbank, and the DAX real-time index introduced at the end of 1987.

The Nikkei is the most widely quoted measure of stock price movements on the Tokyo Stock Exchange, the world's second biggest in terms of market capitalisation. Not strictly an index but an average of 225 shares, it is not weighted according to market capitalisation, so smaller firms can move the index as much as bigger ones. The index is run by the *Nihon Keizai Shimbun*, Japan's main financial daily newspaper. Nikkei is an abbreviation of the newspaper's name. The Nikkei is a benchmark similar to the Dow or the FT 30-Share but is more widely followed than the comprehensive Tokyo Stock Exchange index. The latter provides a more accurate guide to the state of the overall market.

In South Africa, the heavy preponderance of gold shares makes publication of the Gold Index indispensable. Since the index moves very closely in line with the gold price, the Johannesburg Stock Exchange (JSE) Industrial index is used to monitor the rest of the market.

Local indices carry great credibility in their local markets, but do not provide the whole picture for the global investor. For example, they may include equities not freely available to international fund managers or some national issues may be illiquid from the viewpoint of committing funds globally.

THE FT-ACTUARIES WORLD INDICES

The FT-Actuaries World Indices table covers global equity markets, expressing the various market indices in terms of both local and key international currencies (see Figure 7.4).

FT-ACTUARIES WORLD INDICES

Jointly compiled by The Financial Times Limited, Goldman, Sachs & Co. and NatWest Securities Limited in conjunction with the Institute of Actuaries and the Faculty of Actuaries

NATIONAL AND REGIONAL MARKETS	MONDAY JULY 26 1993								FRIDAY JULY 23 1993					DOLLAR INDEX		
Figures in parentheses show number of lines of stock	US Dollar Index	Day's Change %	Pound Sterling Index	Yen Index	DM Index	Local Currency Index	Local % chg on day	Gross Div. Yield	US Dollar Index	Pound Sterling Index	Yen Index	DM Index	Local Currency Index	1993 High	1993 Low	Year ago (approx)
Australia (69)	138.55	−0.6	136.76	93.58	124.22	135.79	−0.8	3.70	139.42	138.08	94.12	124.60	136.82	144.19	117.39	141.33
Austria (17)	159.52	+1.3	157.46	107.75	143.02	143.00	+1.8	1.36	157.44	155.93	106.29	140.71	140.41	159.52	131.16	150.98
Belgium (42)	147.23	−0.2	145.32	99.43	132.00	129.80	+0.3	4.41	147.46	146.04	99.54	131.78	129.46	156.76	131.19	145.74
Canada (108)	124.16	+1.1	122.55	83.85	111.31	115.12	+1.1	2.92	122.80	121.62	82.90	109.74	113.82	130.38	111.41	127.10
Denmark (33)	208.87	−0.1	206.17	141.07	187.26	190.40	+0.1	1.19	209.11	207.10	141.17	186.88	190.27	225.64	185.11	238.61
Finland (23)	95.82	+0.4	94.58	64.72	85.91	87.49	+0.1	1.04	95.42	94.50	64.42	85.28	87.40	100.92	65.50	70.36
France (97)	152.62	+0.2	150.65	103.08	136.82	140.95	+0.5	3.25	152.25	150.78	102.78	136.05	140.25	167.36	142.72	155.84
Germany (60)	116.90	+0.9	115.38	78.96	104.80	104.80	+1.2	2.02	115.89	114.78	78.25	103.57	103.57	117.10	101.59	119.36
Hong Kong (55)	276.00	+1.7	272.43	186.41	247.46	274.79	+1.7	3.45	271.42	268.81	183.23	242.58	270.20	301.61	218.82	235.97
Ireland (15)	157.93	+0.0	155.89	106.67	141.60	158.95	+0.3	3.47	157.90	156.38	106.60	141.12	158.42	170.40	129.28	157.08
Italy (70)	67.91	−0.4	67.03	45.87	60.88	81.35	−0.4	2.00	68.18	67.52	46.02	60.93	81.67	72.82	53.78	61.30
Japan (470)	150.39	+0.5	148.44	101.57	134.85	101.57	+0.5	0.82	149.68	148.24	101.05	133.79	101.05	155.96	100.75	91.87
United Kingdom (218)	173.81	+0.9	171.57	117.39	155.82	171.57	+0.6	4.04	172.26	170.60	116.28	153.93	170.60	181.99	162.00	178.81
USA (520)	183.83	+0.5	181.45	124.16	164.82	183.83	+0.5	2.79	182.97	181.21	123.53	163.53	182.97	186.27	175.38	167.80
Europe (751)	144.27	+0.7	142.41	97.44	129.35	138.82	+0.7	3.22	143.31	141.93	96.75	128.08	137.86	149.02	133.92	145.01
Nordic (114)	162.41	+1.1	160.31	109.69	145.61	168.99	+0.8	1.47	160.70	159.15	108.49	143.62	167.64	171.77	142.13	172.34
Pacific Basin (714)	153.74	+0.5	151.76	103.84	137.84	108.02	+0.5	1.09	153.03	151.56	103.31	136.77	107.48	159.07	105.89	98.55
Euro-Pacific (1465)	149.74	+0.5	147.81	101.13	134.25	120.83	+0.6	1.93	148.93	147.50	100.53	133.09	120.14	154.05	117.26	117.34
North America (628)	180.12	+0.5	177.79	121.67	161.51	179.16	+0.5	2.80	179.23	177.51	121.01	160.21	178.28	182.38	171.51	165.24
Europe Ex. UK (533)	125.71	+0.5	124.08	84.92	112.73	119.57	+0.8	2.66	125.06	123.85	84.44	111.79	118.64	128.65	112.51	124.40
Pacific Ex. Japan (244)	187.25	+0.4	184.83	126.49	167.90	173.02	+0.4	3.20	186.49	184.69	125.92	166.68	172.42	194.08	152.70	164.42
World Ex. US (1652)	150.32	+0.6	148.38	101.54	134.78	122.83	+0.6	1.96	149.45	148.01	100.90	133.57	122.08	154.27	118.51	119.26
World Ex. UK (1954)	159.24	+0.5	157.18	107.56	142.78	138.61	+0.6	2.10	158.45	156.92	106.97	141.62	137.85	161.34	134.22	130.54
World Ex. So. Af. (2112)	160.35	+0.5	158.28	108.31	143.77	141.19	+0.6	2.27	159.48	157.94	107.67	142.54	140.40	162.74	137.29	134.36
World Ex. Japan (1702)	167.87	+0.6	165.70	113.39	150.53	164.15	+0.6	2.94	166.92	165.32	112.70	149.20	163.21	170.05	157.47	158.50
The World Index (2172)	160.54	+0.5	158.47	108.44	143.95	141.69	+0.6	2.28	159.69	158.15	107.81	142.72	140.91	162.86	137.32	134.71

Copyright, The Financial Times Limited, Goldman, Sachs & Co. and NatWest Securities Limited. 1987

Fig. 7.4 FT-Actuaries World Indices

READING THE FIGURES

- Calculated by the FT, Goldman, Sachs and NatWest Securities in conjunction with the Institute and Faculty of Actuaries.

- Launched in March 1987 and based on just under 2,200 equity securities from 24 countries, the indices represent at least 70 per cent of the total market capitalisation of the world's main stock exchanges.

- The complete World series has eleven regional indices. Figures are shown for these and the main country indices. Seven broad economic sectors are made up from more than thirty composite industry indices, derived from over 100 sub-industry categories. For example, the consumer goods/services sector has twelve industry groups and as many as thirty-six subsectors ranging from automobiles to tobacco manufacturers, from health care to the broadcast media.

- The series is calculated nightly in five currencies (the dollar, pound sterling, yen, and deutsche mark plus the local currency) with the percentage change on the previous day shown in terms of the dollar and the local currency. The figures for the five currency indices are shown for the previous trading day plus the highs and lows for the year and the value for the dollar index a year ago .

- Markets, companies and securities are only included where direct holdings of shares and repatriation of dividends by foreign nationals are allowed. Also excluded are companies where 75 per cent or more of the issued capital is controlled by dominant shareholders, or where less than 25 per cent of the shares are available to investors through the local market.

- Each company subset aims to capture at least 70 per cent of the total market value of all shares listed on the domestic exchange, or between 82 and 87 per cent of the eligible universe of stocks. In some countries, this is not possible because of restrictions on foreign shareholdings.

- The indices aim to cover a significant proportion of the stocks listed in each market rather than concentrating merely on the

largest companies, and encompass around 15 per cent of an estimated universe of more than 15,000 listed companies.

- The number of US companies (by far the most broadly based of the world's equity markets) is limited to just over 500 under the rules of the indices.

- To ensure that they reflect a reasonable marketability of shares, companies with a market capitalisation of less than $100 million

MARKETS IN PERSPECTIVE

	% change in local currency †				% change sterling †	% change in US $ †
	1 Week	4 Weeks	1 Year	Start of 1993	Start of 1993	Start of 1993
Austria	+4.82	+8.14	+17.38	+19.61	+13.61	+12.33
Belgium	-1.46	+4.16	+16.56	+18.51	+11.94	+10.68
Denmark	-1.39	+0.35	+2.62	+19.79	+13.63	+12.35
Finland	+0.46	+14.07	+87.96	+53.64	+38.62	+37.08
France	+1.00	+2.28	+15.74	+9.96	+4.62	+3.44
Germany	+0.94	+7.63	+10.60	+18.23	+12.66	+11.39
Ireland	-1.10	+2.90	+26.83	+34.39	+17.61	+16.29
Italy	-0.91	+5.19	+54.47	+35.26	+25.67	+24.26
Netherlands	-0.19	+1.37	+18.89	+16.16	+10.57	+9.33
Norway	-2.00	+5.55	+19.22	+20.73	+15.11	+13.82
Spain	+0.73	+0.27	+24.80	+21.71	+2.89	+1.73
Sweden	+0.21	+6.79	+38.88	+16.93	+3.54	+2.37
Switzerland	-1.64	-0.12	+31.52	+14.85	+12.14	+10.88
UK	-0.18	-1.90	+20.66	+1.08	+1.08	-0.06
EUROPE	**-0.02**	**+1.35**	**+21.02**	**+10.42**	**+6.56**	**+5.73**
Australia	+0.48	+5.84	+7.88	+13.07	+12.70	+11.43
Hong Kong	-2.85	-4.29	+10.44	+22.70	+23.90	+22.50
Japan	-2.62	+1.76	+32.32	+21.91	+44.13	+42.51
Malaysia	+4.45	+7.49	+45.37	+29.89	+33.88	+32.38
New Zealand	+0.76	+3.47	+11.79	+13.86	+23.17	+21.80
Singapore	+3.18	+3.58	+22.88	+17.53	+20.51	+19.16
Canada	-2.13	-5.98	+3.70	+6.90	+7.40	+6.19
USA	+0.24	+0.04	+9.03	+2.73	+3.90	+2.73
Mexico	-2.26	+2.61	+5.97	-7.94	-6.92	-7.97
South Africa	-2.52	-1.12	+17.83	+27.73	+39.68	+38.11
WORLD INDEX	**-0.82**	**+0.82**	**+17.96**	**+10.59**	**+15.68**	**+14.39**

† Based on July 23rd 1993.   Copyright, The Financial Times Limited, Goldman Sachs & Co, and NatWest Securities Limited.

Fig. 7.5 Markets in perspective

are generally excluded. This cut-off level is lowered, however, in the case of countries whose average market capitalisation is less than $100 million.

- Companies and markets are only included where a timely and reliable source of daily price movements is available.

USING THE INFORMATION

The index is designed to represent global equity markets and to reflect the increases in cross-border equity investment, particularly from the United States and Japan. It is designed primarily for such end-users as pension fund managers, consultants and money managers. Its primary function is global equity performance measurement, hence it is essential that shares that make up the index can be purchased and sold, but it is also being used for the creation of derivative products, such as stock index funds. An increasing number of companies are running funds designed to track the FT-A World Indices or one or more of their subseries.

Markets in perspective

Derived from the FT-Actuaries World Indices, a further chart (see Figure 7.5), records movements in leading international market indices in terms of local currencies, dollars and sterling.

- **National markets:** shows percentage changes in market indices in a number of leading markets from a week ago, a month ago, a year ago and from the start of the year. Figures are given in local currencies, and in dollars and sterling for changes from the start of the year.

Evaluating quarterly performance

The FT-A World Indices quarterly valuation (see Figure 7.6) carries quarterly assessments of market capitalisation and relative market size for the major national and regional markets.

- **Market capitalisation:** calculated for each market by multiplying the total number of shares in issue by the market price per share.

FT-ACTUARIES WORLD INDICES QUARTERLY VALUATION

The market capitalisation of the national and regional markets of the FT-Actuaries World indices as at JUNE 30, 1993 are expressed below in millions of US dollars and as a percentage of the World Index. Similar figures are provided for the preceding quarter.
The percentage change for each Dollar index value since the end of the calendar year is also provided.

NATIONAL AND REGIONAL MARKETS Figures in parentheses show number of lines of stock	Market capitalisation as at JUNE 30, 1993 (US$m)	% of World Index	Market capitalisation as at MARCH 31, 1993 (US$m)	% of World Index	% change in $ index since DECEMBER 31, 1992
Australia (68)	103395.7	1.25	107176.6	1.37	+5.27
Austria (18)	10354.4	0.12	9861.5	0.13	+4.79
Belgium (42)	54451.8	0.66	56425.1	0.72	+10.13
Canada (108)	141914.2	1.71	136258.3	1.74	+10.55
Denmark (33)	26551.3	0.32	24917.5	0.32	+17.26
Finland (23)	11782.7	0.14	9464.2	0.12	+34.13
France (97)	252093.3	3.04	270100.3	3.45	+4.18
Germany (62)	252256.8	3.04	264841.2	3.38	+4.54
Hong Kong (55)	140999.5	1.70	124357.7	1.59	+29.61
Europe (761)	1928984.5	23.26	1909694.2	24.37	+5.78
Nordic (114)	107547.4	1.30	99354.8	1.27	+8.77
Pacific Basin (713)	2892341.0	34.87	2479786.1	31.64	+36.96
Euro-Pacific (1474)	4821325.5	58.13	4389480.3	56.00	+22.58
North America (627)	3352031.0	40.41	3332978.5	42.52	+3.76
Europe Ex. UK (542)	1142830.6	13.78	1136756.1	14.50	+8.47
Pacific Ex. Japan (243)	336414.1	4.06	312404.3	3.99	+18.86
World Ex. US (1660)	5084572.1	61.30	4641025.3	59.21	+22.05
World Ex. UK (1960)	7508535.1	90.52	7064807.4	90.14	+15.54
World Ex. So. Af. (2119)	8215414.5	99.04	7767621.5	99.11	+13.96
World Ex. Japan (1709)	5738762.1	69.19	5670363.8	72.35	+5.46
The World Index (2179)	8294689.0	100.00	7837745.5	100.00	+14.13

© The Financial Times Limited, Goldman, Sachs & Co, and NatWest Securities Limited. 1987

Fig. 7.6 FT Actuaries world indices quarterly valuation

- **Percentage of world index:** the relative size of each market to the whole.

EMERGING MARKETS

Each Thursday, the *Financial Times* carries data on the emerging stock markets of Latin America, East and South Asia, Europe and the Middle East, which are attracting increasing investor attention. The tables are prepared by the International Finance Corporation, a subsidiary of the World Bank, as a complement to the much more comprehensive daily coverage of the FT-Actuaries world series (see Figure 7.7).

- **Market and number of stocks**

- **Dollar terms:** the latest value of the local market index, the percentage change over the previous week, and from the end of the previous year.

- **Local currency terms:** the same figures in the local currency.

EMERGING MARKETS: IFC WEEKLY INVESTABLE PRICE INDICES

Market	No. of stocks	Dollar terms			Local currency terms		
		Jul 23 1993	% Change over week	% Change on Dec '92	Jul 23 1993	% Change over week	% Change on Dec '92
Latin America							
Argentina	(11)	606.30	+0.8	+4.5	372,043.54	+0.8	+4.7
Brazil	(44)	188.29	+3.3	+50.6	17,151,437.18	+9.8	+722.4
Chile	(20)	409.92	-0.9	-2.1	663.78	-0.9	+3.5
Colombia[1]	(8)	397.95	+1.9	-6.4	562.18	+2.0	-8.1
Mexico	(59)	661.16	+1.6	-2.2	889.75	+1.4	-2.0
Venezuela[2]	(8)	598.27	+3.1	+15.1	1,241.38	+3.7	+33.0
East Asia							
South Korea[3]	(130)	99.76	-2.5	+1.6	106.01	-2.4	+4.2
Philippines	(11)	152.04	-0.1	+13.9	205.08	+3.1	+26.9
Taiwan, China[4]	(76)	84.12	+1.5	+14.0	83.59	+2.3	+19.9
South Asia							
India[5]	(61)	73.33	+1.6	-21.7	81.09	+1.6	-15.1
Indonesia[6]	(31)	79.11	-0.6	+34.8	89.81	-0.7	+36.6
Malaysia	(61)	210.53	+4.5	+28.7	199.25	+4.3	+26.3
Pakistan[7]	(8)	235.67	+7.7	+17.7	300.21	+11.6	+29.5
Thailand	(52)	245.10	+1.2	+6.4	246.51	+1.0	+5.7
Euro/Mid East							
Greece	(17)	226.75	+2.8	+16.1	362.87	+3.4	+27.4
Jordan	(5)	164.39	-3.2	+40.7	235.71	-3.6	+42.1
Portugal	(16)	90.27	-2.7	+17.0	106.46	0.0	+36.6
Turkey[8]	(31)	127.42	-6.5	+90.5	664.18	-6.5	+147.7

Indices are calculated at end-week, and weekly changes are percentage movement from the previous Friday. Base date: Dec 1988=100 except those noted which are:(1)Feb 1 1991;(2)Jan 5 1990;(3)Jan 3 1992;(4)Jan 4 1991;(5)Nov 6 1992;(6)Sep 28 1990;(7)Mar 1 1991;(8)Aug 4 1989

Fig. 7.7 Emerging markets: IFC weekly investable price indices

8

TRUSTS AND FUNDS
The managed money markets

Managed funds are collective investment vehicles that are run by investment companies to provide professional management of investors' money. These funds in turn may be linked to other financial products. Managed funds are an easy way to get into share-buying for small, private investors.

THE MANAGED FUNDS SERVICE

The FT's managed funds service provides investors with information relating to a substantial number of managed funds. The information is provided by the individual management groups to a specific formula laid down for UK authorised bodies by the regulatory organisations. The address and telephone number of the group are normally given under its name, except in the case of those offshore funds that have not been authorised by the Securities and Investments Board (SIB) or the Department of Trade and Industry (DTI) to be promoted for general sale in the United Kingdom. This does not mean that they are in some way suspect; it merely signifies that the country in which they are based has not applied for designated territory status. This status is only given if the country's regulatory system is deemed to be at least equal to that ruling in the United Kingdom.

Authorised unit trusts

Unit trusts offer professional management of funds pooled together and divided into units whose value is based on the market valuation of the securities acquired by the fund. Hence the value of the units varies in accordance with the movement of the market price of the securities owned by the fund. Authorised unit trusts are unit trusts that have been approved as being suitable for general promotion and sale in the United Kingdom.

The attraction of unit trusts is that they enable small investors to achieve the advantages available to large investors of cheaper dealing costs and a spread of investments to reduce risk. They can also be tailored to meet the particular needs of investors looking for capital growth or income, or to go into specific sectors and overseas markets. They are therefore also widely used by stockbrokers and fund management groups. Since capital gains tax on sales and purchases made within the fund does not have to be paid, unit trusts have the additional advantage of favourable tax treatment.

Under the deed creating the trust, unit trust management groups have an obligation to keep investors properly informed about movements in the value of the underlying units in the investment funds. Instead of having to circulate information to each unit holder individually, it is accepted by the authorities that this obligation can be discharged by regular publication of the unit prices in certain national newspapers, in particular the *Financial Times* (see Figure 8.1).

READING THE FIGURES

- **Name of the investment group, its pricing system and trust name:** each investment group is listed together with its component trusts, and the basis of its pricing system. The price regime for each group is measured at a certain cut-off point, the figure in brackets representing a time, and calculated on a forward (F) or historical (H) basis.

- **Initial charge:** the second column indicates the percentage charge imposed on buyers of the fund to cover the 'front load' costs. If it is five per cent, out of every £100 invested, £5 is retained by the management group to cover its costs, leaving the remaining £95 to be actually invested in the fund.

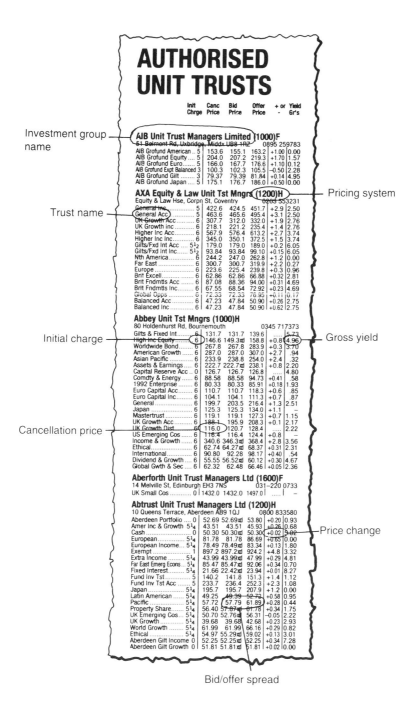

Fig. 8.1 Authorised unit trusts

- **Cancellation price:** the third column shows the lowest estimated bid price available for sellers if there was a large excess of selling, forcing the fund to dispose of units. The fund is put on a pricing (or bid) basis aimed at discouraging sales and encouraging purchases.

- **Bid/offer spread:** the fourth and fifth columns show the gap between the bid price, at which units can be sold, and the offer price, at which they can be bought. These are calculated by the group assessing the value of the underlying securities held at the most recent lowest market dealing price (plus other assets like uninvested income and undistributed income), adding the various costs involved such as dealing charges, and dividing the total by the number of units issued.

- **Price change:** the sixth column compares the mid-point between the bid and offer prices with the previous quotation. It may be unchanged, or show an upward or downward trend, according to changes in the value of the underlying securities or an alteration in the bid/offer spread. Since Saturday's FT carries the price change for the last day's trading of the week, the Monday paper replaces this column with the trust's Cityline number (see page 70).

- **Gross yield:** is the gross income paid by the unit trust as a percentage of the offer price. The quoted yield reflects income earned by the fund during the previous twelve months, and therefore only relates to past performance.

USING THE INFORMATION

The information provided means that investors can calculate how much their unit trust holdings are worth, and how they are performing on a day-to-day basis. Details of charges made by individual fund groups are also provided.

The spread is used by unit trust groups to collect the initial charge imposed to cover the expense of setting up and promoting the fund as well as recouping other costs. It also takes into account the bid/offer spread of the underlying assets. Under the formula laid down by the SIB, the spread for unit trusts can only be moved up and down within a limited scale. If there is a surplus of sellers, the spread tends to be based at the bottom end of the scale, at or near the cancellation price. Conversely, if there is an excess of buyers, the spread is raised to the upper end of the scale, enhancing the value of the fund. It is therefore a useful exercise to compare cancellation and bid prices to get an idea of whether a trust is attracting more buyers than sellers or vice versa.

Unit trusts with low, or even nil yields are those concentrating on capital growth rather than providing income. If there is a yield, UK investors have to deduct their top rate of income tax from this yield to calculate the true (net) return they will receive. Hence a gross yield of 10 per cent is currently only equivalent to 6 per cent for the top-rate taxpayer.

The relationship between risk and return is important to selection, as are investment goals: income, capital growth or total return. Unit trusts should generally be seen as a long-term investment: they need time to recoup the dealing charges.

Other UK unit trusts

These are trusts that are not authorised by the SIB and which are therefore not open to investment by members of the general public. They are available only to specific buyers such as pension funds, charities and local authorities.

INVESTMENT TRUSTS

Investment trusts are companies that exist to invest in the equity of other companies, and their business consists entirely of buying, selling and holding shares. Like unit trusts, they provide an accessible vehicle for small investors to achieve a wide spread of investments. Investment trusts differ from unit trusts, however, in the sense that they issue equity themselves, and hence their shareholders hold a direct stake in the profits of the trust rather than merely the profits of a unit of shareholdings. Their performance is listed in the FT's London Share Service.

The Investment Trust section of the London Share Service (see Figure 8.2) includes the net asset value (NAV) of the trust and the dis-

INVESTMENT TRUSTS

	Notes	Price	+ or –	1993 high	low	Yld Gr's	NAV	Dis or Pm(-)
Authorised by the Inland Revenue								
Aberforth Smllr	.......□	167xd	......	167	121	3.4	155.1	–7.7
Warrants	....	76	......	76	48	–	–	–
Aberforth Split Inc	......	90$\frac{1}{2}$xd	......	95	78	11.6	–	–
Cap	....	157	......	160	115	–	240.4	–34.9
Units	....	249xd	+1	251	195	4.2	250.9	1.0
Abtrust Euro Index ♣N□		74	+$\frac{1}{2}$	74	59	0.5	77.8	4.9
Warrants	....	18	+$\frac{1}{2}$	18	6$\frac{1}{2}$	–	–	–
Abtrust New Dawn..♣□		179xd	+1	183	131	0.5	188.7	5.2
Warrants	....	90	+2	90	46	–	–	–
B Warrants	....	60	+1	60	21	–	–	–
For Abtrust New Euro see Abtrust Euro Index Inv								
Abtrust New Thai.♣□		111	+1	115	82	1.1	121.7	9.2
Warrants	....	36	......	41	18	–	–	–
Abtrust Prf Inc..... ♣M		109	+1$\frac{1}{2}$	109	72	14.1	104.8	–2.2
Zero Div Pf	....	149	......	149	141	–	–	–
Abtrust Scotland .....♣		26	......	26	19	3.0	34.6	24.8
Albany	....	123	......	123	106	4.1	133.3	8.1
Alliance Tst........♣		1731	–2	1733	1548	3.2	1844.7	6.2
American Tst	.........□	262	–2	264	226$\frac{1}{2}$	2.3	279.1	6.0
B	....	250	+2$\frac{1}{2}$	253	218	–	–	–
Amicable Smllr	.......□	116	+1	118	90	3.7	118.8	2.8
Warrants	....	35	......	36	26	–	–	–
Anglo & O'seas ....♣□		379	–1	380	304	2.3	438.4	13.7
Archimedes Inc	....	220	......	235	180	14.2	–	–
Cap	....	300	......	300	240	–	577.1	48.0
BZW Conv	............□	131$\frac{1}{2}$	......	139$\frac{1}{2}$	124	7.3	126.8	–5.1
Eq Ind 96–2	....	147	......	147	133	1.3	–	–
Baillie Giff Jap	........♣	703	+2	703	438	–	749.4	6.5
Baillie Giff Shin ...♣□		158	......	158	86	–	156.8	0.1
Baillie Giff Tech	....	10	......	10	9	–	7.4	–29.1
Bankers'........ .♣†□		170$\frac{1}{2}$	+1	170$\frac{1}{2}$	133$\frac{1}{2}$	2.5	165.0	–3.3
Baring Stratton	....	184	......	186	180	1.6	223.7	18.0
Baring Tribune	....	291xd	......	298	264	2.8	345.5	15.8
Berry Starquest.......♣		179	......	179	131	1.5	202.6	11.9
Beta Global	....	125	......	125	111	–	130.4	4.5
Warrants	....	47	......	47	28	–	–	–
Brazilian Inv Tst	....	62$\frac{1}{4}$	......	69	40$\frac{1}{2}$	0.7	67.2	7.1
Warrants	....	38$\frac{3}{8}$	......	43	21	–	–	–
British Assets......K□		106	–1	107	96$\frac{1}{2}$	5.0	107.6	1.7
Eq Ind 2005 ....□		145	......	145	136	3.7	–	–
Brit Empire..........♣□		76	......	76	57$\frac{1}{2}$	1.5	85.3	11.2
Warrants	....	26	......	26	14	–	–	–
British Inv	....	181	–1	183	156	3.1	207.8	12.9
Broadgate Tst	....	117	......	125	115	–	117.5	0.9
Brunner	.................†	201xd	......	201	174	3.1	234.5	14.3
CU Enviromental ......Z		95	......	106	88	1.1	108.5	12.4
Warrants	....	39	......	40	24	–	–	–
Candover	....	285	......	288	243	4.5	269.1	–5.9
Castle Cairn	....	49	......	50	40	2.0	57.3	15.3
Warrants	....	14$\frac{1}{2}$	......	14$\frac{1}{2}$	9$\frac{1}{2}$	–	–	–
China Inv Tst........□		91	......	100	90	–	–	–
Warrants	....	51	......	53	32	–	–	–
City Mer High Yld ....♣		131	......	131	99	7.5	132.1	0.9
City of Oxford.........□		29	......	30	19	21.6	34.4	17.1
Warrants	....	4$\frac{3}{4}$	......	5	2$\frac{1}{2}$	–	–	–
Zero Div Pf	....	93$\frac{3}{4}$	+$\frac{1}{2}$	93$\frac{3}{4}$	86$\frac{1}{4}$	–	–	–
Contl Assets	....	175	......	175	130	1.7	175.5	0.3

Trust name

Stock type

Net asset value

Discount against net asset value

Closing price   Price change   Gross yield

Fig. 8.2 London Share Service – investment trusts

count at which the share price typically stands in relation to that asset value. The NAV is the market value of the various securities in which the trust has invested, and therefore what, in theory, the trust might be worth if it were liquidated immediately. This figure is of key importance to investors, not least because in recent decades investment trust share prices have tended to trade at a significant discount to net asset value, making them tempting targets for takeovers.

The figures are supplied by a leading broker and are the result of a daily simulation of changes in portfolio values. Calculations of the discount are generally reliable but, in some cases, such as recent new issues with substantial uninvested cash or funds, which have radically restructured their portfolios, the estimates may need to be treated with caution.

INSURANCES

These are funds that are managed by insurance companies and are linked to other savings products such as investment bonds, regular premium policies or pension contracts (see Figure 8.3).

Fig. 8.3 Insurances

Offshore insurances

These are funds that are run by insurance companies which are based in countries with designated territory status for insurance products.

The funds listed are linked to products which the companies are authorised to promote in the United Kingdom. Such authorisation must be sought from the SIB.

Management services

These are funds which are managed mainly by intermediaries. They are often known as 'broker bonds'. Many of them are underwritten by insurance companies.

OFFSHORE AND OVERSEAS

These are funds based in foreign counties, often with a more liberal tax regime that Britain, but effectively operating under the advice or management of groups offering authorised unit trusts in the United Kingdom (see Figure 8.4).

Fig. 8.4 Offshore and overseas

SIB-recognised funds

These are offshore funds that are based in designated territory-status countries and the European Community and for which authorisation for promotion in the United Kingdom has been secured from the SIB. These funds can be sold freely without any restrictions and their full names, addresses and telephone numbers are therefore included in the listing.

Regulated funds

These funds are based in designated territory-status countries which comply with local regulations but have not applied for official SIB recognition for sale in the United Kingdom. They cannot be promoted in the United Kingdom and therefore only the names are listed.

Other offshore funds

These are funds based in countries throughout the world but predominantly in tax havens. They cannot be advertised in the United Kingdom and again only the names are listed.

9

BONDS AND EUROBONDS
The international capital markets

Bonds are debt instruments, securities sold by governments, companies and banks in order to raise capital. They normally carry a fixed
rate of interest, known as the coupon, have a fixed redemption value,
the par value, and are repaid after a fixed period, the maturity. Some
carry little or no interest (deep discount and zero coupon bonds),
rewarding the buyer instead with a substantial discount from their
redemption value and, hence, the prospect of a sizeable capital gain.

As seen in chapter 1, the prices of bonds fluctuate in relation to the
interest rate. The secondary market for bonds provides the liquidity
necessary for a thriving primary market. This now exists not only for
government bonds, but also on an international scale for all kinds of
debt instruments.

National boundaries are no longer an obstruction to lenders and
borrowers meeting in a market to buy and sell securities. It is possible
for borrowers in one country to issue securities denominated in the
currency of another, and for these to be sold to investors in a third
country. Often, such transactions will be organised by financial institutions located in yet another country, usually one of the three primary centres of these international capital markets – London, New
York and Tokyo. These are the Euromarkets.

The International Capital Markets pages of the *Financial Times*
attempt to keep track of developments in the Euromarkets and other
areas which involve the raising of capital across borders. These
include the growing markets in derivative products (such as futures,
options, and interest rate and currency swaps) and in cross-border
new equity issues. The newspaper also tracks developments in impor-

tant government bond markets such as the US Treasury bond market and, of course, the market in UK government bonds, known as gilt-edged stock or gilts.

From Tuesday to Friday, daily reports cover the market in international bonds, including Eurobonds and government bonds. These markets, like the international equity markets, are not compartmentalised. In the interdependent world of international finance, developments in one market will often influence many others. For example, a sharp rally in gilts is likely to prompt a similar rally in Eurosterling bonds, which may in turn encourage borrowers to launch new issues.

GOVERNMENT BONDS

As discussed in chapter 4, the government of a country finances many of its activities through borrowing from lenders by issuing bonds. In the United Kingdom, government bonds are known as gilt-edged securities and they trade in a secondary market run by leading marketmakers, using the Stock Exchange only as a price exporting mechanism.

British funds

Detailed price information on the UK government bond market is contained in the London share service from Tuesday to Saturday under the heading British Funds. These are classified under four headings based on their time to redemption: 'shorts' with lives up to five years, 'medium-dated' with lives from five to fifteen years, 'longs' with lives of over fifteen years, and undated, irredeemable stocks like Consols and War Loan. The classifications reflect the current life of the stock rather than the life when it was issued, and so stocks get reclassified as their date of maturity draws closer. There is also a fifth category, index-linked gilts, whose yield is tied to the rate of inflation.

The gilt market is moved by economic and financial news, notably the movements of interest rates and inflation. The key to understanding it is that as interest rates go up, bond prices go down, making the coupon an effective rate of interest. Since a high rate may be used to support a weak currency, a weakness in the currency may signal future increases in the interest rate, and a damaging effect on gilt prices. Similarly, prospects of inflation may lead to rate increases and bond price falls. Inflation also erodes the value of bonds since their prices and yields, unless index-linked, do not keep pace with rising prices generally. Hence, it is important for investors in bonds to look for changes in expectations about the future rates of interest and inflation. Other price determinants include the degree of risk (credit risk in the case of companies), the opportunity cost of other potential investments, and the time value.

The market for gilts is run by primary dealers, the gilt-edged marketmakers who have an obligation to maintain a market and a right to deal directly with the Bank of England in, for example, bidding for tap stock. Information on gilt prices is carried on SEAQ and transactions are for immediate or cash settlement. Institutional investors generally deal directly with the primary dealers. Figure 9.1 shows FT listings of British funds.

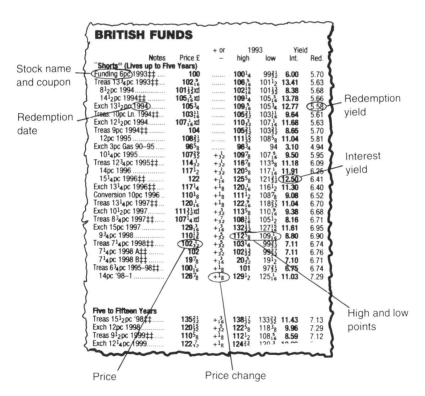

Fig. 9.1 London Share Service – British funds

- **Stock name and coupon:** the name given to a gilt is not important except as a means of differentiating it from others. The coupon, however, indicates how much nominal yield the owner is entitled to receive annually. Most gilts are issued in units of £100 (their par value), and so the percentage is equivalent to the number of pounds the owner receives. The coupon is a good indication of the interest rates the government was obliged to pay at the time of issue, and of the broad movements in the rate over the years.

- **Redemption date:** the year of redemption by the government, the specific date on which repayment of the loan will take place. If there are two dates, there is no specific date for repayment, but the stock will not be redeemed before the first one, and must be by the second one.

- **Price, price change and the year's high and low points:** the price is the middle price between the buying and selling price quoted by marketmakers in pounds and fractions of pounds (usually in thirty-seconds) for a nominal £100 of stock. Each gilt has this par value, and moves of a point mean that it has risen or fallen by £1 in price.

- **Interest yield:** this yield (also known as the income, earnings or flat yield) depends on the current price of the stock. It is calculated by dividing the coupon by the current price. This explains mathematically why bond prices always fall when interest rates rise and vice versa: since the coupon is, by definition, fixed, the price and yield are in an inverse relationship. To maintain a competitive yield when interest rates rise, the price has to fall. Gross redemption yield is the interest rate plus the capital gains or losses.

- **Redemption yield:** this figure indicates the total return to be secured by holding on to a stock until it is finally redeemed by the government. It thus includes the capital gains or losses made at redemption as well as the income from the coupon. If the current price is below £100, the redemption yield will be bigger than the interest yield since, assuming the bond is held to redemption, there will also be a capital gain.

- **Tap stock:** a large black dot in the British funds signals a tap stock. This is a gilt issue of which the Bank of England, performing its role as the government's broker, still holds a part and is ready to supply to the market. When the Bank announces a new stock, part of the issue is often left unsold to release to the market in the future. This minimises any effect of depressing gilt prices overall that a new issue might have.

Also included in the London Share Service are index-linked bonds. These bonds, the interest and redemption value are adjusted to account for movement in the retail prices index with a time lag of eight months. In this way, they maintain their real value, and hedge their owners against inflation. The price of the hedge is the lower nominal coupon rate. The yield columns of the table give two possible redemption yields, one based on the assumption of 10 per cent inflation, the other on the assumption of 5 per cent inflation. The table also indicates the base date for the indexation calculation.

Monday's FT has a variation on the listing for British funds, indicating the percentage price change on the previous week, the total amount of the stock in issue in millions of pounds (a fixed sum since the stock is guaranteed by the government to be redeemed at that amount, the bond equivalent of market capitalisation), the dates on which the interest is paid (twice yearly), the last ex-dividend payment of interest and the Cityline telephone number for real-time updates on the stock price.

The market price of a gilt reflects its redemption value, coupon and other rates. It is not directly determined by its redemption value until the redemption date gets closer. As a gilt approaches redemption, its price will get closer and closer to £100, the amount for which it will be redeemed.

Long-dated stock prices move most in response to expectations of rate changes. Since their maturity value is fixed, they are a good indicator of expected trends in the rate of interest and the rate of inflation. As explained in chapter 1, investors expect higher rates of return for longer-term investments. If short-term rates become higher than long-term, investors will move out of short-term assets. Thus, short- and long-term rates tend to move together. The yield curve is a means of comparing rates on bonds of different maturities, as well as giving an indication of the tightness of monetary conditions. Longer-term yields are usually higher because of the greater degree of risk (time and inflation risk). When short-term rates are higher, there is a negative yield curve.

Interest and redemption yields quoted only apply to a new buyer. The yields for investors already in possession will depend on the price they paid. But, in both cases, the yields can be calculated exactly, in contrast with equities where both the dividend and capital gain or loss are uncertain. This reflects the greater degree of risk associated with investment in equities.

The difference between income yield and redemption yield is important to the investor because of the tax implications. Income from gilts is taxed but capital gains are not. Hence, the net return is determined by the composition of the total return.

The investor will also want to compare bond and equity yields. The yield gap (long-term bond yields minus the dividend yield on shares) is a good indicator of the relative rates, though generally, due to fears of inflation and the opportunities for capital gains on shares, there is a reverse yield gap.

Index-linked stocks are valuable when inflation is feared; they are not so good when the real rates of return on gilts are high, that is, when nominal yields are above the rate of inflation. The difference between the long bond yield and the real yield on index-linked stocks is an indicator of expected inflation.

New government bond issues are often the focus of FT reports on the gilt market as this extract indicates:

> The £3.25 billion sale of 8 per cent stock due 2003 had been aimed at international investors who have been heavy buyers of UK paper on the back of low inflation, low growth and the prospect of sterling appreciation. However, over the past week, gilt prices have risen sharply and the pound has raced ahead against a number of European currencies. Yesterday's auction was covered only 1.1 times, the lowest level since January 1988. (*Financial Times*, 1 July 1993)

This demonstrates the major influences on the gilt market. For example, low inflation implies returns, in terms of both interest and capital appreciation, that are not eroded in value. It also suggests continuing low interest rates which, though not promising for income, do prevent prices from falling. In fact, the corollary of low growth suggests the reverse: the possibility of interest rate cuts to spur growth, and hence of capital appreciation. It also means there will be less of a threat from the inflationary pressures of a boom. The appreciation in sterling itself implies that interest rate increases are unnecessary and that cuts may be possible, which in itself it is of benefit to investors whose home currencies are depreciating against the pound.

At the same time, the second sentence of the extract implies that these benefits may have already been discounted by the market and, indeed, that both prices and the pound may now be highly valued. This leads to the lack of enthusiasm for the new issue: the auction's cover means the factor by which the issue has been oversubscribed. Since the rate of interest typically goes up in a time of economic buoyancy, bond prices tend to fall on the upswing of the business cycle.

Private investors are becoming increasingly interested in bonds and gilts as investments. Banks recognise this and are promoting actively to this group; Saturday's FT now regularly features advertisements and brochures for bond issues clearly directed at the private investor.

Fixed interest indices

As well as individual bond prices, the FT provides indices of a broad range of fixed interest instruments (see Figure 9.2).

• **Government securities (UK):** the movements of a representative

FT FIXED INTEREST INDICES

	July 14	July 13	July 12	July 9	July 8	Year ago	High *	Low *
Govt Secs (UK)	98.46	97.90	98.06	97.89	97.86	89.54	98.46	93.28
Fixed Interest	116.84	116.53	116.21	116.00	115.90	106.22	116.84	108.67

Basis 100: Government Securities 15/10/26; Fixed Interest 1928.
* for 1993. Government Securities high since compilation: 127.40 (9/1/35), low 49.18 (3/1/75)
Fixed Interest high since compilation: 116.84 (14/7/93), low 50.53 (3/1/75)

GILT EDGED ACTIVITY

Indices*	July 13	July 12	July 9	July 8	July 7
Gilt Edged Bargains	110.2	102.3	97.4	92.3	107.3
5-Day average	101.9	101.7	100.4	100.2	106.4

* SE activity indices rebased 1974

Commercial banks needed   council meeting today and will

Fig. 9.2 FT fixed interest indices

cross-section of gilt-edged stocks, the Government Securities Index, over the past five trading days, the value of the index a year ago, and its high and low points for the year to date. This index began from a base of 100 in 1926, and the notes to the table detail its high and low since compilation.

- **Fixed interest:** the movements of a broader range of fixed interest stocks, including those issued by the UK government, local government, public boards and by British industrial companies. As with the gilts index, this charts the index values over the past five trading days, one year ago and at its zenith and nadir both for the year and since compilation.

- **Gilt-edged activity indices:** gilt-edged bargains and five-day average are a measure of the level of gilt-edged activity, the number of transactions on the five previous days and a rolling five-day average. They are an indicator of the liquidity of the market.

The FT-Actuaries fixed interest indices (see Figure 9.3) are designed to perform roughly the same service for professional investors in gilt-

| , ı⁄₀)   180   4   15 17½   9   17   20   (*191)   200   7   15   19   19   24 26½ | Euro FT-SE Calls 706 Puts 5,856 *Underlying security price. † Long dated expiry mths. Premiums shown are based on closing offer prices. |

FT-ACTUARIES FIXED INTEREST INDICES

PRICE INDICES						AVERAGE GROSS REDEMPTION YIELDS			Wed Jul 14	Tue Jul 13	Year ago (approx.)
	Wed Jul 14	Day's change %	Tue Jul 13	Accrued Interest	xd adj 1993 to date	**British Government**					
						1 Low	5 years.........		6.75	6.80	8.24
						2 Coupons	15 years........		7.74	7.83	8.68
						3 (0%-7¾%)	20 years........		7.90	7.98	8.68
British Government						4 Medium	5 years.........		6.90	6.94	9.17
1 Up to 5 years (25) ..	128.61	+0.11	128.46	2.04	5.94	5 Coupons	15 years........		7.84	7.93	8.92
2 5-15 years (23)	151.86	+0.51	151.09	2.57	6.65	6 (8%-10¾%)	20 years........		7.96	8.04	8.87
3 Over 15 years (9) ..	165.56	+0.80	164.25	2.27	5.77	7 High	5 years.........		7.08	7.14	9.39
4 Irredeemables (6) ..	187.96	+0.82	186.43	1.76	7.35	8 Coupons	15 years........		8.09	8.18	9.06
5 All stocks (63)........	147.49	+0.45	146.83	2.34	6.34	9 (11%-)	20 years........		8.13	8.22	8.98
Index-Linked						10 Irredeemables(Flat Yield)	....		8.05	8.12	8.97
6 Up to 5 years (2)...	186.43	+0.09	186.25	1.36	1.92	**Index-Linked**					
7 Over 5 years (11)....	176.80	+0.35	176.18	0.61	2.92	11 Inflation rate 5%	Up to 5yrs.		2.75	2.91	4.01
8 All stocks (13)........	176.98	+0.32	176.42	0.69	2.80	12 Inflation rate 5%	Over 5 yrs.		3.43	3.49	4.35
						13 Inflation rate 10%	Up to 5 yrs.		1.92	2.19	3.22
						14 Inflation rate 10%	Over 5 yrs.		3.24	3.32	4.16
9 **Debs & Loans (65)**	134.73	+0.56	133.98	2.59	5.59	15 **Debs &**	5 years....		8.35	8.46	10.43
						16 **Loans**	15 years....		8.82	8.89	10.19
						17	25 years....		9.01	9.07	10.06

Fig. 9.3 FT-Actuaries fixed interest indices

edged stocks as the corresponding FT-A equity indices have provided for investors in ordinary shares. They are produced at the close of business each day that the Stock Exchange is open and published in the following day's FT, normally Tuesday to Saturday. The indices address British government securities (BGS), index-linked British government securities (I-L) and debentures and loan stocks (DLS), with the number of stocks in each sector on each day shown after the name of that sector. The information displayed falls into two sections: price indices and yield indices.

- **Price indices:** there are nine indices, five covering the market for all conventional UK government stocks (shorts, medium-dated, longs, irredeemable, and all stocks), three for index-linked securities (one each for under and over five years to redemption plus all stocks) and one for corporate debentures and loans.

- **Average gross redemption yields:** there are seventeen indices, three each based on maturity for each of the three categories of coupon (low, medium and high) and one for irredeemables, four for index-linked securities, based on different maturities and inflation assumptions, and three for corporate debentures and loans (five-, fifteen- and twenty-year maturities). The number of yield indices is a compromise between the need for an easily comprehensible snapshot of the market, and the need to represent some of its complexities.

The tables provide the following information:

- **Value:** the first three columns of the price indices list current value, the percentage change on the previous trading day's value and the previous day's value.

- **Accrued interest:** interest on gilt-edged stocks is paid in twice-yearly instalments. Accrued interest simply records the amount of interest included in each day's price index that has accumulated on the stock since the last dividend payment.

- **Ex-dividend adjustment to date:** the amount of income that a holder of a portfolio of stocks proportionate to the index would have received in the year to date, credited on the ex-dividend date for each stock.

- **Redemption yields:** the three columns in this table give the two previous days' value and an approximation of the value a year ago. The whole table, subdividing coupon categories into short, medium and long terms to redemption, provides a representative picture of yields across the market. It indicates the shape of the market's time-related yield curve.

- Saturday's FT adds information on the highs and lows for the year, with dates, for the seventeen categories of stocks listed under average gross redemption yields.

The price indices and the ex-dividend adjustment can be used to work out an appropriate market rate of return, using whatever tax rate is appropriate on income. The indices can provide a basis for performance measurement.

The yields on corporate bonds are generally higher and the prices lower, reflecting the more variable creditworthiness of their issuers and a greater risk of default. These bonds are often classified by rating agencies such as Standard & Poor and Moody, which rate bonds according to the risk they carry (ranging from high-quality *AAA* to below-grade *D*).

Low-grade corporate bonds rated as being below investment quality may be issued offering very high yields. Known colloquially as junk bonds, these essentially unsecured, high-yield debt securities peaked in popularity in the late 1980s, and financed a significant portion of the merger and acquisition boom in the United States.

The FT yield indices can be used to monitor the difference in yield between gilt-edged stocks and equities (the yield gap), as a guide to market rates in making valuations and in setting the terms for new issues. Stocks are divided into low, medium and high coupons because investors' tax liabilities lead to very different yields being established in the market.

Benchmark government bonds

Coverage of government bond markets picks out items of importance or interest from internationally tradeable government bond markets throughout the world, and where relevant, related futures and options activity (see Figure 9.4).

BENCHMARK GOVERNMENT BONDS

		Coupon	Red Date	Price	Change	Yield	Week ago	Month ago
AUSTRALIA		9.500	08/03	117.5238	+0.706	7.04	7.09	7.58
BELGIUM		9.000	03/03	112.8800	+0.150	7.10	7.01	7.07
CANADA *		7.500	12/03	101.5800	+0.200	7.28	7.13	7.33
DENMARK		8.000	05/03	106.3500	+0.550	7.07	7.14	6.86
FRANCE	BTAN	8.000	05/98	107.2737	+0.250	6.18	6.24	6.09
	OAT	8.500	04/03	112.0650	+0.225	6.76	6.78	6.70
GERMANY		6.750	04/03	101.2300	-0.270	6.57	6.57	6.63
ITALY		11.500	03/03	104.3200	+0.070	11.05†	11.10	11.48
JAPAN	No 119	4.800	06/99	104.1661	+0.098	3.93	4.01	4.22
	No 145	5.500	03/02	108.4523	+0.204	4.17	4.22	4.38
NETHERLANDS		7.000	02/03	104.0200	-0.380	6.41	6.37	6.42
SPAIN		10.300	06/02	100.3722	+0.339	10.22	10.32	10.15
UK GILTS		7.250	03/98	102-11	+13/32	6.65	6.81	6.88
		8.000	06/03	103-27	+20/32	7.44	7.52	7.65
		9.000	10/08	110-09	+18/32	7.83	7.86	8.00
US TREASURY *		6.250	02/03	102-22	+4/32	5.87	5.77	5.79
		7.125	02/23	106-03	+12/32	6.65	6.59	6.68
ECU (French Govt)		8.000	04/03	105.1300	+0.140	7.24	7.28	7.07

London closing, *denotes New York closing   Yields: Local market standard
† Gross annual yield (including withholding tax at 12.5 per cent payable by non-residents.)
Prices: US, UK in 32nds, others in decimal   *Technical Data/ATLAS Price Sources*

Fig. 9.4 Benchmark government bonds

- A summary of daily movements in important benchmark bonds in a number of major markets is provided.

- Bonds are described by coupon and redemption date, the price and change on the previous day, the yield according to the local market standard (as standards vary yields are not necessarily comparable) and the yields prevailing one week and one month earlier.

The yield differential is the gap between bond yields in different countries. It is an indication of the relative attractiveness of different currencies.

INTERNATIONAL BONDS

The International Capital Markets pages in Monday to Friday's FT carry reports on new bond issues together with tables of the previous day's prices and issues. These markets have emerged with the growth of what have come to be known as Eurocurrencies. A Eurocurrency is a currency deposited outside its country of origin. For example, an exporter might receive dollars but not convert them. Since the United States, in running persistent trade deficits, exports dollars, banks accumulate these deposits which are then put to work. This stateless money is free of local regulations and London is its centre. Eurocurrencies are borrowed by loans or the issue of various kinds of debt instrument that 'securitise' the money: Euronotes, Eurocommercial paper and Eurobonds.

Eurobonds are the most common. They tap the large stateless pool of cash and are traded in a secondary market of screen and telephone. These are volatile and unregulated markets – they can become illiquid since there is no obligation for anyone to take part.

In many aspects trading activity in these markets is similar to trading in domestic stock markets, particularly in the case of sterling bond issues, industrial debentures and corporate bonds.

New international bond issues

A table of new International bond issues lists the previous week's issues of bonds, broken down according to the issuing currency (see Figure 9.5).

- **All new issues launched the previous day:** the table gives details of the borrower, currency, amount, coupon, price, maturity, the fees payable to the underwriters and the issue's arranger. The table also carries details of bonds on which terms have been altered or finalised subsequent to launch.

- **Book runner:** the issuer gives a mandate to one or more lead banks to manage the issue. The fee is paid in the form of a discount on the issue price.

Monday's *Financial Times* rounds up the issues of the previous week divided according to currency.

Total amount of issue

Lead managers of issue

Gota Bank, the Swedish bank which was rescued by the government in December 1992,

Like a number of other Swedish banks involved in last year's bail-out, it is now

Urban Mortgage Bank, recently completed a similar deal in the private placement market.

NEW INTERNATIONAL BOND ISSUES

Borrower	Amount m.	Coupon %	Price	Maturity	Fees %	Spread bp	Book runner
US DOLLARS							
Keihin Electric Railway(a)Φ	250	1.625	100	Aug.1997	2.25	-	Yamaichi Intl.(Europe)
Gota Bank(b)‡	100	(b)	100	Sep.2001	-	-	Chemical Inv'ment Bank
CSFB Finance (Neths.)(c)‡	50	(c)	99.875R	Aug.2003	0.5R	-	CSFB
STERLING							
Greenalls Group(d)§	109.993	7#	(d)	Sep.2003	-	-	J.Henry Schroder Wagg
YEN							
Mazda Motor Corp.	20bn	5.1	99.925R	Aug.2000	0.35R	-	Nomura International
NSK(e)	20bn	4.05	99.9R	Aug.1997	0.25R	-	Nomura International
Mitsui & Co.	10bn	4.9	100.2R	Nov.2000	0.35R	-	Fuji Intl. Finance
Mazda Motor Corp.‡	10bn	(f)	100R	May.2000	0.25R	-	Sumitomo Finance Intl.
CANADIAN DOLLARS							
Sudwest LB London Cap.Mkts.	200	6.5	99.75R	Aug.1997	0.225R	+28 (g)	Lehman Brothers Intl.
DANISH KRONER							
Finance for Danish Ind.(h)	200	7	102.039	Aug.1998	1.875	-	Morgan Stanley Intl.

Final terms and non-callable unless stated. The yield spread (over relevant government bond) at launch is supplied by the lead manager. §Convertible. ΦWith equity warrants. ‡Floating rate note. #Semi-annual coupon. R: fixed re-offer price; fees are shown at the re-offer level. a) Fixing: 4/8/93. b) Coupon pays 6-month Libor + 1.1% for first 3 years and + 3% thereafter. Callable on 9/9/96 at par. c) Issue launched on 22/7/93 was increased to $200m. Coupon pays 6-month Libor - 0.125%; minimum 5.5%, maximum 9.5%. d) Issue is consideration for the acquisition of J.A. Devenish and amount shown is the maximum that will be issued. Conversion price: £4.65. e) Puttable on 5/8/96 at par. f) Coupon pays 3-month Libor + 0.325%. g) Spread is over the interpolated yield curve. h) Issue launched on 22/7/93 was increased to DKr550m.

Coupon
(rate of interest)

Repayment due
date

Yield
spread

Fig. 9.5 New international bond issues

FT/ISMA international bond service

From Monday to Friday, the FT carries information on the secondary market prices of recently issued and actively traded bonds in the Eurobond market. Provided by the International Securities Market Association (ISMA) at close of business on the previous trading day, it covers Eurobonds picked from the sectors that best represent current market conditions, aiming to include certain 'benchmark' issues. The table (see Figure 9.6) also tries to maintain a selection of securities involving a broad spread of borrowers and currency groups.

READING THE FIGURES

- **'Straights':** fixed interest bonds, differentiated according to currency of denomination: US dollars, Deutsche marks, Swiss francs, yen, and other currencies, including sterling, Australian and Canadian dollars and ecus. Straights are traditional fixed interest bonds with a redemption date and no conversion rights. For straights, the table shows the amount of the bond issue, the prices bid and offered, the changes on the day and week and the yield.

- **Floating rate notes (FRNs):** these pay interest which is adjusted regularly in line with short-term international money rates. There are also FRNs that convert into fixed rate at the option of the investor (debt convertible), become fixed rate at a certain level (droplock) and that have caps and floors. The rates of interest on FRNs are set by reference to the London Inter-Bank Offered Rate (LIBOR), which acts as the benchmark against which rates vary (often so many basis points above the LIBOR).

- **Convertible bonds:** bonds that can be converted into shares of the issuing company at a price set at the time of issue. These are often discounted, meaning the issuing company pays a relatively low rate of interest. Investors gamble on the future success of the company by accepting a lower return in the short term in the expectation that the company will be successful. If it is, the investor will convert the bond into equity providing an income stream in dividend payments and capital growth.

- Monday's FT has an extended listing of secondary market prices and yields for about 500 bonds. The table lists fixed interest bonds under each currency of issue with sections for FRNs, convertibles and equity warrants (options giving the holders of a particular security the right to subscribe for future issues). This shows the amount issued, the bid price, change in price on the previous week and yield.

- **Currency:** borrowers choose the currency that they wish to borrow in. There are dangers of currency risk: borrowers typically choose a country with a lower rate of interest so that the rate paid is less, but if the currency rises, the debt becomes more expensive to repay.

FT/ISMA INTERNATIONAL BOND SERVICE

Listed are the latest international bonds for which there is an adequate secondary market.

Closing prices on July 28

U.S. DOLLAR STRAIGHTS	Issued	Bid	Offer	Chg. day	Yield
ABN $9\frac{1}{8}$ 94	200	$104\frac{5}{8}$	$105\frac{1}{8}$	$-\frac{1}{8}$	4.34
AlbertaProvince $9\frac{3}{8}$ 95	600	$109\frac{1}{2}$	$109\frac{7}{8}$		4.79
Austria $8\frac{1}{2}$ 00	400	$113\frac{1}{2}$	$113\frac{7}{8}$		5.92
Bank of Tokyo $8\frac{3}{8}$ 96	100	$107\frac{3}{8}$	$108\frac{1}{8}$	$+\frac{1}{8}$	5.33
Belgium $9\frac{5}{8}$ 98	250	$116\frac{5}{8}$	117		5.68
BFCE $7\frac{3}{4}$ 97	150	$107\frac{3}{4}$	$108\frac{1}{2}$		5.31
BNP $8\frac{5}{8}$ 94	300	$104\frac{3}{8}$	$104\frac{3}{4}$	$+\frac{1}{4}$	4.13
British Gas 0 21	1500	$11\frac{1}{4}$	12		7.87
Canada 9 96	1000	$109\frac{7}{8}$	$110\frac{1}{4}$		4.82
CCCE $9\frac{1}{4}$ 95	300	$107\frac{1}{4}$	$107\frac{5}{8}$	$-\frac{1}{8}$	4.40
Council Europe 8 96	100	$107\frac{3}{4}$	$108\frac{1}{2}$		5.16
Credit Foncier $9\frac{1}{2}$ 99	300	$117\frac{3}{8}$	$117\frac{3}{4}$		5.75
Denmark $9\frac{1}{4}$ 95	1571	$107\frac{5}{8}$	$107\frac{7}{8}$	$-\frac{1}{8}$	4.33
ECSC $8\frac{1}{4}$ 96	193	$108\frac{3}{4}$	$109\frac{3}{8}$	$+\frac{1}{8}$	5.31
EEC $8\frac{1}{4}$ 96	100	108	$108\frac{3}{4}$	$-\frac{1}{8}$	5.20
EIB $7\frac{3}{4}$ 96	250	$107\frac{1}{4}$	$107\frac{3}{4}$	$+\frac{1}{8}$	5.04
EIB $9\frac{1}{4}$ 97	1000	$114\frac{1}{8}$	$114\frac{1}{2}$	$-\frac{1}{8}$	5.46
Elec de France 9 98	200	$113\frac{1}{4}$	$113\frac{7}{8}$	$+\frac{1}{4}$	5.65
Euro Cred Card Tst 9 94	325	105	$105\frac{1}{2}$	$-\frac{1}{8}$	4.64
Eurofima $9\frac{1}{4}$ 96	100	$110\frac{1}{4}$	111	$+\frac{1}{8}$	4.96
Ex–Im Bank Japan 8 02	500	111	$111\frac{3}{8}$	$+\frac{1}{8}$	6.33

OTHER STRAIGHTS	Issued	Bid	Offer	Chg. day	Yield
Arbed $7\frac{1}{2}$ 95 LFr	600	100	101		7.49
Genfinance Lux $9\frac{1}{8}$ 99 LFr	1000	$108\frac{3}{8}$	$110\frac{1}{2}$		7.27
World Bank 8 96 LFr	1000	$102\frac{1}{4}$	$103\frac{1}{4}$	$+\frac{1}{4}$	7.04
Bank Voor Ned Gem $7\frac{5}{8}$ 02 Fl	1000	$105\frac{3}{8}$	$105\frac{3}{4}$		6.82
Energie Beheer $8\frac{3}{4}$ 98 Fl	500	$110\frac{1}{4}$	$110\frac{1}{4}$		6.39
AlbertaProvince $10\frac{5}{8}$ 96 C$	500	$109\frac{1}{2}$	110	$+\frac{1}{8}$	6.42
Bell Canada $10\frac{5}{8}$ 99 C$	150	$112\frac{5}{8}$	$113\frac{3}{8}$	$+\frac{1}{4}$	7.89
British Columbia 10 96 C$	500	$108\frac{7}{8}$	$109\frac{3}{8}$	$+\frac{1}{8}$	6.47
EIB $10\frac{1}{8}$ 98 C$	130	$111\frac{5}{8}$	$112\frac{3}{8}$	$+\frac{1}{4}$	7.07
Elec de France $9\frac{3}{4}$ 99 C$	275	$110\frac{3}{8}$	$110\frac{7}{8}$	$+\frac{1}{4}$	7.56
Ford Credit Canada 10 94 C$	100	$103\frac{7}{8}$	$104\frac{1}{4}$	$+\frac{1}{8}$	6.02
Gen Elec Capital 10 96 C$	300	$108\frac{3}{8}$	109	$+\frac{1}{8}$	6.68
KfW Int Fin 10 01 C$	400	$112\frac{1}{8}$	$112\frac{5}{8}$	$+\frac{1}{4}$	7.81
Nippon Tel Tel $10\frac{1}{4}$ 99 C$	200	$112\frac{1}{4}$	$112\frac{3}{4}$	$+\frac{1}{4}$	7.69
Ontario Hydro $10\frac{7}{8}$ 99 C$	500	$114\frac{1}{2}$	115	$+\frac{1}{4}$	7.61
Oster Kontrollbank $10\frac{1}{4}$ 99 C$	150	$112\frac{3}{4}$	$113\frac{3}{8}$	$+\frac{1}{4}$	7.53
Quebec Prov $10\frac{1}{2}$ 98 C$	200	$112\frac{3}{4}$	$113\frac{3}{8}$	$+\frac{1}{8}$	7.50
Belgium $9\frac{1}{8}$ 96 Ecu	1250	$105\frac{3}{8}$	$105\frac{1}{2}$	$+\frac{1}{8}$	6.80
Council Europe 9 01 Ecu	1100	$108\frac{7}{8}$	$109\frac{1}{8}$	$+\frac{1}{8}$	7.51
Credit Lyonnais 9 96 Ecu	125	104	$104\frac{7}{8}$	$+\frac{1}{8}$	7.34

DEUTSCHE MARK STRAIGHTS	Issued	Bid	Offer	Chg. day	Yield
Austria $5\frac{7}{8}$ 97	500	$99\frac{1}{8}$	$99\frac{1}{2}$	$+\frac{1}{8}$	6.14
Belgium $7\frac{3}{4}$ 02	500	$105\frac{1}{4}$	$105\frac{1}{2}$		6.91
Credit Foncier $7\frac{1}{4}$ 03	2000	$102\frac{3}{4}$	$102\frac{7}{8}$	$-\frac{1}{8}$	6.84
Denmark $6\frac{1}{8}$ 98	2000	$99\frac{1}{8}$	$99\frac{1}{4}$	$-\frac{1}{8}$	6.34
Deutsche Finance $7\frac{1}{2}$ 95	1000	$101\frac{1}{2}$	$101\frac{5}{8}$		6.37
ECSC $8\frac{5}{8}$ 96	700	$106\frac{5}{8}$	$106\frac{7}{8}$		6.37
EEC $6\frac{1}{2}$ 00	2900	$100\frac{1}{4}$	$100\frac{3}{8}$	$-\frac{1}{8}$	6.44
EIB $7\frac{1}{2}$ 99	400	$104\frac{7}{8}$	$105\frac{1}{4}$	$-\frac{1}{8}$	6.53
Finland $7\frac{1}{2}$ 00	3000	$103\frac{3}{8}$	$103\frac{1}{2}$	$-\frac{1}{4}$	6.83
Ireland $7\frac{3}{4}$ 02	500	$105\frac{3}{8}$	$105\frac{7}{8}$		6.94
Italy $7\frac{1}{4}$ 98	5000	$102\frac{3}{8}$	$102\frac{1}{2}$		6.61
Spain $7\frac{1}{4}$ 03	4000	$102\frac{7}{8}$	103	$-\frac{1}{8}$	6.82
Sweden 8 97	2500	$105\frac{3}{8}$	$105\frac{7}{8}$	$-\frac{1}{8}$	6.50
Tokyo Elec Power $7\frac{5}{8}$ 02	1000	$105\frac{1}{4}$	$105\frac{5}{8}$		6.83
United Kingdom $7\frac{1}{8}$ 97	5500	103	$103\frac{3}{8}$	$+\frac{1}{2}$	6.29
Volkswagen Intl Fin 7 03	1000	$101\frac{1}{8}$	$101\frac{3}{8}$		6.83
World Bank 0 15	2000	23	$23\frac{1}{2}$		6.78
World Bank $5\frac{3}{4}$ 96	300	$99\frac{7}{8}$	$100\frac{1}{4}$	$+\frac{1}{8}$	5.79
World Bank $8\frac{3}{4}$ 00	1250	$112\frac{3}{8}$	$112\frac{7}{8}$	$+\frac{3}{8}$	6.42

SWISS FRANC STRAIGHTS	Issued	Bid	Offer	Chg. day	Yield
Asian Dev Bank 6 10	100	108	109		5.28
Council Europe $4\frac{3}{4}$ 98	250	$101\frac{1}{2}$	$101\frac{5}{8}$		4.37
EIB $8\frac{1}{4}$ 04	300	$112\frac{1}{4}$	$112\frac{1}{2}$		5.27
Elec de France $7\frac{1}{4}$ 06	100	$114\frac{1}{2}$	115	$+\frac{1}{4}$	5.60
Finland $7\frac{1}{4}$ 99	300	112	$112\frac{1}{2}$		4.95
General Motors $7\frac{1}{2}$ 95	100	103	$103\frac{1}{2}$	$+\frac{1}{4}$	5.56
Hyundai Motor Fin $8\frac{1}{2}$ 97	100	109	$109\frac{1}{2}$		5.96
Iceland $7\frac{5}{8}$ 00	100	$112\frac{1}{2}$	$113\frac{1}{2}$	$+\frac{1}{4}$	5.43
Kobe $6\frac{3}{8}$ 01	240	$109\frac{1}{2}$	110		4.91
New Zealand $4\frac{7}{8}$ 99	200	$100\frac{1}{4}$	101	$-\frac{1}{4}$	4.82
Ontario $6\frac{1}{4}$ 03	400	$107\frac{3}{8}$	$107\frac{3}{4}$	$-\frac{1}{8}$	5.24
Quebec Hydro 5 08	100	$96\frac{1}{2}$	$97\frac{1}{2}$	$-\frac{1}{2}$	5.35
SNCF 7 04	450	$116\frac{1}{8}$	$116\frac{1}{4}$	$+\frac{1}{8}$	5.07
World Bank 5 03	150	102	103		4.74
World Bank 7 01	600	$111\frac{7}{8}$	$113\frac{1}{4}$	$+\frac{1}{8}$	5.07

YEN STRAIGHTS	Issued	Bid	Offer	Chg. day	Yield
Belgium 5 99	75000	$102\frac{1}{4}$	$102\frac{1}{2}$	$+\frac{1}{8}$	4.58
Denmark 7 95	40000	$105\frac{1}{4}$	$105\frac{1}{2}$	$-\frac{1}{8}$	3.35
EIB $6\frac{5}{8}$ 00	100000	$111\frac{1}{4}$	$111\frac{1}{2}$	$+\frac{1}{8}$	4.61
Elec de France $5\frac{5}{8}$ 96	20000	$105\frac{1}{4}$	$105\frac{3}{4}$	$+\frac{1}{8}$	3.86
Finland $6\frac{3}{4}$ 96	50000	$106\frac{7}{8}$	$107\frac{1}{8}$		3.96
Inter Amer Dev $7\frac{1}{4}$ 00	30000	$115\frac{1}{8}$	$115\frac{3}{8}$	$+\frac{1}{8}$	4.60
Japan Dev Bk 5 99	100000	$103\frac{1}{2}$	$103\frac{5}{8}$	$+\frac{1}{8}$	4.34
Japan Dev Bk $6\frac{1}{2}$ 01	120000	$112\frac{1}{4}$	$112\frac{1}{2}$		4.66
Nippon Tel Tel $5\frac{7}{8}$ 96	50000	$106\frac{5}{8}$	$106\frac{7}{8}$	$+\frac{1}{8}$	3.61
Norway $5\frac{1}{4}$ 95	50000	$102\frac{5}{8}$	$102\frac{7}{8}$		3.48
SNCF $6\frac{3}{4}$ 00	30000	$111\frac{3}{4}$	112	$+\frac{1}{8}$	4.63
Sweden $5\frac{5}{8}$ 95	20000	$103\frac{7}{8}$	$104\frac{3}{8}$		3.72
World Bank $6\frac{3}{4}$ 00	50000	$112\frac{1}{8}$	$112\frac{3}{8}$	$+\frac{1}{8}$	4.58

FLOATING RATE NOTES	Issued	Bid	Offer	C.cpn
Banco Roma 0 99	200	99.40	99.67	3.3438
Belgium $\frac{1}{16}$ 97 DM	500	100.04	100.14	8.0000
BFCE −0.02 96	350	99.79	99.90	3.2500
Britannia 0.10 96 £	150	99.59	99.71	6.1625
CCCE 0 06 Ecu	200	98.93	99.26	7.4844
Citicorp Bkg $\frac{1}{4}$ 96	400	99.96	100.29	5.2500
Credit Foncier $-\frac{1}{16}$ 98	200	100.40	100.81	5.0000
Credit Lyonnais $\frac{1}{16}$ 00	300	100.11	100.60	5.0000
Denmark $-\frac{1}{8}$ 96	1000	99.48	99.59	3.0625
Dresdner Finance $\frac{1}{32}$ 98 DM	1000	99.85	99.96	6.9688
Elec de France $\frac{1}{8}$ 99	400	101.94	102.78	5.2500
Ferro del Stat $\frac{1}{16}$ 97	420	99.15	99.39	3.2875
Finland 0 97	1000	99.55	99.66	3.5000
Halifax BS $\frac{1}{16}$ 95 £	350	99.91	100.00	6.0625
Ireland 0 98	300	99.64	99.79	3.4400
Italy $\frac{1}{4}$ 98	2000	99.92	99.99	3.6016
Leeds Permanent $\frac{1}{8}$ 96 £	200	99.85	99.98	6.0000
Lloyds Bank Perp S 0.10	600	79.50	80.75	3.3710
Malaysia $\frac{1}{16}$ 05	650	99.86	100.21	5.2500
Nationwide 0.08 96 £	300	99.53	99.64	6.1425
New Zealand $\frac{1}{8}$ 96	250	100.02	100.15	4.4380
Renfe 0 98	500	99.17	99.33	3.1250
Societe Generale 0 96	300	99.39	99.55	3.2500
State Bk Victoria 0.05 99	125	99.20	99.48	3.5500
Sweden 0 98	1500	99.79	99.87	3.3125
United Kingdom $-\frac{1}{8}$ 96	4000	99.88	99.94	3.1250

CONVERTIBLE BONDS	Issued	Conv. price	Bid	Offer	Prem.
Browning–Ferris $6\frac{3}{4}$ 05	400	$52\frac{1}{2}$	$98\frac{7}{8}$	$99\frac{3}{4}$	
Chubb Capital 6 98	250	86	118	119	+11.98
Eastman Kodak $6\frac{3}{8}$ 01	300	50.67	$105\frac{3}{4}$	$106\frac{5}{8}$	+5.07
Gold Kalgoorlie $7\frac{1}{2}$ 00	65	1.0554	$114\frac{1}{8}$	$115\frac{1}{8}$	+45.82
Hanson $9\frac{1}{2}$ 06 £	500	2.5875	$113\frac{1}{8}$	$113\frac{3}{4}$	+25.09
Hawley Pref 6 02	400	19.1	$131\frac{5}{8}$	$133\frac{3}{8}$	
Land Secs $6\frac{3}{4}$ 02 £	84	6.72	$102\frac{3}{8}$	$103\frac{3}{8}$	+11.14
Lasmo $7\frac{3}{4}$ 05 £	90	5.64	$87\frac{5}{8}$	$88\frac{1}{2}$	
Mitsui Bank $2\frac{5}{8}$ 03	200	2332.6	$99\frac{1}{8}$	$101\frac{1}{8}$	+13.42
Mount Isa Fin $6\frac{1}{2}$ 97	100	2.283	$100\frac{3}{4}$	$101\frac{5}{8}$	+61.78
Ogden 6 02	85	39.077	$94\frac{3}{4}$	$95\frac{3}{4}$	+43.79
Smith Nephew 4 02 £	90	1.775	$132\frac{1}{2}$	$133\frac{1}{2}$	+64.47
Sumitomo Bank $3\frac{1}{8}$ 04	300	3606.9	$94\frac{3}{8}$	$95\frac{5}{8}$	+21.32
Sun Alliance $7\frac{1}{4}$ 08 £	155	3.9	$109\frac{5}{8}$	$110\frac{1}{2}$	+15.55
Tesco Capital 9 05 £	200	2.51	$115\frac{1}{8}$	116	+40.96
Texas Instruments $2\frac{3}{4}$ 02	300	$82\frac{7}{8}$	$103\frac{1}{2}$	$104\frac{3}{8}$	+17.10
Thorn EMI $5\frac{3}{4}$ 04 £	103	7.16	$131\frac{7}{8}$	$132\frac{7}{8}$	−0.71

* No information available – previous day's price
‡ Only one market maker supplied a price

Fig. 9.6 FT/ISMA international bond service

USING THE INFORMATION

This market offers an alternative method of raising money for companies who do not want to issue stock or accept the conditions of a bank loan. It grew up because of the restraints of government regulations in traditional equity and money markets.

It also offers opportunities for interest rate and currency swaps. When a company which can, for instance, easily raise money in sterling because of local reputation needs dollars to fund an acquisition or expansion, it may find an American company in the opposite position and swap debt.

For investors the markets are international and anonymous – there is no register of creditors – and tax efficient. It offers a chance to use currencies, debt, equity and interest rates simultaneously but because of its complexity is generally restricted to large investment banks.

10

CASH AND CURRENCY
The foreign exchange and money markets

The currency markets are global markets for foreign exchange. Their primary purposes are to allow companies and other organisations to purchase goods from abroad, and for foreign investment or speculation. Hence they are markets largely of concern to companies and financial institutions or investors in stocks that are particularly sensitive to currency or interest rate movements.

The money markets include the foreign exchange markets but also cover the domestic UK market for short-term loans essentially between the major institutions of the City: banks, accepting houses, discount houses and the Bank of England.

One page of the *Financial Times*, the Currencies, Money and Capital Markets page, is given over largely to recording dealing rates and brief reports of trading in the foreign exchange (forex) and money markets. It is headed by a brief report describing the major events in the foreign exchange markets during the previous day's trading. In addition, there are more detailed descriptions of the experiences of individual major currencies, both on the previous day and over a rather longer time-span. These items generally discuss the main factors affecting exchange rates.

With the exception of the domestic money markets in its various forms, these are international markets in which business is conducted twenty-four hours a day by telex, telephone and computer screen. As the London markets close in the evening, business is handed over to New York, which overlaps with Tokyo for a couple of hours each afternoon. Thus, there are no official closing rates in these international markets. The FT takes a representative sample of rates from major participants in the London markets at around 5pm local time each trading day.

Foreign exchange markets exist to facilitate international trade, and allow companies involved in international trade to hedge transactions through the forward purchase of relevant currency at a fixed rate, designed to counteract any potential losses through future rises in its value. In practice however, the bulk of turnover in these markets is attributable to speculation, and while speculation provides the markets with necessary liquidity, it can also destabilise those markets, hence creating a further need for hedging.

As in all markets the value of currencies in the international market is determined by supply and demand. The main players are the foreign exchange dealers of commercial banks and foreign exchange brokers. However, the market is often significantly affected by the intervention of central banks on behalf of governments. So, in this marketplace there is considerable interaction between the authorities and market professionals.

Speculation provides liquidity but makes the markets volatile and prediction difficult. Currency swings can be vast and not often very attached to fundamentals. They are particularly damaging for companies which rely heavily on exports or imported raw materials.

The core determining factor of a currency's value is the health of the real national economy, especially the balance of payments (current account). If there is a surplus on the current account, that is, a country sells more goods than it buys, then buyers have to acquire that currency to purchase goods. This adds to foreign reserves and bids up the price of that currency. As it rises, exports rise in price, fall in quantity and the currency falls again.

The currency's value is also affected by the level of inflation and the domestic rate of interest. High rates of interest and low inflation make a currency attractive for those holding assets denominated in it or lending it to borrowers. So typically one country raising interest rates while others remain the same will raise the value of that currency as money flows into the country. This will have a limited effect if the fundamentals are wrong; that is, if there is a persistent deficit on the current account.

A significant factor determining short-term currency values is market sentiment. There is a self-fuelling process in which enthusiasm for a currency, or the lack of it, drives the rate. Speculators might

Ecu central rates set by the European Commission. Currencies are in descending relative strength. Percentage changes are for Ecu; a positive change denotes a weak currency. Divergence shows the ratio between two spreads: the percentage difference between the actual market and Ecu central rates for a currency, and the maximum permitted percentage deviation of the currency's market rate from its Ecu central rate. (17/9/92) Sterling and Italian Lira suspended from ERM. Adjustment calculated by Financial Times.

POUND SPOT - FORWARD AGAINST THE POUND

Jul 26	Day's spread	Close	One month	% p.a.	Three months	% p.a.
US	1.4940 - 1.5055	1.5015 - 1.5025	0.41-0.39cpm	3.20	1.06-1.03pm	2.78
Canada	1.9145 - 1.9275	1.9225 - 1.9235	0.40-0.34cpm	2.31	0.97-0.84pm	1.88
Netherlands .	2.9020 - 2.9200	2.9075 - 2.9175	PAR-$\frac{1}{4}$cdis	-0.52	$\frac{1}{8}$-$\frac{1}{4}$dis	-0.26
Belgium	53.35 - 53.90	53.65 - 53.75	9-15cdis	-2.68	21-31dis	-1.94
Denmark	10.0225 - 10.0835	10.0625 - 10.0725	N/A	N/A	N/A	N/A
Ireland	1.0700 - 1.0755	1.0720 - 1.0730	0.03-0.07cdis	-0.56	0.10-0.15dis	-0.47
Germany	2.5870 - 2.5950	2.5875 - 2.5925	$\frac{1}{8}$-$\frac{3}{8}$pfdis	-1.16	$\frac{1}{2}$-$\frac{3}{4}$dis	-0.97
Portugal	257.40 - 260.00	259.00 - 260.00	172-197cdis	-8.53	391-471dis	-6.64
Spain	205.90 - 208.55	207.45 - 207.75	141-190cdis	-9.57	316-381dis	-6.71
Italy	2404.50 - 2418.20	2408.75 - 2409.75	8-10liredis	-4.48	20-24dis	-3.65
Norway	11.0125 - 11.0670	11.0300 - 11.0400	par-1$\frac{1}{4}$oredis	-0.68	$\frac{3}{4}$-2$\frac{1}{4}$dis	-0.54
France	8.8105 - 8.8635	8.8375 - 8.8475	4$\frac{1}{8}$-5cdis	-6.19	7$\frac{1}{8}$-8$\frac{1}{2}$dis	-3.53
Sweden	12.0055 - 12.1800	12.0725 - 12.0825	2$\frac{3}{8}$-3$\frac{1}{2}$oredis	-2.92	5$\frac{7}{8}$-7$\frac{3}{8}$dis	-2.19
Japan	159.20 - 161.00	160.00 - 161.00	$\frac{1}{2}$-$\frac{3}{8}$ypm	3.27	1$\frac{1}{4}$-1pm	2.80
Austria	18.10 - 18.26	18.20 - 18.23	$\frac{7}{8}$-1$\frac{7}{8}$grodis	-0.91	2-4dis	-0.66
Switzerland .	2.2735 - 2.2900	2.2800 - 2.2900	$\frac{3}{8}$-$\frac{1}{8}$cpm	1.31	$\frac{7}{8}$-$\frac{5}{8}$pm	1.31
Ecu	1.3290 - 1.3360	1.3330 - 1.3340	0.31-0.35cdis	-2.97	0.70-0.76dis	-2.19

Commercial rates taken towards the end of London trading. Six-month forward dollar 1.81-1.76pm . 12 Month 3.00-2.90pm.

Fig. 10.1 (a) Pound spot – forward against the pound

£ IN NEW YORK

Jul 26	Close	Previous Close
£ Spot	1.5000-1.5010	1.5040 1.5050
1 month	0.40-0.39pm	0.38 0.37pm
3 months	1.04-1.02pm	1.07 1.05pm
12 months ...	3.00-2.90pm	3.05 2.98pm

Forward premiums and discounts apply to the US dollar

Fig. 10.1 (b) £ in New York

FORWARD RATES AGAINST STERLING

	Spot	1 mth	3 mths	6 mths	12 mths
US Dollar	1.4815	1.4778	1.4714	1.4640	1.4515
D-mark	2.5500	2.5531	2.5587	2.5658	2.5670
French Fr.	8.6675	8.6694	8.6720	8.6740	8.6745
Swiss Fr.	2.2675	2.2649	2.2604	2.2535	2.2369
Yen	162.50	162.10	161.38	160.36	158.51

Fig. 10.1 (c) Forward rates against sterling

decide, as they did with the pound sterling on Black Wednesday, that a currency is over-valued or simply that there are speculative gains to be made. Short selling will then cause it to fall, often in spite of government intervention.

Currencies are measured in terms of one another or a trade weighted index, a basket of currencies. The value of a currency in a trade-weighted index is assessed on a basis which gives a value appropriate to the volume of trade conducted in that currency. The FT provides detailed information on two primary currencies in the world: the pound and the dollar. A large number of international contracts are struck in these currencies and the dollar particularly is used globally as a reserve currency.

Figure 10.1(a) lists spot and forward prices for the pound against the currencies of the other major industrialised countries.

READING THE FIGURES

- **The previous day's prices for the pound spot and forward:** these are prices for immediate delivery, and prices on contracts struck for settlement one month or three months ahead and, in the case of the sterling/dollar rate, six and twelve months ahead. Since sterling is the largest currency unit, all prices are given in so many deutsche marks, francs, dollars, etc. to the pound.

- **Spread:** the highest and lowest prices at which dealings have taken place in the spot currency during the European trading day and a representative spread on the price at the close. Different banks may quote slightly different rates at the same time, particularly if the market is moving in a very volatile fashion.

- **Forward:** the premium or discount to the spot rate at which forward market dealings are being struck. These premiums and discounts are quoted in two different ways: as an absolute amount to be added to or subtracted from the spot rate (a premium is subtracted, a discount added), and as a percentage of the spot price at an annual rate. The second method is a reminder that forward currency rates and interest rates are intimately connected. A bank given an order to supply dollars against pounds in three months' time will in theory (out of simple prudence) purchase the dollars at once and leave them on deposit for three months. If dollars are yielding less than pounds, it will lose interest by switching from pounds to dollars. It naturally passes this cost on to the customer by charging more for three months dollars than it would for spot dollars. The forward dollars are sold at a premium.

- **Pound in New York:** figure 10.1(b) details the rates for the pound in the New York market on a spot basis and one, three and twelve months ahead, plus the close on the previous trading day.

- **Forward rates against sterling:** Saturday's FT carries this supplement (Figure 10.1(c)) to the daily tables of one and three months' rates against sterling with six and twelve months' rates for five major currencies. Unlike the daily rates, these are expressed as actual rates by subtracting the premiums and adding the discounts to the spot rate. The curve of forward rates, at a premium or a discount, is essentially determined by the interest rates available for deposit of these currencies relative to sterling. The lower the interest rate available, the higher the effective cost of buying that currency in advance, and this is reflected in the forward rates.

USING THE INFORMATION

It is possible that by the time the rates are consulted the markets may have moved quite sharply. The rates in the newspaper cannot guarantee to be up to the minute; what they do provide is a daily record of the market's activities for reference purposes.

The rates are frequently used by exporters and importers striking contracts in more than one currency at an agreed published rate.

Businesses frequently need to hedge against currency risk. Typically a UK business with significant dollar income might sell dollars forward at a particular rate. This protects it against the pound weakening (though it also means gains from it strengthening would be missed) but more importantly makes the exchange rate predictable for that company to aid planning.

The dollar, spot and forward

The dollar has long been the dominant currency in world trade and the United States has often been able to pay for its imports with dollars. Given that fact and the persistent twin deficits of the current account and government budget, the US is consistently exporting dol-

DOLLAR SPOT - FORWARD AGAINST THE DOLLAR						
Jul 26	Day's spread	Close	One month	% p.a.	Three months	% p.a.
UK†	1.4940 - 1.5055	1.5015 - 1.5025	0.41-0.39cpm	3.20	1.06-1.03pm	2.78
Ireland†	1.3950 - 1.4010	1.3995 - 1.4005	0.45-0.42cpm	3.73	1.16-1.11pm	3.24
Canada	1.2795 - 1.2810	1.2800 - 1.2810	0.09-0.11cdis	−0.94	0.26-0.32dis	−0.91
Netherlands .	1.9375 - 1.9440	1.9390 - 1.9400	0.61-0.64cdis	−3.87	1.52-1.58dis	−3.20
Belgium	35.65 - 35.85	35.70 - 35.80	18.50-21.00cdis	−6.63	45.00-52.00dis	−5.43
Denmark	6.6850 - 6.7140	6.7000 - 6.7050	N/A	N/A	N/A	N/A
Germany	1.7220 - 1.7285	1.7240 - 1.7250	0.62-0.64pfdis	−4.38	1.61-1.63dis	−3.76
Portugal	172.70 - 173.05	172.75 - 172.85	163-178cdis	−11.84	395-435dis	−9.61
Spain	137.30 - 138.90	138.40 - 138.50	132-147cdis	−12.09	310-340dis	−9.39
Italy	1599.25 - 1615.00	1603.75 - 1604.25	9.80-10.30liredis	−7.52	25.00-26.50dis	−6.42
Norway	7.3410 - 7.3735	7.3450 - 7.3500	2.10-2.60oredis	−3.84	5.90-6.70dis	−3.43
France ...⌐....	5.8800 - 5.9090	5.8850 - 5.8900	N/A	N/A	N/A	N/A
Sweden	7.9925 - 8.1260	8.0375 - 8.0425	3.80-4.40oredis	−6.12	9.70-10.70dis	−5.07
Japan	106.15 - 107.00	106.80 - 106.90	par-0.01ydis	−0.06	0.03-0.01pm	0.07
Austria	12.1290 - 12.1600	12.1375 - 12.1425	3.95-4.25grodis	−4.05	9.80-10.70dis	−3.38
Switzerland .	1.5150 - 1.5235	1.5205 - 1.5215	0.20-0.24cdis	−1.74	0.53-0.59dis	−1.47
Ecu†	1.1230 - 1.1275	1.1265 - 1.1275	0.58-0.57cpm	6.12	1.45-1.38pm	5.02

Commercial rates taken towards the end of London trading. † UK, Ireland and Ecu are quoted in US currency. Forward premiums and discounts apply to the US dollar and not to the individual currency.

Fig. 10.2 Dollar spot – forward against the dollar

lars which then move around world markets and economies. Hence the importance of the dollar spot and forward rates published in the FT (see Figure 10.2).

- The previous day's prices for the dollar spot and forward. The equivalent range of information as the pound spot and forward.

- All prices, except for sterling and the Irish pound, are quoted in terms of francs, guilders, etc to the dollar. Since sterling and the Irish pound are quoted in dollars rather than in so many units to the dollar, a forward discount means that the dollar, not the pound, is at a discount.

OTHER CURRENCIES

- The table in Figure 10.3 gives sterling and dollar rates for second-rank currencies in which some sort of free market exists. In some cases, there may be a considerably higher degree of official exchange rate control.

```
  Morgan  Guaranty  changes:  average
1980-1982=100.  Bank  of  England  (Base
Average 1985=100) **Rates are for Jul 23
```

OTHER CURRENCIES

Jul 26	£	$
Argentina	1.4990 - 1.5000	0.9980 - 0.9990
Australia	2.2115 - 2.2135	1.4730 - 1.4740
Brazil	101641 - 101643	67671.0 - 67672.0
Finland	8.7415 - 8.7525	5.8325 - 5.8525
Greece	352.500 - 359.650	235.500 - 240.200
Hong Kong ..	11.6405 - 11.6525	7.7545 - 7.7555
Iran	2345.00 - 2355.00	1580.00 - 1590.00
Korea(Sth) ...	1206.15 - 1225.60	805.50 - 811.90
Kuwait	0.45270 - 0.45370	0.30160 - 0.30210
Luxembourg	53.65 - 53.75	35.70 - 35.80
Malaysia	3.8535 - 3.8605	2.5660 - 2.5670
Mexico	4.6875 - 4.6905	3.1210 - 3.1230
N.Zealand ...	2.7180 - 2.7215	1.8095 - 1.8120
Saudi Ar	5.6285 - 5.6400	3.7495 - 3.7505
Singapore ...	2.4270 - 2.4335	1.6165 - 1.6175
S.Af (Cm)	5.0405 - 5.0515	3.3580 - 3.3695
S.Af (Fn)	6.7290 - 6.7440	4.4800 - 4.4900
Taiwan	40.40 - 40.55	26.90 - 27.00
U.A.E.	5.5125 - 5.5255	3.6715 - 3.6735

Fig. 10.3 Other currencies

Currencies of the world

More obscure currencies, many of them fixed against the dollar and nearly all of them very strictly controlled by the local monetary authorities, are not openly dealt on world foreign exchange markets (see Figure 10.4).

- A weekly table which shows the value of these currencies in terms of sterling, the dollar, the deutsche mark and the yen.

Currency movements and currency rates

- **Movements:** there are two trade-weighted measures (see Figure 10.5(a)). The Bank of England index shows the relative trade-weighted position of currencies compared to a base value of 1985 = 100. So a figure of 121.9 for the deutsche mark would indicate that it has strengthened by 21.9 per cent against the currencies of its trading partners, weighted by volume of trade since 1985. The second column shows the percentage changes in the currency as calculated by Morgan Guaranty, also on a trade-weighted basis, but based on an average 1980–82 = 100.

FT GUIDE TO WORLD CURRENCIES

COUNTRY		£ STG	US $	D-MARK	YEN (X 100)
Gambia	(Dalasi)	13.3545	8.8911	5.1561	8.3205
Germany	(D-Mark)	2.5900	1.7243	1	1.6137
Ghana	(Cedi)	987.90	657.723	381.429	615.514
Gibraltar	(Gib £)	1.00	0.6657	0.3861	0.623
Greece	(Drachma)	356.075	237.067	137.481	221.854
Greenland	(Danish Krone)	10.0675	6.7027	3.887	6.2725
Grenada	(E Carr $)	4.05	2.6964	1.5637	2.5233
Guadaloupe	(Local Fr)	8.8425	5.8871	3.414	5.5093
Guam	(US $)	1.5020	1	0.5799	0.9358
Guatemala	(Quetzal)	8.5865	5.7167	3.3152	5.3498
Guinea	(Fr)	1218.84	811.478	470.595	759.402
Guinea-Bissau	(Peso)	7502.50	4995.01	2896.72	4674.45
Guyana	(Guyanese $)	189.06	125.872	72.9961	117.794
Haiti	(Goude)	18.0060	11.988	6.9521	11.2186
Honduras	(Lempira)	10.2409	6.8181	3.954	6.3806
Hong Kong	(HK $)	11.6465	7.7539	4.4967	7.2563
Hungary	(Forint)	142.7876	95.0649	55.1303	88.9642
Iceland	(Icelandic Krona)	108.20	72.0372	41.776	67.4143
India	(Indian Rupee)	47.0972	31.3563	18.1842	29.344
Indonesia	(Rupiah)	3155.65	2100.97	1218.4	1966.14
Iran	(Rial)	2350.00	1564.58	907.336	1464.17
Iraq	(Iraqi Dinar)	0.4664	0.3105	0.18	0.2905
Irish Rep	(Punt)	1.0725	0.714	0.414	0.6682
Israel	(Shekel)	4.2925(3)	2.8578	1.6573	2.6744
Italy	(Lira)	2409.25	1604.03	930.212	1501.09

Fig. 10.4 FT guide to world currencies

- **Bank rates:** a guide to the discount rates at which central banks are prepared to buy bills of exchange from the discount houses. Although often the most significant interest rates in domestic economies, they are not all strictly comparable and in some countries other market rates set by the central bank have more influence on the level of market interest rates than the bank rate itself.

- **Rates:** the table (Figure 10.5(b)) provides the previous day's value in seventeen major currencies and two international currency substitutes, the Special Drawing Right (SDR) of the International Monetary Fund and the European currency unit (ecu). Both of these are currency baskets made up of a predetermined amount of a number of different currencies: five in the case of the SDR, the unit in which the IMF accounts are denominated; rather more for the ecu which comprises currencies in which transactions concerning the European monetary system are administered. Their composite character means that these currency substitutes are less volatile than the individual units, and they are being used to an increasing extent for commercial purposes.

CURRENCY MOVEMENTS

Jul 26	Bank of England Index	Morgan ** Guaranty Changes %
Sterling	82.0	-27.96
U.S Dollar	66.0	-11.80
Canadian Dollar	94.4	-7.81
Austrian Schilling	113.1	+15.45
Belgian Franc	113.3	+0.15
Danish Krone	114.9	+9.64
D–Mark	121.9	+30.04
Swiss Franc	112.0	+21.11
Dutch Guilder	117.2	+19.73
French Franc	106.7	-8.64
Lira	79.9	-34.56
Yen	183.2	+123.81
Peseta	85.8	-33.72

Morgan Guaranty changes: average 1980-1982=100. Bank of England (Base Average 1985=100) **Rates are for Jul 23

Fig. 10.5 (a) Currency movements

CURRENCY RATES

Jul 26	Bank ♣ rate %	Special * Drawing Rights	European † Currency Unit
Sterling	–	0.927673	0.751161
U.S Dollar	3.00	1.38984	1.12802
Canadian $	4.53	1.77900	1.44443
Austrian Sch	6.25	16.8046	13.7088
Belgian Franc	6.00	49.3984	40.4169
Danish Krone	9.25	9.28413	7.56054
D–Mark	6.75	2.38983	1.94786
Dutch Guilder	6.00	2.68712	2.19095
French Franc	10	8.16114	6.65193
Italian Lira	9.00	2241.10	1810.22
Japanese Yen	2.50	147.740	120.021
Norway Krone	–	10.2139	8.30278
Spanish Peseta	–	191.256	156.298
Swedish Krona	11.50	11.2615	9.07322
Swiss Franc	4.50	2.10728	1.71515
Greek Drach	19	N/A	268.243
Irish Punt	–	N/A	0.806996

♣ Bank rate refers to central bank discount rates. These are not quoted by the UK, Spain and Ireland.
† European Commission Calculations.
* All SDR rates are for Jul 23

Fig. 10.5 (b) Currency rates

STERLING INDEX

	Jul 26	Previous
8.30 am	81.8	81.8
9.00 am	81.9	81.8
10.00 am	81.9	81.8
11.00 am	82.0	81.9
Noon	82.1	81.8
1.00 pm	82.1	81.7
2.00 pm	82.1	81.7
3.00 pm	82.0	81.8
4.00 pm	82.0	81.7

Fig. 10.5 (c) Sterling index

- **Sterling index:** is an hourly value on the past two trading days. The index is weighted by the importance of trade with the United Kingdom (see Figure 10.5(c)). It is not a monetary value but a measure of the strength or weakness of the pound against all currencies. It is also known as the Bank of England index and is compiled by the Bank.

Exchange cross rates

EXCHANGE CROSS RATES

Jul 26	£	$	DM	Yen	F Fr.	S Fr.	N Fl.	Lira	C$	B Fr.	Pta.	Ecu
£	1	1.502	2.590	160.5	8.843	2.285	2.913	2409	1.923	53.70	207.6	1.334
$	0.666	1	1.724	106.9	5.887	1.521	1.939	1604	1.280	35.75	138.2	0.888
DM	0.386	0.580	1	61.97	3.414	0.882	1.125	930.1	0.742	20.73	80.15	0.515
YEN	6.231	9.358	16.14	1000.	55.10	14.24	18.15	15009	11.98	334.6	1293	8.312
F Fr.	1.131	1.699	2.929	181.5	10.	2.584	3.294	2724	2.175	60.73	234.8	1.509
S Fr.	0.438	0.657	1.133	70.24	3.870	1	1.275	1054	0.842	23.50	90.85	0.584
N Fl.	0.343	0.516	0.889	55.10	3.036	0.784	1	827.0	0.660	18.43	71.27	0.458
Lira	0.415	0.623	1.075	66.63	3.671	0.949	1.209	1000.	0.798	22.29	86.18	0.554
C $	0.520	0.781	1.347	83.46	4.599	1.188	1.515	1253	1	27.93	108.0	0.694
B Fr.	1.862	2.797	4.823	298.9	16.47	4.255	5.425	4486	3.581	100.	386.6	2.484
Pta	0.482	0.724	1.248	77.31	4.260	1.101	1.403	1160	0.926	25.87	100.	0.643
Ecu	0.750	1.126	1.942	120.3	6.629	1.713	2.184	1806	1.442	40.25	155.6	1

Yen per 1,000: French Fr. per 10: Lira per 1,000: Belgian Fr. per 100: Peseta per 100.

Fig. 10.6 Exchange cross rates

- The reciprocal values of the world's eleven principal trading currencies plus the ecu, quoted in a grid displaying each currency's value in terms of the others (see Figure 10.6).

Eurocurrency interest rates

The FT's currencies page gives a fairly full list of interest rates on deposits in various currencies in markets outside their countries of origin, the so-called Euromarket rates (see Figure 10.7). Outside the United States, for example, banks are not bound by any considerations of reserve requirement on their holding of dollars, and outside France French francs are not affected by French controls. These then are free market rates at which banks lend and borrow money to and from each other.

- **Eurocurrencies:** interest rates are quoted for thirteen currencies and the so-called 'Asian' dollar, that is, offshore dollars traded in the Far East before the European market opens. A short-term rate is given (generally referring to the day after next), and also rates for

Switzerland .	1.5150 - 1.5235	1.5205 - 1.5215	0.20-0.24cdis	-1.74	0.53-0.59dis	-1.47
Ecu†	1.1230 - 1.1275	1.1265 - 1.1275	0.58-0.57cpm	6.12	1.45-1.38pm	5.02

Commercial rates taken towards the end of London trading. † UK, Ireland and Ecu are quoted in US currency. Forward premiums and discounts apply to the US dollar and not to the individual currency.

EURO-CURRENCY INTEREST RATES

Jul 26	Short term	7 Days notice	One Month	Three Months	Six Months	One Year
Sterling.................	$6 - 5\frac{3}{4}$	$6 - 5\frac{3}{4}$	$6\frac{1}{16} - 5\frac{15}{16}$	$6\frac{1}{16} - 5\frac{15}{16}$	$6 - 5\frac{7}{8}$	$6 - 5\frac{7}{8}$
US Dollar...............	$3\frac{3}{16} - 3\frac{1}{16}$	$3\frac{1}{8} - 3$	$3\frac{3}{16} - 3\frac{1}{16}$	$3\frac{5}{16} - 3\frac{3}{16}$	$3\frac{9}{16} - 3\frac{7}{16}$	$3\frac{7}{8} - 3\frac{3}{4}$
Can. Dollar............	$3\frac{3}{4} - 3\frac{1}{2}$	$4 - 3\frac{3}{4}$	$4\frac{1}{8} - 3\frac{7}{8}$	$4\frac{5}{16} - 4\frac{1}{16}$	$4\frac{11}{16} - 4\frac{7}{16}$	$5 - 4\frac{3}{4}$
Dutch Guilder..........	$6\frac{1}{2} - 6\frac{1}{8}$	$6\frac{7}{8} - 6\frac{3}{4}$	$6\frac{3}{4} - 6\frac{5}{8}$	$6\frac{9}{16} - 6\frac{7}{16}$	$6\frac{3}{8} - 6\frac{1}{4}$	$6\frac{1}{8} - 6$
Swiss Franc...........	$4\frac{3}{4} - 4\frac{1}{2}$	$4\frac{3}{4} - 4\frac{1}{2}$	$4\frac{11}{16} - 4\frac{9}{16}$	$4\frac{11}{16} - 4\frac{7}{16}$	$4\frac{5}{8} - 4\frac{1}{2}$	$4\frac{7}{16} - 4\frac{5}{16}$
D–Mark.................	$7\frac{1}{8} - 7$	$7\frac{1}{16} - 6\frac{15}{16}$	$7\frac{1}{16} - 6\frac{15}{16}$	$6\frac{15}{16} - 6\frac{13}{16}$	$6\frac{3}{4} - 6\frac{5}{8}$	$6\frac{3}{8} - 6\frac{1}{4}$
French Franc..........	$11\frac{1}{2} - 10\frac{1}{2}$	$13 - 12$	$11\frac{1}{2} - 11\frac{1}{4}$	$9\frac{1}{2} - 9\frac{1}{4}$	$8\frac{1}{8} - 7\frac{7}{8}$	$7\frac{1}{8} - 6\frac{7}{8}$
Italian Lira.............	$11 - 9$	$10\frac{1}{2} - 10$	$10\frac{1}{4} - 9\frac{3}{4}$	$9\frac{3}{4} - 9\frac{3}{8}$	$8\frac{1}{2} - 9\frac{1}{8}$	$9\frac{1}{2} - 9$
Belgian Franc.........	$9\frac{3}{4} - 9\frac{1}{2}$	$9\frac{1}{2} - 9\frac{3}{8}$	$9\frac{1}{2} - 9$	$9 - 8\frac{3}{4}$	$8\frac{1}{4} - 8$	$7\frac{1}{4} - 7$
Yen......................	$3\frac{1}{4} - 3\frac{3}{16}$	$3\frac{3}{32} - 3\frac{7}{32}$	$3\frac{1}{4} - 3\frac{3}{16}$	$3\frac{1}{4} - 3\frac{3}{16}$	$3\frac{3}{16} - 3\frac{1}{8}$	$3\frac{3}{16} - 3\frac{1}{8}$
Danish Krone..........	$11 - 9$	$13 - 11$	$19 - 16$	$12\frac{1}{2} - 11\frac{1}{2}$	$10\frac{1}{2} - 10$	$8\frac{3}{4} - 8\frac{1}{8}$
Asian $Sing............	$3\frac{1}{2} - 2\frac{1}{2}$	$3\frac{1}{2} - 2\frac{1}{2}$	$3\frac{1}{2} - 2\frac{1}{2}$	$4 - 3$	$4 - 3$	$4\frac{1}{4} - 3\frac{1}{4}$
Spanish Peseta.......	$13\frac{1}{2} - 12\frac{1}{2}$	$15 - 14\frac{1}{4}$	$14\frac{3}{8} - 14\frac{1}{8}$	$12\frac{13}{16} - 12\frac{9}{16}$	$11\frac{3}{8} - 11\frac{1}{8}$	$10\frac{5}{8} - 10\frac{3}{8}$
Portuguese Esc.......	$13\frac{3}{4} - 12\frac{3}{4}$	$14\frac{1}{2} - 13\frac{1}{2}$	$14\frac{3}{8} - 13\frac{3}{8}$	$13\frac{3}{8} - 12\frac{3}{8}$	$12\frac{1}{2} - 11\frac{1}{2}$	$11\frac{3}{4} - 10\frac{3}{4}$

Long term Eurodollars: two years $4\frac{7}{16}$-$4\frac{5}{16}$ per cent; three years $4\frac{7}{8}$-$4\frac{3}{4}$ per cent; four years $5\frac{1}{4}$-$5\frac{1}{8}$ per cent; five years $5\frac{1}{2}$-$5\frac{3}{8}$ per cent nominal. Short term rates are call for US Dollar and Japanese Yen; others, two days' notice.

Fig. 10.7 Eurocurrency interest rates

one week, and one, three, six and twelve months. Rates are also quoted for Eurodollar certificates of deposit (CDs). These are, in essence, marketable bank deposits: a depositor who buys a three-month CD from a bank may sell it to a third party if liquidity is needed before the maturity date. Because CDs can be sold on, unlike ordinary deposits, they carry slightly lower interest rates.

The Eurocurrency interest rates follow but do not necessarily match domestic rates. The rates are lowest for the strongest currencies. The key rate is the LIBOR (London Inter-Bank Offered Rate), the heart of the interbank market, which is in turn the core of the money markets.

Interbank fixing

In connection with the Eurocurrency rates, the *Financial Times* publishes the FT London Interbank Fixing (see Figure 10.8). These are three- and six-month Eurodollar deposit rates representing the average of rates collected from five leading banks (National Westminster Bank, Bank of Tokyo, Deutsche Bank, Banque National de Paris and Morgan Guaranty Trust) at 11am London time every trading day.

Belgian Fr. per 100: Peseta per 100.		Spot 1.5020	1-mth. 1.4980	3-mth. 1.4916	6-mth. 1.4842	12-mth. 1.4725

FT LONDON INTERBANK FIXING

(11.00 a.m. Jul 26) 3 months US dollars		6 months US Dollars	
bid $3\frac{3}{16}$	offer $3\frac{5}{16}$	bid $3\frac{7}{16}$	offer $3\frac{9}{16}$

The fixing rates are the arithmetic means rounded to the nearest one-sixteenth, of the bid and offered rates for $10m quoted to the market by five reference banks at 11.00 a.m. each working day. The banks are National Westminster Bank, Bank of Tokyo, Deutsche Bank, Banque National de Paris and Morgan Guaranty Trust.

Fig. 10.8 FT London interbank fixing

- **LIBOR:** the rates are intended to be used as a reference point by borrowers or lenders of floating-rate money when the rate of interest is linked to Eurodollar LIBOR (London Inter-Bank Offered Rate). LIBOR, a major reference point for the international financial markets, is not calculated in any universal way or at a universally recognised time. These figures, published daily by the *Financial Times* since June 1980, are intended to fill this gap by providing an internationally acceptable standard rate.

While the LIBOR represents the rate at which banks in London lend wholesale to each other, the equivalent rate for deposits is covered by the London Interbank Bid Rate (LIBID). Different LIBORs apply to different key currencies, and similar sets of interbank rates exist in certain other financial centres, for example the Paris Inter-Bank Offered Rate (PIBOR) in France.

THE MONEY MARKETS

The money markets are the markets in deposits and short term financial instruments, places for money that is available for short periods and where money can be converted into longer period loans. It is a wholesale market for professionals only, though its operations have an impact on the price of money and liquidity generally. Its main functions are:

- those banks temporarily short of funds can borrow while those with a surplus can put it to work;
- it is a source of liquidity;
- banks can borrow wholesale funds as do companies and governments;
- it corrects imbalances between the banking system as a whole and the government.

The FT's reports describe monetary conditions and central bank money market intervention in a number of countries, especially the United Kingdom. The choice of market centres will depend on the amount of activity in each on the preceding day.

London money rates

The UK money market report is designed to be read in conjunction with the London money rates table (see Figure 10.9). It describes the flows of funds between the government and the banks on the previous day, the resulting state of credit (whether it is abundant or in short supply) and the actions of the Bank of England in the market. When, as is usual, the market is short of credit, the way in which and the price at which the Bank chooses to supply it can sometimes be a significant pointer to the direction in which monetary policy is moving. For example:

> The Bank of England forecast a small shortage of £850 million in the morning which was later revised to £900 million. This was despatched by early afternoon in discount market dealing. Overnight rates fell to 4 per cent. Further out, rates were mostly unchanged. The 3 month interbank rate continued to reflect a very slight easing of monetary policy by the autumn.
> (*Financial Times*, 13 JULY 1993)

This quotation shows how the Bank influences monetary conditions and the relationship between the interest rates of loans of different maturities.

The London money rates table in Figure 10.9 provides details of interest rates for overnight deposits and other short-term instruments. These are representative interest rates taken by the FT from major market participants near the end of the London trading day.

LONDON MONEY RATES

Jul 26	Overnight	7 days notice	One Month	Three Months	Six Months	One Year
Interbank Offer	$6\frac{1}{8}$	$5\frac{15}{16}$	$6\frac{1}{16}$	$6\frac{1}{16}$	6	6
Interbank Bid	$3\frac{1}{2}$	$5\frac{11}{16}$	$5\frac{15}{16}$	$5\frac{15}{16}$	$5\frac{7}{8}$	$5\frac{7}{8}$
Sterling CDs.	–	–	$5\frac{31}{32}$	$5\frac{31}{32}$	$5\frac{13}{16}$	$5\frac{13}{16}$
Local Authority Deps.	$5\frac{1}{2}$	$5\frac{3}{4}$	$5\frac{15}{16}$	$5\frac{15}{16}$	$5\frac{15}{16}$	$5\frac{15}{16}$
Local Authority Bonds	–	–	–	–	–	–
Discount Mkt Deps	6	$5\frac{7}{8}$	–	–	–	–
Company Deposits	–	–	–	–	–	–
Finance House Deposits	–	–	$5\frac{15}{16}$	$5\frac{15}{16}$	$5\frac{31}{32}$	$5\frac{7}{8}$
Treasury Bills (Buy)	–	–	$5\frac{11}{16}$	$5\frac{3}{8}$	$5\frac{3}{8}$	–
Bank Bills (Buy)	–	–	$5\frac{11}{16}$	$5\frac{31}{32}$	$5\frac{9}{16}$	–
Fine Trade Bills (Buy)	–	–	–	–	–	–
Dollar CDs.	–	–	3.01	3.08	3.29	3.58
SDR Linked Dep. Offer	–	–	$4\frac{7}{16}$	$4\frac{7}{16}$	$4\frac{3}{8}$	$4\frac{3}{8}$
SDR Linked Dep. Bid	–	–	$4\frac{5}{16}$	$4\frac{5}{16}$	$4\frac{1}{4}$	$4\frac{1}{4}$
ECU Linked Dep. Offer	–	–	9	$8\frac{5}{16}$	$7\frac{1}{16}$	$7\frac{1}{8}$
ECU Linked Dep. Bid	–	–	$8\frac{1}{2}$	$7\frac{13}{16}$	$7\frac{5}{16}$	$6\frac{5}{8}$

Treasury Bills (sell); one-month $5\frac{5}{8}$ per cent; three months $5\frac{5}{16}$ per cent; six months $5\frac{5}{16}$ per cent; Bank Bills (sell): one-month $5\frac{21}{32}$ per cent; three months $5\frac{5}{8}$ per cent; Treasury Bills; Average tender rate of discount 5.1338 p.c. ECGD Fixed Rate Sterling Export Finance. Make up day June 30 ,1993 . Agreed rates for period July 26, 1993 to Aug. 24, , 1993 Schemes II & III: 7.18 p.c. Reference rate for period May 29, 1993 to June 30 , 1993, Scheme IV&V: 5.939 p.c. Local Authority and Finance Houses seven

Fig. 10.9 London money rates

- **Loan period:** rates are given for a number of maturities, varying from overnight to one year, for a number of different instruments.

- **Interbank offer and bid: offer (lend) and bid (borrow) rates for interbank deposits:** this is a measure of short-term swings in rates; a constantly changing indicator of the cost of money in large amounts for banks themselves. The interbank market exists to allow banks to lend and borrow surplus liquidity in substantial amounts; in practice, very large company depositors should be able to deal at or near interbank rates when they are placing money in the market. Rates for different maturities produce the yield curve; when interest rates might drop, the yield curve will be negative. This is the case in this example, where the longer the money is lent, the lower the rate of interest, reflecting an easing of monetary policy.

- **Sterling CDs:** certificates of deposit issued in sterling by UK banks and in which a secondary market exists. These carry a slightly higher rate than interbank loans.

- **Deposits:** money lent to local authorities (offered rate for deposits) and finance houses, as well as the rates at which discount houses (the institutions with which the Bank of England carries out the bulk of its operations in the money market) accept the secured money from banks. Banks are required to maintain a certain amount of cash with the discount market, and these rates are generally below interbank levels.

- **Bills:** the rates at which various bills of exchange are discounted. Bills of exchange are securities issued by companies, banks or governments with a fixed maturity value. Discounting them means buying them at a discount from face value with the discount rate being the difference between purchase price and face value as a percentage of the face value.

- **Currency-linked deposits:** offer and bid rates for deposits linked to the Special Drawing Rights of the IMF and the European currency unit.

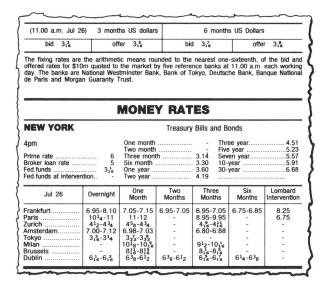

Fig. 10.10 Money rates

International money rates

The money rates table in Figure 10.10 lists representative interest rates from nine major domestic markets outside London.

- **The key rates:** the prime rate, the rate at which US banks lend to highly creditworthy customers, and the equivalent of the UK's base lending rate; and the Federal Funds rate, which is the overnight rate paid on funds lent between the member banks of the US Federal Reserve System. The latter is highly volatile and the most sensitive reflection of the day-to-day cost of money in the United States. Treasury bills and bonds are government securities, the equivalent of UK Treasury bills and gilts. They range in maturity term from one month to the thirty years of the benchmark long bond, and in this case have a positive yield curve indicating that investors expect a premium for holding investments over the longer term.

- **Rates elsewhere:** overnight and one- two- three- and six-month rates or rate spreads in Germany, France, Switzerland, the Netherlands, Japan, Italy, Belgium and Ireland.

- **Lombard intervention:** the rate at which the central bank in Germany intervenes in the interbank market to manage day-to-day liquidity lending to German commercial banks. France too has an official intervention rate of this kind.

WEEKLY CHANGE IN WORLD INTEREST RATES

	Jul 16	change		Jul 16	Change
LONDON			**NEW YORK**		
Base rates	6	Unch'd	Prime rates	6	Unch'd
7 day Interbank	6	$-\frac{1}{8}$	Federal Funds	$2\frac{15}{16}$	Unch'd
3-month Interbank	$5\frac{15}{16}$	$-\frac{1}{16}$	3 Mth. Treasury Bills	3.08	+0.01
Treasury Bill Tender	5.1341	-0.0155	6 Mth. Treasury Bills	3.22	+0.01
Band 1 Bills	$5\frac{7}{8}$	Unch'd	3 Mth. CD	3.03	-0.04
Band 2 Bills	$5\frac{7}{8}$	Unch'd			
Band 3 Bills	-	-	**FRANKFURT**		
Band 4 Bills	-	-	Lombard	8.25	Unch'd
3 Mth. Treasury Bill	$5\frac{11}{32}$	$-\frac{1}{32}$	One mth. Interbank	7.30	-0.175
1 Mth. Bank Bills	$5\frac{21}{32}$	$-\frac{1}{32}$	Three month	7.20	-0.175
3 Mth. Bank Bills	$5\frac{15}{32}$	$-\frac{1}{32}$	**PARIS**		
TOKYO			Intervention Rate	6.75	Unch'd
One month	$3\frac{1}{4}$	-	One mth. Interbank	$8\frac{1}{16}$	Unch'd
Three month	-	-	Three month	$7\frac{9}{16}$	Unch'd
BRUSSELS			**MILAN**		
One month	$8\frac{1}{4}$	$+1\frac{3}{16}$	One month	$9\frac{11}{32}$	$-\frac{1}{32}$
Three month	$7\frac{1}{2}$	$+\frac{5}{8}$	Three month	$9\frac{5}{16}$	$-\frac{1}{32}$
AMSTERDAM			**DUBLIN**		
One month	7.005	Unch'd	One month	$6\frac{3}{4}$	$+\frac{1}{16}$
Three month	6.840	Unch'd	Three month	$6\frac{1}{16}$	$+\frac{1}{16}$

Fig. 10.11 Weekly changes in world interest rates

Global interest rates

A weekly table in Monday's FT summarises the state of key global money markets (see Figure 10.11).

- **Rates:** Friday's latest rates plus changes over the previous week in the main financial centres around the world.

Interest rates and currency rates are two of the most volatile features of world financial markets. To protect against their fluctuations and other price movements, many investors and companies employ a variety of risk management techniques which in turn offer speculative opportunities. This leads to the subject of the next chapter, the market for futures, options and other derivative assets.

11

FUTURES AND OPTIONS
The derivatives markets

The market for futures and options is concerned with the management and transfer of risk. Like the currency market, the market for derivatives, as futures, options and their variants are collectively known, is valuable for those wishing to hedge transactions and a source of speculative opportunity.

THE INTERNATIONAL MARKETS FOR DERIVATIVES

Over the past fifteen years or so, financial futures and options have established themselves as an integral part of the international capital markets. While futures and options originated in the commodities business, the concept was applied to financial securities in the United States in the early 1970s. Currency futures grew out of the collapse of the Bretton Woods fixed exchange rate system, and heralded the growth of a wide variety of financial instruments designed to capture the advantages or minimise the risks of an increasingly volatile financial environment. Now these products are traded around the world by a wide variety of institutions.

The underlying cash instruments, be they bonds, equities or foreign exchange, are becoming ever more closely linked in price and trading patterns to the derivative instruments. In some markets, the turnover in derivatives is many times greater than turnover in the underlying products. The importance of derivatives is undoubtedly set to grow.

Essentially, futures and options provide alternative vehicles both for trading and for the management of a diverse set of financial risks.

They are thus of benefit to financial market participants ranging from securities houses, which are trading government bonds for their own accounts, to multinational companies which wish to manage their foreign exchange exposure.

Options

Options are derivative securities: they derive their value from the value of underlying assets. In the case of financial options, these underlying assets may be bonds, currencies, individual stocks, stock groupings or indices such as the FT-SE 100. An option on an asset represents the right to buy or sell that asset at a predetermined price (the striking or exercise price) at a predetermined future date (in the case of a European-style option) or by a predetermined future date (in the case of an American-style option). It is important to note that an option conveys the right, but not the requirement, to buy or sell.

The seller (generally known as the writer) of a put (an option to sell) or a call (an option to buy) receives a premium upfront from the option buyer. Other than this premium, there is no further exchange of money until and unless the option is exercised, either at or before expiration. If, say, over the life of a European-style call option, the price of the underlying asset rises above the striking price of the option, the option is said to be 'in the money': the buyer can exercise the option at expiration and receive a profit equal to the difference between the option striking price and the actual price of the underlying assets, less the premium paid to the option writer. An in the money option is said to have intrinsic value.

If the call is 'out of the money' or 'at the money', that is, the underlying asset price is below or at the striking price, the option buyer will generally choose not to exercise the option. Nothing will be earned from the option position, and a loss will be incurred equal to the premium paid to the option writer. Before expiry, any option still has time value, the possibility that it will be worth exercising; at expiry it only has intrinsic value left and if it is out of the money it has no intrinsic value.

On the other side of the transaction, the option writer receives the premium paid by the buyer. This represents clear profit if the option remains unexercised. On the other hand, the option writer also

LIFFE EQUITY OPTIONS

Option		CALLS Jul	Oct	Jan	PUTS Jul	Oct	Jan
Allied-Lyons	500	34½	50½	58½	2½	12	19
(*529)	550	5½	22½	31	25½	35	43½
Argyll	300	17	28	34	4	11	17
(*311)	330	2	12	20	22	27	33
ASDA	57	9	11	–	1½	4	–
(*64)	67	1½	5	–	4½	8½	–
Brit Airways	287	27½	38½	43	2½	9	14½
(*310)	316	7	21	26½	13½	21	28
SmKl Bchm A	420	16½	32	41½	10½	23	30
(*424)	460	3	15	25	38½	47½	53½
Boots	420	15	31½	38½	7½	17	25½
(*426)	460	2	14	21	36	42½	48½
BP	280	18	24½	29½	2½	10½	15
(*293)	300	5	14	19½	12	19½	23½
British Steel	80	11½	15	18	1	4	5½
(*89)	90	4	9	13	4½	8	10
Bass	460	21	37	45	5½	14½	27
(*471)	500	3½	18	25	30	36½	49½
Cable & Wire	750	24½	42	53½	14½	29½	38
(*764)	800	3½	21	33	51	60	68
Courtaulds	500	55	67½	74½	1½	8	16½
(*548)	550	12	34	47½	14	26½	36
Comm Union	600	2	14	–	52½	57	–
(*612)	650	1	5½	–	103	103	–
GKN	420	36½	43	–	2½	12½	–
(*452)	460	9	18	–	17½	32½	–
ICI	633	17½	32	58	13½	34½	41½
(*635)	657	7	22	37	28	49½	55½
Kingfisher	584	23½	41	76½	7	22	–
(*597)	632	3½	18	–	37½	48½	–
Land Secur	550	30	44½	50½	2½	11	19
(*576)	600	2½	17	22	27½	34½	44½
Marks & S	330	18	29	34	3½	9½	14½
(*343)	360	3½	13½	19½	20	25	29½
NatWest	460	28	36	48½	5	12½	22
(*480)	500	6½	16½	29	25½	37	45½
Sainsbury	420	38	50	56½	1½	7	12½
(*455)	460	9	24½	32½	14	22	29
Shell Trans.	600	19½	31	41½	6½	21½	27½
(*611)	650	2	9	19½	41	53	57
Storehouse	180	19	25	30	1	1½	9
(*196)	200	5	12	18	7½	13	18
Trafalgar	101	7	13½	–	3	6½	–
(*105)	110	3½	9	13	7½	11½	15
Unilever	1000	20½	51	66½	17½	33	44½
(*1000)	1050	4	27	42	56	65	73½
Zeneca	600	28½	43	57½	6	25	35
(*619)	650	5	21	33½	35	57	64

Option		Jul	Oct	Feb	Jul	Oct	Feb
Grand Met	420	10½	24½	34½	13½	23½	34½
(*420)	460	1½	11	20½	47½	51	60
Ladbroke	180	11	21½	27	4	13½	16
(*187)	200	3	11½	18	15½	25½	30

Option		CALLS Aug	Nov	Feb	PUTS Aug	Nov	Feb
Brit Aero	360	40½	57	69½	8½	25	32½
(*386)	390	22½	42½	55½	43	58½	65½
BAT Inds	400	23½	31	42	7	20½	24½
(*413)	425	9½	19	28	19½	34	38
BTR	360	14	22	28	6½	15½	18
(*365)	390	2½	8½	14	26	34	35
Brit Telecom	390	33	36½	39	3	12	17½
(*418)	420	12	18½	23	12½	25½	32
Cadbury Sch	420	41½	51½	60	2½	11	13
(*455)	460	13	26½	36	15½	27	31
Eastern Elec	460	32	37½	44½	7½	16½	23
(*488)	500	5½	18	24½	32	38½	44½
Guinness	460	25½	41½	52½	8½	21	26½
(*472)	500	6½	22	32½	32	43½	48½
GEC	300	26	34	38	3	6	9½
(*321)	330	6	15½	20	14	18	22
Hanson	220	12	17	21	4	8½	13½
(*226)	240	3	8	12½	15	21	24½
Lasmo	140	20½	26½	32	2½	8	11
(*157)	160	7½	16	21½	9½	16	21
Lucas Inds	140	8	14½	18½	7	14½	17
(*140)	160	2½	7	11	22½	28	30
P & O	600	25	41	53½	14	36½	46
(*606)	650	6	19	32	47	69	76
Pilkington	120	9½	15½	17	3½	7½	12
(*124)	130	4½	10½	12	8½	13	17
Prudential	330	11½	21	27½	9½	19	23
(*330)	360	2½	9	15	32½	39	41
RTZ	650	38	61½	82½	8	22½	33½
(*675)	700	11½	34½	55½	33½	46½	58½
Redland	460	21½	37	44½	13½	31½	36½
(*464)	500	5½	20	28	40	55½	60
Royal Insce	288	29	37½	45½	3	9	13½
(*311)	317	9½	20½	29½	13½	22	27
Scot & New	420	43½	46	–	3½	10½	–
(*459)	460	11½	21	–	21½	28½	–
Tesco	200	12	19	25	5	12	15
(*205)	220	4	10	15	17	23	26
Vodafone	420	29	46	54	8	19	25
(*437)	460	8½	26	34	30	40½	45½
Williams	300	26½	32½	39	3½	11½	15
(*319)	330	7½	16½	23½	16	28	31

Option		Aug	Nov	Jan	Aug	Nov	Jan
BAA	700	35½	56½	63	8	18½	26½
(*724)	750	9	30½	36	34	44	51½
Thames Wtr	460	22	34½	38	6½	17½	21
(*471)	500	5	14½	18½	31	39½	43

Option		Sep	Dec	Mar	Sep	Dec	Mar
Abbey Natl	390	31½	34½	52	9	14	19½
(*414)	420	14	27	35	23½	27½	33½
Amstrad	30	5	6	7	2	3	4½
(*32)	35	2½	4	5	4½	5½	6
Barclays	460	30½	44	52	14½	21½	26½
(*476)	500	11	24½	32	37½	44½	48½

Option		CALLS Sep	Dec	Mar	PUTS Sep	Dec	Mar
Eurotunnel	390	44	60½	–	19½	32	–
(*410)	420	27½	46½	–	34½	48	–
Glaxo	500	63	71	–	9	22	–
(*546)	550	31	42	–	28½	47½	–
Hillsdown	140	13	18	21½	7½	13	15
(*143)	160	5	9	13	21	25½	27
Lonrho	120	11½	17½	20½	8½	12½	15½
(*124)	130	7	13	16	14½	18	21
HSBC 75p shs	650	38½	58½	–	31	44	–
(*654)	700	17½	36	–	61½	72½	–
Natl Power	360	19½	30	35	11	18	22
(*364)	390	7½	16½	21½	30	34	38½
Reuters	1400	69	105	–	55	80	–
(*1415)	1450	42	80	–	85	105	–
Rolls-Royce	140	12	17½	19	8	14½	15½
(*141)	160	4½	9½	10½	21½	27	27½
Scot Power	310	12½	19	–	12	16	–
(*315)	330	3½	10	14	26	28½	32
Sears	90	12½	14	16	2	3½	4½
(*99)	100	5	7½	10	5	7½	8½
Forte	220	19	26½	32	10½	17½	21½
(*226)	240	9½	17	23	22	29	32½
Tarmac	130	11½	15½	19	8½	14½	16½
(*130)	140	7	11½	15	14½	21	23
Thorn EMI	900	28	45	55	41	48	58½
(*903)	950	9½	26	34	77½	83½	91
TSB	180	16	21	25	6½	10½	14½
(*190)	200	5½	11½	15½	18	21	26
Tomkins	220	14½	22	26½	8½	13	17
(*228)	240	5½	14	17½	22	25	28½
Wellcome	600	66½	84½	95	15½	29	36½
(*645)	650	36	56	67	34	52½	61

EURO FT-SE INDEX (*2838)

	2775	2825	2875	2925	2975	3025	3075	3125
CALLS								
Jul	61	25	8	3	1½	1	1	1
Aug	86	54	32	18	8	4	2	1½
Sep	104	75	51	30	19	11	6	3
Dec	–	128	–	81	–	46	–	24
Mar †	–	167	–	118	–	78	–	48
PUTS								
Jul	8	22	55	100	149	200	250	300
Aug	29	48	75	111	152	196	245	295
Sep	40	59	84	116	155	197	242	289
Dec	–	96	–	147	–	212	–	289
Mar †	–	119	–	167	–	225	–	293

FT-SE INDEX (*2838)

	2800	2850	2900	2950	3000	3050	3100	3150
CALLS								
Jul	42	15	5	1½	1	½	½	½
Aug	70	42	24	12	6	3	2	1½
Sep	90	63	41	26	15	8	5	3
Oct	107	79	57	40	26	16	11	6½
Dec †	144	–	93	–	57	–	31	–
Jun †	214	–	166	–	120	–	36	–
PUTS								
Jul	13	38	79	129	179	229	279	329
Aug	37	60	93	135	180	229	279	329
Sep	52	75	107	143	185	230	280	330
Oct	66	88	116	150	189	233	281	331
Dec †	89	–	140	–	206	–	289	–

Fig. 11.1 LIFFE equity options

assumes the risk of having to sell the underlying asset at a striking price significantly below actual market price or to buy the underlying asset at a striking price significantly above the actual market price. In either of these cases, the loss suffered by the option writer at the exercise of the option can overwhelm any premium received for writing the option. It is potentially limitless.

LIFFE EQUITY OPTIONS

The London International Financial Futures and Options Exchange (LIFFE) is the primary market for options and futures in the United Kingdom. It provides facilities for trading in derivatives contracts on stocks, stock indices, bonds, currencies and interest rates. Until 1992, the London Traded Option Market was a separate entity that dealt in equity option contracts, but it is now a part of LIFFE. Nevertheless, the *Financial Times* continues to list price and trading data on equity and financial derivatives separately. LIFFE equity options are shown in Figure 11.1.

READING THE FIGURES

- **Option:** the first column lists the security from which the options are derived and its closing price in the cash market on the previous day. For example, in this table, the British Aerospace stock closed at 386 pence.

- **Striking price:** the second column gives the option series quoted. For British Aerospace, there are two series, one with a striking price of 360 pence, the other with a striking price of 390 pence. Thus, one is lower than the current cash market price, the other higher.

- **Calls:** the third, fourth and fifth columns give the price or premiums payable for call options that can be exercised on three different dates. For British Aerospace, the price of a 360 pence call option that expires in November is 57 pence, while a 390 option that expires in the same month costs $42\frac{1}{2}$ pence.

- **Puts:** the final three columns give the premiums payable for put options that can again be exercised on three dates in the future.

- **FT-SE index:** this table provides prices for eighty different options, six calls and six puts with up to eight striking prices.

USING THE INFORMATION

The buyer of an option is willing to risk a limited amount (the premium) in exchange for an uncertain reward (the possibility of buying at some level below or selling at some level above the market price), whereas the option writer is willing to accept an offsetting, uncertain risk (having to sell at some level below or buy at some level above the market price) in return for a certain reward (the option premium).

Option contracts, like insurance policies, are used to protect the investor, whether writer or buyer, from unacceptable risk. The option buyer is in a position analogous to that of the owner of an insurance policy; the uncovered option writer is like the insurance underwriter who accepts risk in return for premium income.

For most investors and companies, options are protection against wide price fluctuations. For dealers and speculators they are an opportunity for big profits.

As an investment, call options are highly geared so that a small change in the underlying asset value has a significant effect on the option value.

Put options on the other hand are more of a hedging strategy protecting against the fall of stock or portfolio value by establishing a floor price below which they cannot fall.

As in the currency markets, it is important in the options markets to have liquidity and so the FT reports often focus on the turnover in the option markets as in this example:

> Good business in Asda stock options boosted total option turnover yesterday to 30,686 contracts. It traded 7,640 lots, with most of the total coming from the July 67 puts. (*Financial Times*, 6 July 1993)

TRADITIONAL OPTIONS

Whereas traded options are a standardised product that may be bought and sold and are transferable within the confines of the exchange, traditional options are bargains struck between two parties that are not readily transferable. Unlike traded options, however, they are available on any security on which the brokers involved care to make a price.

As with shares, transactions in traditional options are made within two-week account dealing periods. Details of the current period for standard three-month options are listed in a chart that appears in the *Financial Times* from Tuesday to Saturday (see Figure 11.2):

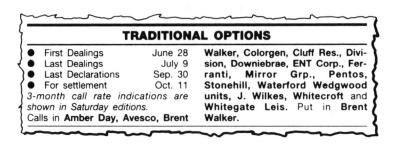

TRADITIONAL OPTIONS

● First Dealings	June 28	Walker, Colorgen, Cluff Res., Divi-
● Last Dealings	July 9	sion, Downiebrae, ENT Corp., Fer-
● Last Declarations	Sep. 30	ranti, Mirror Grp., Pentos,
● For settlement	Oct. 11	Stonehill, Waterford Wedgwood
3-month call rate indications are		units, J. Wilkes, Whitecroft and
shown in Saturday editions.		Whitegate Leis. Put in Brent
Calls in **Amber Day, Avesco, Brent**		Walker.

Fig. 11.2 Traditional options

- **First and last dealings:** the beginning and end dates for the current period of issuing or buying three-month call, put or double options. Double options give the right, but not the obligation, to buy or sell the underlying stock.

- **Last declarations and settlement:** the last day but one on which traditional options bought in this account period must be declared. Declaration means that the option is on the point of expiring and the owner must state whether or not the option to buy or sell the underlying security will be exercised. The actual settlement day is then seven business days after the last declarations date. The account dealing-dates chart (discussed in chapter 5) includes the declaration days for traditional options expiring in the next three account periods.

- **Calls and puts in:** a list of some of the traditional options available in this account period.

Saturday's FT adds a chart of the prices of three-month call options in a range of stocks (including industrials, property, oils and mines), but this tailored market provides a whole variety of prices that must be sought by telephoning individual brokers (see Figure 11.3):

TRADITIONAL OPTION 3-month call rates

INDUSTRIALS	p								
llied-Lyons	50	Cadburys	36	HSBC (75p shs)	39	Ratners	3	Brit Land	7
mstrad	3½	Charter Cons.	52	Hanson	20	Reed Intl	52	Land Sec.	40
stec (BSR)	3½	Comm Union	52	ICI	75	Sears	9	MEPC	30
AT Inds	75	Courtaulds	48	Ladbroke	15	SmKl Bchm A	40	■ OILS	
OC	56	Eurotunnel	30	Legal & Gen	38	TI	28	Arcon Intl.	6
T	28	FKI	12	Lex Service	19	TSB	12	Aviva Pet	5
TR	41	FNFC	7	Lloyds Bank	45	Tesco	20	BP	21
arclays	30	Forte	14	Lonhro	7	Thorn EMI	70	Burmah Castrol	60
ue Circle	22	GKN	40	Lucas Inds	13	Tomkins	22	Premier Cons	3
oots	42	Gen Accident	31	Marks Spencer	25	T & N	15	Shell	36
owater	40	GEC	22	NatWest Bank	30	Unilever	72	■ MINES	
rit Aerospace	24	Glaxo	55	P & O Dfd	40	Vickers	9	RTZ	52
itish Steel	6	Grand Met	40	Racal Elect	12	Wellcome	75		
		GRE	15	Rank Org	53	■ PROPERTY			

Fig. 11.3 Traditional options – three-month call rates

FINANCIAL FUTURES AND OPTIONS

A financial futures contract is an agreement to buy or sell a standard quantity of a certain financial instrument or foreign currency at a future date and at a price agreed between two parties. Trades are usually executed on an exchange floor with buyers and sellers grouped together in a pit shouting at each other in what is termed 'open outcry'. Some exchanges have developed automated systems which allow trading to take place on computer screens. The financial guarantee is generally provided by a central clearing house which stands between buyer and seller and guarantees the trade.

Futures and options are leveraged instruments. This means that for a relatively small down payment (margin for futures, premium for options), participants gain a disproportionately large exposure to price movements in the underlying cash market, hence their appeal as a trading vehicle. They are also used to a large extent as a hedging mechanism. For example, if a US multinational company incurs a significant exposure to the deutsche mark through the nature of its export markets, but also believes that the dollar will appreciate against the German currency over coming months, the treasurer might wish to sell deutsche mark futures to cover the company's risk. Losses incurred by lower revenues should then be at least partially offset by gains from selling the future.

An investor might also use futures to hedge a portfolio, most commonly using index futures, which are futures on major market indices. For example, if the market is expected to fall, selling stock index futures can protect portfolio value: if the market does fall, the loss on the actual stocks is compensated by the profits of buying back the futures at a reduced price.

The relationship between the futures and cash markets is kept stable by the arbitragers who seek out discrepancies between the

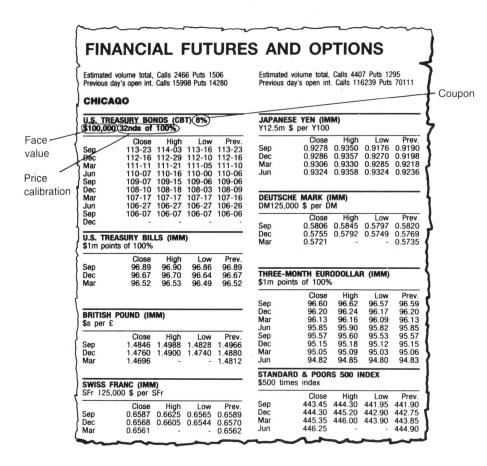

Fig. 11.4 Financial futures and options

prices. Generally, futures trade a little above the cash price, reflecting the time and risk premiums. If, for example, there are expectations of a market rise and the future and cash prices are equivalent, money goes into the futures, driving up its price relative to the cash price.

The primary FT focus in derivatives is on financial futures and options, the most commonly traded types of derivative.

There is some variation in the format of the financial futures and options tables, but contracts in the Chicago Board of Trade US Treasury bonds are a good example (see Figure 11.4).

Information on closing prices and highs and lows is displayed for each contract:

- **Coupon, face value and calibration:** the coupon on the bond is specified at eight per cent, the face value at a nominal $100,000, and the price is calibrated in thirty-seconds (i.e. the price can move by a minimum of one 32nd of one per cent).

A typical report on the market looks like this, an analysis of a key index future and its relationship with other markets:

> In mid-morning trading the September contract on the FT-SE 100, which opened the day at 2,841, touched a low of 2,828. ... Its generally poor fortunes were exacerbated by one trader selling 500 contracts. There was also some unwinding by arbitragers. But as dealers began to anticipate a reasonable early performance from yesterday's Wall Street session, the contract mustered a slight rally. ... There was additional bolstering of confidence with the steady performance of US bonds. The contract continued to trail its fair value premium to cash of 7 points, ending 4 points below. (*Financial Times*, 8 July 1993)

This demonstrates how an index future price is determined. In this case it has fallen because of the impact of one particular market player and arbitragers taking profits. The extract indicates the impact of the underlying cash markets and the performance of the overall economy as reflected in the bond market. The extract also illustrates the direct relationship between the FT-SE 100 future and the cash instrument, the index itself. A future is generally assumed to be at a fair value premium, the correct reflection of its value as determined by the time to maturity and the risk. Here it is below fair value suggesting it might go up perhaps as arbitragers buy it and sell the index.

As the extract makes clear, other financial markets are crucial in determining futures market behaviour. Similarly, their ability to spread risk and deliver exceptional profits makes the derivatives markets increasingly central to financial activity and a major influence on the world economy.

12

PRIMARY PRODUCTS
The commodities markets

Commodities are basic raw materials, primary products and food-stuffs that are homogeneous and generally traded on a free market. Commodity contracts may represent cash transactions for immediate delivery, or, more commonly, forward contracts for delivery at a specified time in the future. The bulk of such contracts are bought and sold on a commodities exchange by dealers and commodity brokers or traders. Their homogeneity, coupled with fast communications and an efficient system of quality grading and control, means that they can be traded without an actual transfer of the goods. This allows enormous scope for hedging and speculative activity as traders buy and sell rights of ownership in spot and futures markets. Commodities were in fact the origin of the derivative markets discussed in the previous chapter.

As in all free markets, the prices of commodities are determined by the forces of demand and supply. And because of the nature of the conditions of demand and supply for commodities, their prices tend to swing more violently than prices of manufactured goods. A small but persistent surplus of the supply of, say, tin, over demand can cause a dramatic slump in prices; similarly, disastrous weather conditions and a poor harvest can drive up a crop price.

Commodities are primarily of interest to industrial users. Oil is the one with the most widespread potential impact since almost all businesses have some energy needs, but there are plenty of other examples. Prospective cocoa prices, for instance, are critical to chocolate makers, while certain metal prices will affect such companies as producers of cars, ships and manufactured goods, as well as the construction industry.

Companies whose profitability is partly dependent on the cost of their raw materials will naturally seek protection from potential surges in primary commodity prices. It is this need to hedge that gives rise to the futures markets.

The *Financial Times'* Commodities and Agriculture page appears from Tuesday to Friday with the upper section devoted to reports on the markets and the lower section to a presentation of the previous day's trading and price data from markets in London, New York and Chicago. The lower section also appears on Saturday with a separate review of the week in the markets.

SPOT MARKETS

Price coverage begins with the markets for spot goods – commodities available for delivery within two days. Generally, these figures represent the cost of actual physical material, exceptions being the London daily sugar prices and the cotton index which are guide prices based on a selection of physical price indications. An example of spot markets is shown in Figure 12.1.

London Markets

SPOT MARKETS

Crude oil (per barrel FOB)(Aug)		+ or -
Dubai	$14.55-4.60	-.245
Brent Blend (dated)	$16.86-6.88	-0.27
Brent Blend (Aug)	$16.91-6.93	-0.25
W.T.I (1 pm est)	$17.98-8.00	-.405

Oil products (NWE prompt delivery per tonne CIF		+ or -
Premium Gasoline	$198-200	
Gas Oil	$163-164	-0.5
Heavy Fuel Oil	$60-62	
Naphtha	$170-171	-0.5
Petroleum Argus Estimates		

Other		+ or -
Gold (per troy oz)♣	$394.00	+2.25
Silver (per troy oz)♣	508.5c	
Platinum (per troy oz)	$406.25	+2
Palladium (per troy oz)	$140.00	-0.25

Fig 12.1 World commodities prices – London markets

- **Prices and changes in price from the previous trading day:** figures are given for the principal crude oils, oil products, metals, meat, sugar, grains, rubber, vegetable oils and oilseeds, cotton and wool.

- **Weekly price changes:** Saturday's paper adds figures on prices at the close of trading for the week, the change on the previous week, prices one year ago and the highs and lows for the year to date.

FUTURES MARKETS

As indicated, futures markets are chiefly used by consumers of physical commodities to avoid the risks of adverse price movements during the periods between contracting purchases and receiving deliveries. This hedging involves the opening of parallel but opposite futures contracts when physical orders are made, so that physical 'profits' or 'losses' made by the time the commodity is delivered will be cancelled out by losses or profits on the futures markets.

The futures markets are basically paper markets, not be confused with forward physical prices, which are simply quotations for physical material for delivery some time in the future. Speculators take on the risk consumers wish to avoid in the hope of accruing the potential profits that the consumer has relinquished.

Coffee, cocoa and sugar

The main futures market for 'soft' commodities (foodstuffs) is the London Commodity Exchange (formerly the London Futures and Options Exchange, FOX). Its core contracts are in coffee, cocoa and sugar, but it also features other agricultural products and some traded options (see page 178). World commodity prices for coffee, cocoa and sugar are shown in Figure 12.2.

- **Date:** the first column lists the expiry dates for the futures contracts currently in issue.

- **Close:** the second column indicates the closing offer prices in the brokers' bid/offer spreads, the price at which they are prepared to sell commodities. As usual with a spread, the bid prices will have been somewhat lower.

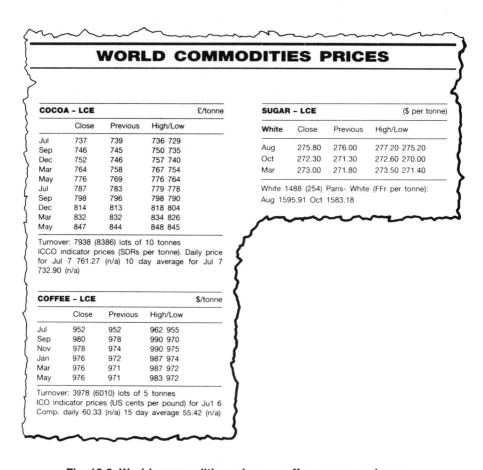

WORLD COMMODITIES PRICES

COCOA – LCE   £/tonne

	Close	Previous	High/Low
Jul	737	739	736 729
Sep	746	745	750 735
Dec	752	746	757 740
Mar	764	758	767 754
May	776	769	776 764
Jul	787	783	779 778
Sep	798	796	798 790
Dec	814	813	818 804
Mar	832	832	834 826
May	847	844	848 845

Turnover: 7938 (8386) lots of 10 tonnes
ICCO indicator prices (SDRs per tonne). Daily price for Jul 7 761.27 (n/a) 10 day average for Jul 7 732.90 (n/a)

COFFEE – LCE $/tonne

	Close	Previous	High/Low
Jul	952	952	962 955
Sep	980	978	990 970
Nov	978	974	990 975
Jan	976	972	987 974
Mar	976	971	987 972
May	976	971	983 972

Turnover: 3978 (6010) lots of 5 tonnes
ICO indicator prices (US cents per pound) for Ju1 6 Comp. daily 60.33 (n/a) 15 day average 55.42 (n/a)

SUGAR – LCE   ($ per tonne)

White	Close	Previous	High/Low
Aug	275.80	276.00	277.20 275.20
Oct	272.30	271.30	272.60 270.00
Mar	273.00	271.80	273.50 271.40

White 1488 (254) Paris- White (FFr per tonne):
Aug 1595.91 Oct 1583.18

Fig. 12.2 World commodities prices – coffee, cocoa and sugar

- **Previous:** the third column indicates the closing offer prices on the preceding trading day.

- **High/low:** the final columns show the highest and lowest levels at which trades were executed during the day. It is possible for prices to close outside these ranges because they may move further near the end of the day without any business actually being done.

- **Turnover:** the figures at the ends of the tables show the number of lots or trading units that changed hands during the day.

- **Indicator prices:** these are calculated by the International Cocoa Organisation and the International Coffee Organisation. These are related to price support systems, affecting changes in export quotas and buffer stock sales or purchases. Cocoa indicator prices are denominated in Special Drawing Rights (see chapter 10) to prevent them from being too susceptible to currency movements.

- **Sugar futures:** the market for white (refined) sugar operates on an automated trading system, in which dealers operate from their offices via screens linked to a central computer. The Paris figures derive from a market that trades on the more traditional 'open outcry' system in which dealers physically gather together on the market floor.

A typical report on these soft commodity markets looks like this:

> At the renamed London Commodity Exchange robusta coffee futures put in the strongest performance since mid-May ... by news of agreement over the weekend by Latin American producers to withhold 20 per cent of their exports from the start of October ... prices were given an extra lift yesterday by reports that frost was possible in Brazilian growing areas this weekend. (*Financial Times*, 10/11 July 1993)

In this case, the futures prices for coffee have benefited from the likelihood of future scarcity of this commodity. The prices are following the simple laws of supply and demand: as supply falls, the price rises.

Other commodities

The FT also carries information on the International Petroleum Exchange: indeed the North Sea oil price features daily on the front page of the FT in its key market summary. The Commodities and Agriculture page also periodically provides coverage of certain minor markets such as tea, jute and spices.

THE LONDON METAL EXCHANGE

The main non-ferrous metals (aluminium, copper, lead, nickel, tin and zinc) are traded on the London Metal Exchange (LME). Although it has always operated as a futures market, the LME has traditionally had a closer relationship with the physical trade than other London

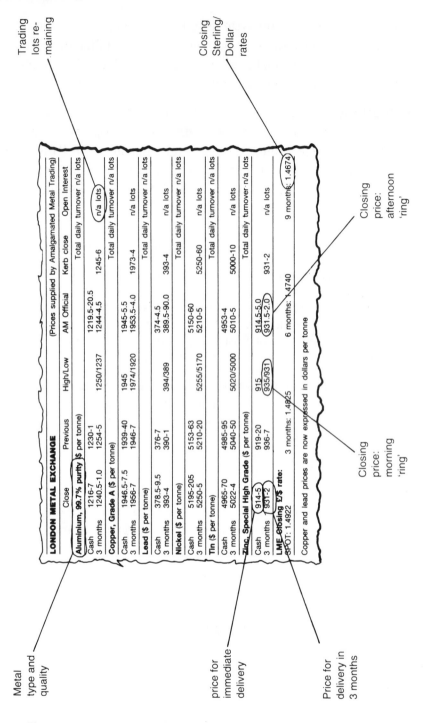

Fig. 12.3 World commodities prices – London Metal Exchange

markets. It claims to account for 70 to 80 per cent of its turnover. Only in 1987 did new investor protection legislation force the LME to abandon its cherished principal trading system in favour of the central clearing system used by the other commodity futures markets. Figure 12.3 shows the LME listing from the world commodity prices.

- **Close and previous, high and low:** these are price indicators as on the London Commodity Exchange (LCE), except that for close and previous, both bid and offer prices are shown. The prices are for immediate delivery and for delivery in three months. The futures price is for a standard contract of metal of a defined grade. It is generally higher than the spot price, a phenomenon known as 'contango' or 'forwardation'. The reverse, where the spot price exceeds the futures price, is called 'backwardation'.

- **AM Official:** these are the values of the metals at the end of the morning 'ring'. The ring opens at 11.50am and closes at 1pm with a ten minute interval starting at 12.20pm. It is followed by twenty-five minutes of after hours dealing, known as the kerb session because it used to be conducted on the street outside the exchange. Prices at the close of the official ring are widely used for industrial supply contract pricing.

- **Kerb close:** the afternoon 'unofficial' ring begins at 3.20pm and ends at 4.30pm. Kerb trading continues until 5pm with each metal phasing out from 4.45pm. This column carries the final prices from this session.

- **Open interest:** this is the number of trading lots that remain to be covered by opposite transactions or physical delivery. Lot sizes are twenty-five tonnes except for nickel which is six tonnes.

- **Closing:** the last line of the LME table gives the sterling/dollar rates published by the exchange at the unofficial close. This can be used to translate LME prices for contract purposes.

GOLD

Twice a day at 10.30am and 3pm, representatives of the major bullion dealers meet at the offices of NM Rothschild to set the fixing price of a troy ounce of gold, and a substantial number of transactions tends to take place at the fixing sessions. Figure 12.4 shows the London bullion market listing.

LONDON BULLION MARKET
(Prices supplied by N M Rothschild)

Gold (troy oz)	$ price	£ equivalent
Close	393.75-394.25	
Opening	396.00-396.50	
Morning fix	397.25	264.041
Afternoon fix	395.80	263.042
Day's high	398.75-399.50	
Day's low	393.00-393.50	

Loco Ldn Mean Gold Lending Rates (Vs US$)

1 month	2.46	6 months	2.51
2 months	2.48	12 months	2.54
3 months	2.50		

Silver fix	p/troy oz	US cts equiv
Spot	343.35	516.75
3 months	348.35	520.70
6 months	352.75	524.70
12 months	362.50	534.65

GOLD COINS

Fig. 12.4 World commodities prices – London bullion market

- **Fix:** these are morning and afternoon fixing prices in dollars per ounce (with sterling conversions), as well as early and late prices for the London market. As with currency markets, there is no official close although the word is used to describe the late price.

READING THE FIGURES

- **Loco London Mean Gold Lending Rates:** familiarly known as 'Gold Libor', these are the interest rates at which large gold holders, principally central banks, will lend gold held in their reserves to approved borrowers, principally miners, who repay the loans from future production. The low rates on offer reflect the highly secure nature of the loans and the extra cost to the borrower of the spread between the bid and offer price on the gold market, usually about $2.50 an ounce.

- **Silver fix:** prices at the morning silver fix in pence per troy ounce, with US cents equivalents.

- **Gold coins:** prices for a representative selection of gold coins. Gold coin prices are for large quantities and are exclusive of value added tax.

USING THE INFORMATION

The gold market can be attractive for investors and speculators. The price of gold is affected by a wide range of factors as this extract suggests:

> The gold market bulls were in full cry at the end of this week as an accumulation of constructive signals prompted a surge in the London bullion market price to a two and a half year high. ... Investors seemed to be interested only in bullish developments, such as European interest rate cuts, signs of a quickening in US inflation and an announcement by international financier Sir James Goldsmith that he planned to swap gold mine shares for gold bullion. (*Financial Times*, 3 July 1993)

The extract refers to European interest rates showing how the price of gold moves up and down with bond yields. Gold does not pay interest and it implies a currency risk for non-US investors since its price is always denominated in dollars. It also demonstrates that gold is often a safer asset when there is upward pressure on inflation. Given the relatively small number of players the price can be significantly influenced by individuals.

Other metals

On Wednesday, the *Financial Times* lists minor metals prices, covering what are known as the strategic metals (because of their importance in high technology and military applications). The metals are antimony, bismuth, cadmium, cobalt, mercury, molybdenum, selenium, tungsten ore, vanadium and uranium. Another minor metal market features in the following story, a further example of how and why commodities prices might move:

The platinum market ... was outperformed by its sister metal, palladium, which rose $16.75 to a four-year high of $146 an ounce. Traders attributed palladium's impressive performance of late ... to very strong physical demand from Japan, almost certainly from the electrical goods sector, and from US electrical goods producers. (*Financial Times*, 3 July 1993)

This indicates a market affected by the actual users of the commodity as an input in their production processes.

TRADED OPTIONS

Traded options appear in a number of commodity futures contracts. Options confer on holders the right, but not the obligation, to trade at a predetermined price, the striking price, within a pre-set time-span. For this, they pay a non-returnable premium. Since the premium is the only money the investor can lose, options represent a relatively low-risk way of speculating in commodities.

TRADED OPTIONS

Aluminium (99.7%)	Calls		Puts	
Strike price $ tonne	Aug	Oct	Aug	Oct
1225	39	65	22	44
1250	26	52	34	57
1275	17	40	40	73

Copper (Grade A)	Calls		Puts	
1900	82	109	30	60
1950	54	83	52	84
2000	33	62	81	112

Coffee	Sep	Nov	Sep	Nov
850	131	134	3	10
900	87	96	9	22
950	52	65	24	41

Cocoa	Sep	Dec	Sep	Dec
725	38	54	18	33
750	24	41	29	45
775	15	32	45	61

Brent Crude	Aug	Sep	Aug	Sep
1700	19	53	32	46
1750	7	24	65	
1800		11		

Fig. 12.5 World comodities prices – traded options

Traded options differ from straight options only in that they can be bought and sold rather than just operated by the original buyer. Figure 12.5 gives the FT's traded options listing.

- A range of striking prices and call (buy) and put (sell) premiums for the two most traded maturity prices.

THE MARKETS IN NEW YORK AND CHICAGO

The *Financial Times* also covers commodities futures markets in the United States since many of them are of interest to European readers, including traders in the commodities and outside speculators following the markets on both sides of the Atlantic. These markets are also, of course, the original futures markets and are still very influential because of that. Extracts from the New York and Chicago exchanges are shown in Figure 12.6.

In New York, the exchanges covered are:

- The Commodity Exchange (Comex) for copper, silver and gold. The price of gold on the Comex is a widespread reference, and is noted daily on the front page of the newspaper.
- The Mercantile Exchange (Nymex) for platinum, crude oil and heating oil.
- The Cocoa, Sugar and Coffee Exchange.
- The Cotton Exchange, which also trades frozen concentrated orange juice.

In Chicago, prices are quoted from:

- The Mercantile Exchange (CME or Merc) for live cattle, live hogs and pork bellies.
- The Chicago Board of Trade (CBoT) for maize, wheat, soyabeans, soyabean meal and soyabean oil.

New York

COTTON 50,000; cents/lbs

	Close	Previous	High/Low	
Jul	56.19	54.85	57.00	54.45
Oct	57.35	57.47	57.50	56.81
Dec	57.80	58.15	58.05	57.40
Mar	58.95	59.05	59.05	58.45
May	59.25	59.62	59.25	59.25
Jul	59.95	60.15	60.25	60.00
Oct	60.30	60.50	0	0
Dec	61.00	60.60	60.50	60.50

ORANGE JUICE 15,000 lbs; cents/lbs

	Close	Previous	High/Low	
Jul	122.25	124.20	124.00	122.00
Sep	125.25	126.55	127.00	125.00
Nov	127.45	129.50	129.50	127.40
Jan	128.50	131.50	131.00	128.50
Mar	130.10	133.00	133.00	131.00
May	132.95	133.45	133.00	133.00
Jul	132.95	133.45	132.00	132.00
Sep	131.95	133.45	0	0
Nov	131.95	133.45	0	0

Chicago

LIVE HOGS 40,000 lb; cents/lbs

	Close	Previous	High/Low	
Jul	48.775	49.125	49.100	48.700
Aug	47.950	47.925	48.250	47.650
Oct	44.125	43.750	44.225	43.725
Dec	44.750	44.850	44.975	44.250
Feb	45.150	45.100	45.200	44.350
Apr	43.725	43.900	43.900	43.200
Jun	49.300	49.750	49.400	49.000
Jul	48.850	49.200	48.850	48.700
Aug	48.700	0	0	0

PORK BELLIES 40,000 lbs; cents/lb

	Close	Previous	High/Low	
Jul	37.275	37.275	37.450	36.500
Aug	36.100	36.525	36.525	35.400
Feb	46.475	45.675	47.100	45.300
Mar	45.900	45.150	46.750	45.000
May	47.000	45.500	47.000	0
Jul	43.600	43.600	45.600	0
Aug	46.000	46.000	48.000	0

Fig. 12.6 World commodities prices – New York: cotton and orange juice; Chicago: live hogs and pork bellies

The many other US markets are not covered because they are too small or primarily of interest to domestic US consumers.

COMMODITY INDICES

The final item in the commodities section of the newspaper is a record of two separate indices (see Figure 12.7):

- The Reuters index is calculated from sterling prices for seventeen primary commodities, weighted by their relative importance in international trade.

- The Dow Jones spot and futures indices are calculated from the dollar prices of cattle, coffee, copper, corn (maize), cotton, gold, hogs, lumber, silver, soyabeans, sugar and wheat.

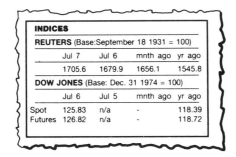

Fig. 12.7 World commodities prices – indices

The two extracts below from FT reports demonstrate the significance of commodity price movements:

> ...equity and bond prices moved solidly lower as surging commodities prices left investors increasingly nervous about inflation. (*Financial Times*, 7 July 1993)

> A retreat in commodity prices eased investors' inflation fears yesterday and helped leading US stocks post solid gains. (*Financial Times*, 8 July 1993)

The commodities markets are dominated by a limited range of players but are important to all markets and the wider economy particularly as a leading indicator of trends and expectations in inflation and equity and bond prices.

Part III

UNDERSTANDING THE ECONOMIES

13

UK ECONOMIC INDICATORS

Every country needs to keep track of its economic progress and the United Kingdom is no exception. Each month a welter of figures is produced by the Central Statistical Office (CSO), the government department responsible for compiling economic statistics, that together throw light on the health of the economy. These official figures – many with track records that go back decades – tell businesses, consumers and the government whether the economy is stuck in recession, growing or hovering at a turning point. The *Financial Times* tracks much of this monthly and quarterly data, together with unofficial but tried-and-tested economic surveys produced by bodies such as the Confederation of British Industry.

The data, which usually refer to the previous month, are collected through nationwide surveys. The results are analysed by teams of statisticians at the CSO's centre in Newport, Gwent, and by the time the figures are announced to the public they have generally been 'smoothed' to take account of seasonal patterns and give a clearer picture of the underlying trend. For example, average earnings figures are seasonally adjusted for the extra hours worked in retailing and postal services in the run up to Christmas.

Many of the figures are presented as indices, assuming constant prices from a given date, usually 1990=100. The reference date is arbitrary and merely provides a convenient landmark for comparison. When this happens what matters is not the index numbers themselves but the change from one period to the next. The more esoteric government figures are rarely reported by the financial press. Unemployment, inflation, output and GDP figures are more likely to make the headlines, particularly when the monthly or quarterly changes are sharp.

Economic news reports appear in the first section of the *Financial Times* the day after they are released by the CSO. For easy reference, a table of UK economic figures appears every Thursday. The following are the figures most likely to be reported in the press and the ones that generally provoke the most public interest.

THE MACROECONOMY

The UK Economic Indicators table, appearing in the *Financial Times* every Thursday, gathers together a range of key economic statistics to give an instant overview of activity in the UK economy. The figures are broken down into five principal sets of values, indices and rates of change for Economic Activity, Output, External Trade, Financial and Inflation indicators.

The economic activity table in Figure 13.1, for example, addresses various indices of manufacturing and retail performance together with unemployment and unfilled vacancies, over two years on a monthly or quarterly basis.

Industrial output

Each month the CSO estimates the output of UK manufacturing industry and the level of energy production in the previous month. These come together as the index of output of the production industries. The two components are usually quoted separately because oil and gas output is often erratic and can easily distort the underlying performance of manufacturing industry. Reparations of oil installations in the North Sea, for example, can bring energy production sharply down in one month. The index for manufacturing output is broken down to show the performance of various sectors such as engineering, chemicals, textiles, and food and drink.

As well as monthly rises in output, the CSO compares output with the levels of a year ago and output in the latest three months (compared with the previous three months) to give a better idea of underlying trends.

ECONOMIC ACTIVITY- Indices of industrial production, manufacturing output (1985=100); engineering orders (£ billion); retail sales volume and retail sales value (1990=100); registered unemployment (excluding school leavers) and unfilled vacancies (000s).

	Indl. prod.	Mfg. output	Eng. order*	Retail vol.	Retail value*	Unem- ployed	Vacs.	
1992								**1992**
1st qtr.	105.4	111.1	30.8	98.6	99.6	2,635	119.8	1st qt
2nd qtr.	105.0	111.6	31.0	99.4	104.5	2,708	117.0	2nd q
3rd qtr.	105.9	111.5	30.4	99.6	104.8	2,805	115.9	3rd qt
4th qtr.	106.8	111.2	31.2	100.3	125.0	2,918	118.1	4th qt
March	105.2	111.6	30.8	98.3	100.5	2,648	120.2	March
April	105.7	111.8	31.1	99.4	105.7	2,690	117.8	April
May	104.6	111.3	31.0	99.4	104.0	2,712	117.1	May
June	104.6	111.8	31.0	99.4	103.9	2,723	116.1	June
July	105.8	111.8	31.4	98.6	105.1	2,758	119.0	July
August	105.7	111.5	31.2	99.6	104.5	2,816	117.1	August
September	106.1	111.2	30.4	100.4	104.8	2,841	111.5	Septen
October	107.4	111.5	31.2	100.7	109.4	2,868	113.5	Octobe
November	106.7	111.1	31.4	100.6	118.0	2,913	117.3	Novem
December	106.5	111.1	31.2	99.8	143.1	2,972	123.4	Decem
1993								**1993**
1st qtr.	107.0	113.5	31.9	102.0	105.2	2,967	121.3	1st qtr
January	106.4	112.7	31.5	101.7	104.1	2,992	120.3	Januar
February	107.9	114.0	31.4	102.0	104.4	2,967	120.5	Februa
March	106.8	113.8	31.9	102.2	106.6	2,941	123.2	March
April	106.6	114.5	32.1	102.1	110.8	2,940	123.5	April
May	108.7	116.5		102.0	109.4	2,917	123.6	May
June				103.3	110.2	2,909	119.7	

*Not seasonally adjusted   †Net changes in amounts outstanding, excluding bank

Fig. 13.1 UK economic indicators – economic activity

Retail sales

These figures, which come from the CSO, show the volume and value of retail sales over the previous month and over the previous quarter. The CSO breaks down the total by category of shops, such as food retailers, clothing and footwear, and so on.

Labour market statistics

Figures for unemployment, vacancies, average earnings and unit wage costs (see Figure 13.2, showing UK unemployment 1985–93) are provided by the Department of Employment. Each month it publishes the total number of people that were out of work and claiming unemployment benefit in the previous month. The figure is then seasonally adjusted to take account of annual fluctuations in the labour market, such as at the end of the academic year when school-leavers flood the jobs market.

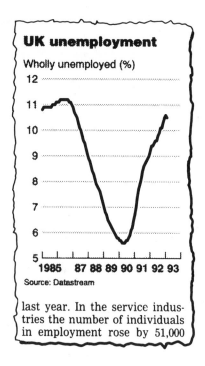

UK unemployment

Wholly unemployed (%)

1985   87 88 89 90 91 92 93

Source: Datastream

last year. In the service industries the number of individuals
in employment rose by 51,000

Fig. 13.2 UK unemployment

This measure of unemployment, known as the claimant-count, is often criticised for excluding large numbers of people who cannot find jobs but who are not eligible for unemployment benefit. Thus women seeking to return to work, the self-employed and 16 and 17 year-old school-leavers do not show up in the official count.

However, every quarter, the Department of Employment carries out a survey of the labour force, designed to capture those unemployed people who are left out of the claimant count. The Labour Force Survey (LFS) uses the International Labour Office measure of unemployment, an internationally recognised definition. It refers to people who were available to start work in the two weeks following their LFS interview and had either looked for work in the four weeks prior to interview or were waiting to start a job they had already obtained.

There is often a difference between the unemployment total revealed by the claimant-count measure and the total arrived at by the

LFS. The discrepancy between the two measures is usually greatest at a time of economic expansion when people feel encouraged to go out and look for work.

The Department also publishes vacancies notified to Job Centres, about one-third of the total vacancies in the economy. The change in the number of vacancies is seen as an important indicator of future employment trends.

Average earnings

The monthly labour market statistics include figures for growth in average earnings in the whole economy and the service and manufacturing sectors. The average earnings index measures the monthly level of earnings of employees in the United Kingdom relative to the average level in the base year of 1988. The index is compiled from a monthly sample survey of the gross wages and salaries paid to the employees of over 8,000 companies and organisations in the private and public sectors. In addition to basic wages, earnings also include overtime payments, grading increments, bonuses and other incentive payments. For this reason earnings increases usually exceed settlement increases and wage claims.

Because the earnings figures are affected by special factors such as back pay and changes in the timing of pay settlements, the Department also publishes its estimate of the underlying trend in earnings. Other figures published on the same day include the following:

- Hours of overtime worked.

- Productivity – output per head.

- Unit wage costs – wages per unit of output. Unit wage costs are an important indicator of inflationary pressures in an economy. If wages increase faster than productivity then unit wage costs rise.

- Days lost through industrial disputes.

- Hours of work and employment.

Inflation

INFLATION-Indices of earnings (1988=100); basic materials and fuels; wholesale prices of manufactured products (1985=100); retail prices and food prices (Jan 1987=100); Reuters commodity index (Sept 18th 1931 =100); trade weighted value of sterling (1985=100)

	Earn-ings	Basic matls.*	Whsale. mnfg.*	RPI*	Foods*	Reuters cmdty.*	Sterling*
1991							
4th qtr.	132.4	102.5	134.6	135.5	126.5	1,625	90.9
1992							
1st qtr.	135.8	102.9	136.5	136.2	129.0	1,599	90.6
2nd qtr.	136.1	102.2	137.9	139.1	129.1	1,598	92.3
3rd qtr.	137.5	100.7	138.5	139.0	127.3	1,542	90.9
4th qtr.	139.3	106.6	139.1	139.6	127.7	1,648	79.8
March	137.6	102.2	137.3	136.7	129.4	1,615	90.1
April	135.5	102.7	137.8	138.8	128.9	1,614	91.4
May	136.6	102.2	137.9	139.3	129.5	1,583	92.8
June	136.3	101.6	138.1	139.3	129.0	1,586	92.9
July	136.4	101.0	138.4	138.8	127.2	1,555	92.5
August	138.0	100.0	-138.5	138.9	127.5	1,530	92.0
September	138.2	101.0	138.6	139.4	127.1	1,540	88.2
October	140.1	103.7	138.7	139.9	127.4	1,610	80.8
November	139.0	107.0	139.2	139.7	127.3	1,656	78.3
December	138.9	109.1	139.5	139.2	128.4	1,675	80.0
1993							
1st qtr.	141.2	110.4	141.5	138.7	130.1	1,740	78.5
January	140.1	109.8	140.7	137.9	128.8	1,703	80.6
February	141.5	110.5	141.4	138.8	130.2	1,759	76.8
March	142.1	110.8	142.3	139.3	131.3	1,758	78.2
April	140.8	110.0	143.1	140.6	130.8	1,672	80.5
May		109.7	143.4	141.1	132.2	1,669	80.5

Fig. 13.3 UK economic indicators – Retail prices index

The rate of change of prices in the UK economy is dealt with in the Economic Indicators – Inflation table in Thursday's *Financial Times* (see Figure 13.3).

In addition to the retail prices index, indices are provided for key inflation in indicators covering earnings, consumer and manufacturing goods, commodities and currency.

The retail prices index (RPI)

A number of different measures of UK inflation are published but the most widely reported is the retail prices index, sometimes referred to as the headline rate of inflation. The change in the index, published by the CSO every month, represents the average change in the prices of millions of consumer purchases.

The CSO says it gets more queries from the public about the RPI than any other statistic, a reflection of the influence inflation has on people's lives. It determines the real value of savings, affects increases in pensions and other state benefits and plays an important part in wage-bargaining.

The index is compiled by tracking the prices of a 'basket' of goods which represents spending by the typical British family. All types of household spending are represented by the basket (see Figure 13.4) apart from a few exceptions. These include savings and investments, charges for credit, betting and cash gifts. Indirect taxes such as VAT are included but income tax and national insurance payments are excluded. (Direct taxes are accounted for in a separate index – the tax and price index. See below.)

The average change in the price of the basket is calculated from the findings of government price collectors. Each month, they visit or telephone a variety of shops gathering about 130,000 prices for different goods and services. They go to the same places and note the

Inflation reflects high street price cuts

UK inflation rate (+1.2%) RPI: 141.0 in June

Component	Rate
Housing (164)	-6.6%
Motoring (136)	+4.7%
Food (non-seasonal) (123)	+2.8%
Alcoholic drink (78)	+4.5%
Household goods (79)	+1.0%
Clothing & footwear (58)	-0.1%
Household services (47)	+3.0%
Leisure goods (46)	+1.6%
Catering (45)	+5.3%
Fuel & light (46)	-2.0%
Personal goods, serv. (39)	+3.7%
Tobacco (35)	+7.3%
Leisure services (62)	+4.1%
Food (seasonal) (21)	-4.1%
Fares & travel costs (21)	+5.2%

Fig. 13.4 Annualised inflation rates of RPI components

prices of the same things each month so that over time they compare like with like. Information on charges for gas, water, newspapers, council rents and rail fares are obtained from central sources. Some big chain stores, which charge the same prices at their various branches, help by sending information direct from their headquarters to the CSO.

The components of the RPI are weighted to ensure that the index reflects average household spending. Thus housing expenditure has much bigger weighting than cinema tickets. The biggest weightings currently go to housing, food and motoring. The weights are obtained from a number of sources but mainly from the CSO's Family Expenditure survey. For this a sample of 7,000 households across the country keep records of what they spend over a fortnight plus details of big purchases over a longer period. The spending of two groups of people is excluded on the grounds that their pattern of spending is significantly different from most people's. These are families with the top 4 per cent of incomes and low-income pensioners who mainly depend on state benefits.

Every year the components and the weightings of the RPI are reviewed to take account of changing habits. Over the past few years microwave ovens, video recorders and compact discs have been introduced, while black and white televisions were dropped when sales declined.

The headline figure for inflation – the one most widely quoted – is the change in the RPI compared with a year ago. If inflation is 3.6 per cent this means the RPI has risen by 3.6 per cent since the same month of the previous year; the average basket of goods is 3.6 per cent dearer. Monthly average price changes are also quoted.

The RPI excluding mortgage interest payments

In addition to the all-items index, the CSO publishes the RPI excluding mortgage interest payments (see Figure 13.5), an underlying measure of inflation favoured by the Treasury. It does this because a cut or rise in interest rates automatically influences mortgage interest payments. These have a higher weighting than any other component of the RPI and hence a strong bearing on the direction of the index.

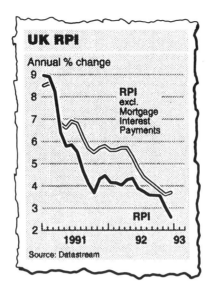

Fig. 13.5 RPI and RPI excluding morgage interest on payments

Excluding mortgage interest payments from the all-items index prevents interest rate changes muddying the underlying pattern of price changes.

The tax and price index (TPI)

The TPI shows how much taxpayers' gross incomes need to change in order to maintain their spending power after taking account of the tax that has been deducted as well as changes in prices. It was introduced after the Budget of 1979 when VAT increased but income tax was reduced. The rise in VAT, a component of the RPI, was duly reflected in the inflation figures. Income tax, however, is not accounted for by the all-items index, so the TPI was introduced to show the balancing effect of the cut in income tax.

Producer prices index (PPI)

Every month the CSO publishes two other inflation indicators. One set of figures tracks the prices of raw materials and fuels used by UK industries, the other tracks the prices of manufactured goods as they leave

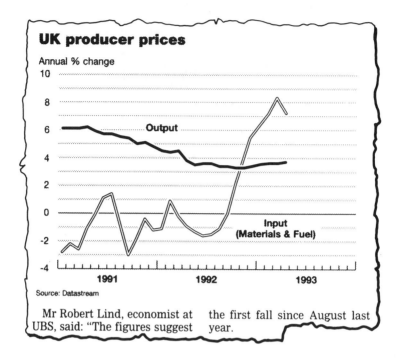

Fig. 13.6 Producer price input and output indices on the same
axis, 1990–1993

factories. The first indicators are referred to as producer input prices,
and the second as producer output prices see (Figure 13.6). Both are
expressed in terms of an index and are regarded as important forward
indicators of retail price inflation. For example, a big leap in raw material prices may be absorbed by manufacturers for a while, but they are
likely, at some stage, to raise prices to restore their profit margins. When
they do, retailers will eventually respond by raising shop prices.

During the recession of 1990/1992, prices of raw materials and fuels
used by UK manufacturers began to fall, reflecting depressed economic
conditions abroad and domestically, as well as the strength of sterling.
But this trend was reversed suddenly in September 1992 when sterling
left the European exchange rate mechanism and devalued. Input price
inflation leapt from being flat in September to a year-on-year growth
rate of over 4 per cent in November, reflecting the higher cost of
imported raw materials as a result of the weaker pound.

Trade

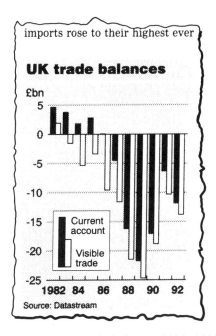

imports rose to their highest ever

UK trade balances

£bn

Current
account

Visible
trade

1982 84   86   88   90   92

Source: Datastream

Fig. 13.7 UK trade balance, 1982–1992

Each month the CSO publishes figures (see Figure 13.7) showing how much the United Kingdom imported and exported in the previous month and consequently how much the United Kingdom is in deficit or surplus with the rest of the world. The monthly figures are mainly concerned with trade in visible items (merchandise goods) which is simpler to measure than invisible trade (services, transfer payments, interest payments, profits and dividends).

Trade in visible items is presented both in current values and in volume terms with adjustments made for items such as erratic items, such as aircraft, and precious stones that are likely to distort the underlying trend. When the United Kingdom imports more visible items than it exports (a perennial problem for the UK) it is said to have a 'trade gap'. This may be of no particular concern provided it is offset by surpluses elsewhere on the balance of payments, such as in invisible items.

By bringing together the balances in visible and invisible trade, the CSO provides the current account. A complete statement of the

United Kingdom's trade and financial transactions with the rest of the world. The full picture is known as the balance of payments which is published every quarter.

The CSO also publishes the United Kingdom's terms of trade with the monthly figures – a price index which shows the UK's export prices in relation to its import prices. An improvement in the terms of trade occurs when export prices rise at a faster rate than import prices.

The principal figures relating to trade and the balance of payments are dealt with by the *Financial Times* in Thursday's Economic Indicators – External Trade table (see Figure 13.8).

EXTERNAL TRADE- Indices of export and import volume (1985=100); visible balance (£m); current balance (£m); oil balance (£m); terms of trade (1985=100); official reserves (end period)

	Export volume	Import volume	Visible balance	Current balance	Oil balance	Terms of trade*	Reserves US$bn	
1991								1991
4th qtr.	128.8	139.2	-2,873	-1,951	+453	97.5	44.13	4th qtr
1992								1992
1st qtr.	127.1	143.1	-3,000	-2,907	+422	99.4	44.31	1st qtr.
2nd qtr.	129.4	147.9	-3,130	-3,206	+355	100.9	45.70	2nd qtr.
3rd qtr.	130.5	148.2	-3,287	-2,241	+367	101.7	42.68	3rd qtr.
4th qtr.	132.2	146.2	-4,354	-3,560	+340	96.6	41.65	4th qtr.
March	129.9	145.1	- 810	- 779	+168	99.4	44.31	March
April	128.0	150.8	-1,275	-1,300	+117	100.2	45.77	April
May	133.2	146.9	- 883	- 909	+167	101.1	45.80	May
June	127.1	146.0	- 972	- 997	+ 71	101.5	45.70	June
July	129.2	149.1	-1,119	- 770	+ 43	101.6	45.75	July
August	132.4	149.8	-1,174	- 826	+246	102.5	44.45	August
September	129.9	145.7	- 994	- 645	+ 78	101.1	42.68	Septembe
October	134.3	144.9	-1,108	- 843	+168	97.2	42.14	October
November	133.3	145.7	-1,361	-1,097	+ 87	96.4	42.09	November
December	129.0	147.9	-1,885	-1,620	+ 85	96.2	41.65	December
1993								1993
1st qtr.			-4,500				40.90	1st qtr
January							42.56	January
February							43.45	February
March							40.90	March
April							41.66	April
May							41.73	May
June							41.90	June

FINAI and inflov

Fig. 13.8 UK economic indicators – external trade

Indices are provided for the various components of the balance of payments in addition to the terms of trade and domestic reserves.

Official reserves

The figures for the United Kingdom's official gold and foreign currency reserves, held by the Bank of England, are published by the Treasury. The monthly data show the change in the total reserves, and the underlying change in reserves, during the previous month.

Economists are interested in the reserves figures mainly because they can act as a guide to the extent of Bank of England intervention on the foreign currency markets to support or undermine the value of the pound during the previous month. In fact it is difficult to get an accurate picture from the figures because of other Bank transactions including new borrowing and repayment of debt by the public sector, official transactions for government departments and foreign central banks. The reserves total is expressed in dollars.

Public sector borrowing requirement (PSBR)

The PSBR shows how much the government has borrowed or paid back in one month. When tax revenues are weak and government spending high – the usual state of affairs during a recession – the PSBR is likely to grow. It will narrow once the economy picks up and tax revenues rise again as more people find jobs. Thus the state of public sector finances is, in large part, dependent on the state of economic activity. Part, or even all, of the deficit is therefore referred to as the 'cyclical' deficit.

However, governments also run-up persistent debts by systematically spending more than they collect in tax revenues. That part of the deficit which exsits regardless of economic activity is referred to as the 'structural' deficit.

When the government collects more revenues that it spends the PSBR becomes known as the public sector debt repayment.

Gross domestic product

A month after the end of each quarter the CSO produces a provisional estimate of gross domestic product. GDP measures economic activity in a country and is reached by adding together the total value of a country's annual output of goods and services. The provisional estimate of GDP is based on output data, such as industrial production and retail sales, but a month later the CSO provides a further estimate taking account of income, output and expenditure data.

When GDP falls compared with the previous quarter, the economy is said to be contracting. Two consecutive quarterly falls, and it is said to be in recession. When GDP rises quarter-on-quarter the economy is expanding. A month later the full national accounts are produced based on complete information. As well as revisions to the provisional GDP figures, the national accounts show a full breakdown of economic activity during the previous quarter and in particular identify the following trends.

- Personal disposable income: the amount of income available to households after payment of income taxes and national insurance contributions.

- Personal savings: the difference between consumer income and consumer spending. Thus savings can be either actual savings held in a deposit account or repayments of debt. The savings ratio is the proportion of income which is saved expressed as a percentage of personal disposable income.

- Fixed investment and stock building.

Cyclical indicators

The cyclical indicators, produced once a month by the CSO, monitor and predict changes in the UK economy. The leading indices, based on series that are good indicators of turning points in GDP, such as share indices and consumer confidence surveys, provide early indications of cyclical turning points in economic activity.

MONEY AND BORROWING

Credit business

This series gives a useful snapshot of consumer behaviour by measuring how much consumers have borrowed from retailers, finance houses, building societies and on the main bank credit cards. It does not cover mortgages and thus accounts for only around 15 per cent of total private sector debt.

The money supply

Every month the Bank of England publishes figures showing the amount of money in circulation in the UK economy. The total value of money in circulation depends on the definition of the money supply. In the United Kingdom there are two main measures, one broad and one narrow.

- **M0, or narrow money:** M0 is almost entirely notes and coins in circulation. Growth in M0 indicates that consumer spending is buoyant. A contraction in M0 suggests consumers are behaving more cautiously.

- **M4 or broad money:** M4 is M0 plus bank and building society deposits.

Sometimes monetary authorities choose to target growth in the money supply as part of an anti-inflationary strategy. Rapid growth in the amount of money circulating in the economy is a sign that inflationary pressures are building up.

- **M4 lending:** This is bank and building society lending to the private and corporate sectors. Sluggish growth in M4 lending indicates that consumers and companies are reluctant to borrow, while strong M4 growth is indicative of a stronger economy. On the same day that the Bank of England publishes the M4 lending figures, the British Bankers Association puts out its own monthly statement about lending by the main retail banks.

FINANCIAL-Money supply (annual percentage change), M0, new M2 (retail deposits and cash), M4; bank sterling lending to private sector; building societies' net inflow; consumer credit†; Clearing Bank base rate (end period).

	MO %	M2 %	M4 %	Bank lending £m	BS inflow* £m	Cnsmer. credit† £m	Base rate %
1992							
1st qtr.	1.9	7.6	6.0	+ 4,861	266	+142	10.50
2nd qtr.	2.2	5.9	5.3	+ 9,750	77	+ 5	10.00
3rd qtr.	2.4	5.3	5.3	+ 5,944	-262	- 11	9.00
4th qtr.	2.7	5.0	4.4	+ 4,890	214	+226	7.00
March	2.3	7.1	5.9	+ 988	-172	- 27	10.50
April	2.4	6.2	5.6	+ 4,195	212	+ 16	10.50
May	2.7	5.9	5.1	+ 2,689	179	+ 45	10.00
June	1.5	5.6	5.2	+ 2,866	-314	- 56	10.00
July	2.6	5.6	5.6	+ 2,900	-325	+ 83	10.00
August	2.5	5.7	5.4	+ 2,338	327	- 69	10.00
September	2.2	4.7	4.8	+ 706	-264	- 25	9.00
October	2.4	5.1	5.1	+ 3,612	281	+ 72	8.00
November	3.0	4.6	4.3	+ 107	-184	+ 17	7.00
December	2.8	5.2	3.7	+ 1,171	117	+137	7.00
1993							
1st qtr.	4.4	4.8	3.3	+ 2,298	820	+400	6.00
January	3.9	4.6	3.1	+ 2,921	363	+150	6.00
February	4.5	5.1	3.3	+ 657	208	+ 54	6.00
March	4.9	4.8	3.6	- 1,280	249	+196	6.00
April	4.8	5.5	3.5	+ 2,984	1,069	+194	6.00
May	3.3	5.9	3.8	+ 2,013	700	+118	6.00
June	4.4				-56		6.00

Fig. 13.9 UK economic indicators – financial

These and other indicators of the money supply appear in the FT's Economic Indicators – Financial table (see Figure 13.9). Indices are also provided for levels of lending, consumer borrowing and base rates of interest.

OTHER OFFICIAL PUBLICATIONS

The Pink Book gives detailed balance of payments data including the City of London's contributions to the United Kingdom's overseas earnings, total transactions with the rest of the European Community and details of the UK's overseas assets and liabilities.

Economic Trends brings together all the main economic indicators.

Financial Statistics provides data on a wide range of financial topics including financial accounts for sectors of the economy, government income and expenditure, public sector borrowing, banking statistics, monetary aggregates, institutional investment, company finance and liquidity, security prices and exchange and interest rates.

OTHER ECONOMIC INFORMATION

Surveys

A number of surveys, produced by bodies such as the Confederation of British Industry (CBI), supplement the FT's regular reporting of UK economic statistics. One of the most important is the CBI's quarterly industrial trends survey of manufacturers, which gives a strong indication of future tends in manufacturing output by asking industrialists about the state of their order books. The CBI also does a monthly inquiry into the state of the distributive trades sector – mainly wholesalers and retailers. This supplements official information on retail sales.

The British Chamber of Commerce carries out a quarterly economic survey of its members which, unlike the CBI industrial trends survey, includes the service sector.

Forecasts of economic growth

As well as the Treasury's forecasts for the UK economy, produced at the time of the Budget, hundreds of other bodies produce their own forecasts, ranging from City analysts to independent think-tanks. The Paris-based Organisation for Economic Cooperation and Development also produces a forecast for the UK economy.

14

THE EUROPEAN ECONOMY

INTEGRATING MARKETS AND ALIGNING CURRENCIES

On 1 January 1993 the single market of the European Community came into effect. The remaining obstacles to the free flow of goods, services and labour between the twelve member states of the EC were removed and the Community moved significantly closer to its goal of becoming a genuine 'common market'.

In spite of upheavals in European currency markets, the EC's long-term goal is to establish a full economic union involving a close harmonisation of member countries' general economic policies, the centralisation of fiscal and monetary control procedures and a single currency.

One of the most important steps towards full economic and monetary union (EMU) was taken in 1979, when the EC set about creating a 'zone of currency stability' known as the European Monetary System.

The European Monetary System and the exchange rate mechanism

The idea behind the European Monetary System was to achieve currency stability through coordinated exchange rate management. This would facilitate intra-Community trade and set the stage for a single currency towards the end of the 1990s.

The European exchange rate mechanism (ERM), a system of fixed but flexible exchange rates, was the central plank of the EMS. Countries participating in the ERM would keep the value of their currencies within margins of 2.25 per cent either side of agreed central rates

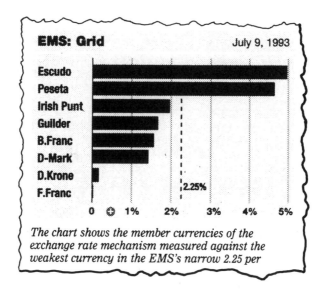

Fig. 14.1 ERM grid (before 15 per cent bands introduced)

against the other currencies in the mechanism. Sterling, the peseta and the escudo, which joined the ERM several years after its inception, were allowed to move within margins of 6 per cent (see Figure 14.1)

The ERM worked by requiring members to intervene in the foreign exchange markets in unlimited amounts to prevent currencies breaching their ceilings or floors against the other currencies. For example, if the peseta fell to its floor against the D-Mark, the Bank of Spain was required to buy pesetas and sell D-Marks. Other members could help by intervening on behalf of the weak currency. This, in theory, would prop up the peseta before it fell through its floor.

As a second resort the country whose currency was under fire could raise its short-term interest rates to make its currency more attractive to investors.

If intervention on the foreign exchanges and adjustment of short-term rates failed to stop a currency from sliding too low or rising too high, an absolute last resort was a realignment of the central rates to relieve the tensions in the system.

In the early years of the ERM there were several realignments but from 1987 until 1993, when the ERM was effectively suspended, there were none. Many economists argue that it was the failure of the mechanism to realign in response to the strength of the D-Mark that led to the tensions of the autumn of 1992, and the summer of 1993 (see below).

Why though, after five years of relative calm, did the currency markets in Europe erupt? The answer lies in German reunification at the end of the 1980s. To pay for unification the German government had to borrow substantial amounts of money. This forced up the cost of borrowing in Germany. High German interest rates coincided with low US interest rates and the result was strong international demand for D-Marks, forcing German rates even higher.

This happened just as the rest of Europe, heading into recession, needed low interest rates to stimulate economic activity. However, since all the other currencies were committed to maintaining their central rates against the D-Mark, they were forced to keep their interest rates at levels that were damaging their economies. So long as Germany's rates were high, countries like the UK and France were unable to lower their lending rates without causing a run on the pound and the franc.

In the case of the UK, the tensions became too much for the system in September 1992. The UK was suffering its longest recession since the 1950s yet had interest rates of 10 per cent. With inflation low, the real cost of borrowing was exceptionally high. The markets took the view that such high lending rates at a time of recession were unsustainable. Pressure on the pound mounted over August, but the UK government, mindful of the hardship being caused by the high cost of borrowing, was unwilling to raise rates further in order to protect the pound. Its only weapons were intervention on the foreign exchanges and repeated assurances by ministers that there would be no devaluation.

Events came to a head on 'Black Wednesday', 16 September 1992, when sterling and the Italian lira were forced out of the mechanism. Investors, losing confidence in the currencies, shifted vast funds out of sterling and the lira into the D-Mark. Both sank well below their ERM floors as soon as the authorities gave up the struggle to keep them within their old bands.

On the day, the UK government tried to save the pound by intervening heavily and by announcing an increase in interest rates to 15 per cent. But this was not enough to stem the flow against sterling and after a steady drain on reserves the government pulled out.

For the next eleven months relative calm returned to what was left of the mechanism. However, in August 1993 tensions arose once more, this time centred on the French franc. The problems were familiar. France was in a recession with high unemployment yet was unable to cut its very high interest rates.

One solution would have been for Germany to ease its lending rates, but the Bundesbank, the German central bank, would not contemplate such a move for fear of encouraging inflation at home. It is worth mentioning that the prime duty of the Bundesbank, as set out in its constitution, is to monitor domestic monetary policy. Thus it was required by law to put the need for low German inflation before the travails of the ERM.

As pressure mounted, EC finance ministers met to find a solution. The answer was to widen the currency bands for all except the D-Mark and the Dutch guilder to 15 per cent. The bands were so wide that although the ERM survived in name, the currencies were effectively floating. With the new bands a currency could theoretically devalue by 30 per cent – from its ceiling to its floor – against another member without falling out of the system.

Economic and monetary union

Following the upheavals of the ERM, plans to introduce a single currency in Europe by 1999 look somewhat optimistic. EMU will only be possible after participating countries have achieved a broadly similar economic performance. It was hoped that the discipline of the ERM would help European economies to converge but, without it, countries will be freer to pursue their own monetary and fiscal policies.

For EMU to take place convergence would be required in a number of key areas including:

- **Interest rates:** these should be at broadly similar levels across countries.
- **Inflation:** this would have to be at comparably low and sustainable levels. With a system of irrevocably fixed exchange rates, or a

single currency, persistent differences in inflation could lead to certain countries experiencing significant competitiveness problems and hence employment losses.
- **Government deficits:** high fiscal deficits would have to be avoided by all member states both to counter inflation and guard against the emergence of excessive real interest rates for the EC as a whole.

During the 1980s while the ERM was in place, EC inflation rates converged to a large extent. Big divergences remain, however, in the spheres of fiscal balances and unemployment. There is significant scepticism about the EC's abilities to bring the different economies into line by the end of the decade.

Enlarging the European Community

The EC currently has twelve members but Norway, Austria, Finland and Sweden have applied to join. Some EC governments, notably the UK, believe enlargement of the EC should be given priority over rapid moves towards economic and monetary union.

THE WORLD ECONOMY

The collapse of communism at the end of the 1980s was expected to usher in a new era of prosperity for the 1990s, but so far this decade global growth has proved disappointing.

According to the International Monetary Fund world output stagnated in 1991, did little better in 1992 and is unlikely to have grown by much in 1993. Unemployment in the twenty-four industrialised nations of the Organisation for Economic Cooperation and Development has jumped from less than 25 million three years ago to over 30 million today. Latest OECD forecasts suggest it will have risen to 36 million by the first half of 1994.

The good news on the global scene is that Latin America appears to be resolving its economic problems after a decade of low growth and falling living standards, triggered by the Mexican debt crisis of 1982. The dynamic economies of south-east Asia should also notch up more growth this decade although at a slower pace than in the boom years of the 1980s.

Meanwhile, Eastern Europe is finding that the struggle to adapt to the market economy is far more difficult than expected. Worse still is the position of the former Soviet Union. Russia's economic reform efforts have run into ever greater problems while the break-up of the single Comecon trading bloc has greatly increased the adjustment problems of all the former communist states. Africa continues to lag economically behind the rest of the globe.

A number of international forums exist to discuss global economic issues and the FT reports on most of their activities. The main ones are:

- The International Monetary Fund (IMF)

The IMF was set up by the Bretton Woods agreement of 1944 and came into operation in March 1947. It was established to encourage international cooperation on monetary issues. The aim of the Fund is to tide members over temporary balance of payments difficulties. It does this by making hard currency loans to members while trying to enforce structural adjustment of the economies.

The fund has more than 140 members who pay subscriptions according to the size of their economies. They pay 75 per cent of the quota in their own currency and 25 per cent in international reserve assets. Members are then given borrowing rights with the Fund which they can use to help finance a balance of payments deficit. Countries in difficulty can also negotiate standby credit on which they can draw as necessary. Members are required to repay their drawings over a three-to-five year period.

The IMF produces an annual report which is a mine of information and is especially useful for its global economic statistics.

- The World Bank

The World Bank was established at the same time as the IMF, and was originally intended to finance Europe's post-war reconstruction. Since then it has concentrated on loans to poor countries to become one of the largest single sources of development aid. The Bank has traditionally supported a wide range of long-term investments including infrastructure projects such as roads, telecommunications and electricity supply. Its funds come mainly from the industrialised nations but it also raises money on international capital markets. The Bank operates according to business principles, lending at commercial rates of interest only to those governments it feels are capable of servicing and repaying their debts.

- Group of Ten

The ten leading capitalist countries – the US, the UK, Germany, France, Belgium, Holland, Italy, Sweden, Canada, and Japan. Switzerland is an honorary member. The G10, originally came together to lend $6 billion to the IMF in 1962, but now exists as a discussion forum for international monetary arrangements. It also meets through its central bank, the Basle-based Bank for International Settlements.

- Group of Seven

The G7 dates back to 1975 when French president, Valery Giscard d'Estaing invited the leaders of the US, West Germany, Japan and Britain to discuss economic problems following the first oil price shock. Since then the summits have grown to include political and foreign issues which form the subject of a political declaration issued on the penultimate day of talks. The sixth and seventh members are Italy and Canada.

- Organisation for Economic Cooperation and Development

The OECD is sometimes referred to as the rich countries' club. Its membership consists of the twenty-four industrialised nations of the world – soon to be twenty-five when Mexico joins – and it has a secretariat in Paris. It too goes back to the end of the Second World War when it was set up to organise Europe's recovery. It is now more of a think-tank to discuss economic issues of mutual interest.

It is a particularly valuable source of publications. It does an annual survey of each of the member countries and publishes a biannual

Economic Outlook which looks at prospects for the industrialised world as a whole.

- European Bank for Reconstruction and Development

The EBRD was set up in 1990 to help the countries of Eastern Europe develop market-based economies. An EC initiative, it resembles existing multinational regional development banks, such as the African Development Bank, and was the first institution specifically designed to muster Western economic help for Eastern Europe in the wake of the collapse of their communist regimes. EC states and institutions have a 53.7 per cent stake. Most other European countries are also shareholders and the US has the biggest single stake of 10 per cent. Japan's 8.5 per cent shareholding matches those of Britain, Germany, France and Italy.

- Trade

One of the most important global issues is trade. Since the end of the Second World War big advances have been made in reducing barriers to the free flow of goods but there is still a long way to go, and the recent world recession has threatened a renewed bout of protectionism as countries have looked inwards to deal with their own problems. The main forum for addressing trade issues is the General Agreement on Tariffs and Trade.

- GATT

The General Agreement on Tariffs and Trade is a multinational institution set up in 1947 to promote the expansion of international trade through a coordinated programme of trade liberalisation and prevent a return to the protectionist days of the 1930s. GATT's two-pronged approach has been to eliminate quotas and reduce tariffs.

GATT has supervised several conferences on tariff reductions and is currently bringing to a completion the Uruguay round.

A successful conclusion to the talks is likely to enhance the growth prospects of industrial and developing countries alike. In the summer of 1993, the world's leading nations agreed a potentially far-reaching tariff-cutting deal to expand market access for manufactured goods.

- Free Trade Agreements

A free trade agreement is an agreement between countries to eliminate all trade barriers among themselves on goods and services, but each continues to operate its own particular barriers against trade with the rest of the world.

A number of regional free trade agreements exist, most notably the North American Free Trade Agreement (NAFTA) and the Association of South East Asian Nations (ASEAN). NAFTA, which includes the US, Canada and Mexico, is due to be completed by 1994. ASEAN was set up in 1967 by Indonesia, Malaysia, the Philippines, Singapore and Thailand.

- World Statistics

INTERNATIONAL ECONOMIC INDICATORS: **BALANCE OF PAYMENTS**

	■ UNITED STATES					■ JAPAN					■ GERMANY				
	Exports	Visible trade balance	Current account balance	Ecu exchange rate	Effective exchange rate	Exports	Visible trade balance	Current account balance	Ecu exchange rate	Effective exchange rate	Exports	Visible trade balance	Current account balance	Ecu exchange rate	Effective exchange rate
1985	279.8	−174.2	−159.7	0.7623	100.0	230.8	76.0	64.5	180.50	100.0	242.8	33.4	21.7	2.2260	100.0
1986	230.9	−140.6	−150.0	0.9836	80.2	211.1	96.2	86.9	165.11	124.4	248.6	53.4	40.3	2.1279	108.8
1987	220.2	−131.8	−141.6	1.1541	70.3	197.3	86.1	75.5	166.58	133.2	254.3	56.8	39.8	2.0710	115.3
1988	272.5	−100.2	−107.0	1.1833	66.0	219.8	80.7	66.6	151.51	147.3	272.6	61.6	42.9	2.0739	114.6
1989	330.2	−99.3	−91.8	1.1017	69.4	245.3	70.5	52.4	151.87	141.9	310.2	65.3	52.3	2.0681	113.5
1990	309.0	−79.3	−70.9	1.2745	65.1	220.0	50.1	28 3	183.94	126.0	323.9	51.8	37.2	2.0537	119.1
1991	340.5	−53.5	−3.0	1.2391	64.5	247.4	83.1	62.9	166.44	137.0	327.4	11.2	−16.2	2.0480	117.7
1992	345.8	−64.1	−51.2	1.2957	62.9	254.8	101.8	89.8	164.05	142.9	330.3	16.4	−19.9	2.0187	121.2
2nd qtr.1992	86.8	−16.9	−14.4	1.2717	63.6	63.9	26.1	23.1	165.60	139.9	81.1	3.6	−5.2	2.0511	118.7
3rd qtr.1992	80.6	−17.7	−12.8	1.3831	60.1	61.5	23.7	20.1	172.79	139.6	83.9	6.4	−6.4	2.0221	122.1
4th qtr.1992	91.5	−17.4	−18.7	1.2658	64.2	65.2	26.9	24.8	155.57	149.7	82.1	3.4	−4.1	1.9593	125.0
1st qtr.1993	95.1	−21.8	−17.5	1.1920	66.4	72.3	29.7	30.4	144.38	158.5			−4.8	1.9476	125.6
June 1992	29.2	−5.2	n.a.	1.3039	62.3	21.3	8.3	6.3	165.32	141.7	25.1	0.6	−2.1	2.0498	119.1
July	27.3	−5.5	n.a.	1.3693	60.5	20.5	8.1	6.9	172.22	139.2	28.3	1.0	−3.8	2.0410	120.7
August	25.9	−6.2	n.a.	1.4014	59.8	19.9	7.4	5.9	177.11	137.0	27.7	3.1	−0.7	2.0326	122.0
September	27.3	−6.0	n.a.	1.3786	60.2	21.1	8.2	7.2	169.05	142.5	27.8	2.3	−1.8	1.9927	123.6
October	29.4	−5.5	n.a.	1.3210	62.1	21.3	8.9	7.7	159.93	148.2	28.6	2.4	−1.3	1.9564	125.7
November	30.5	−6.3	n.a.	1.2372	65.1	22.1	9.1	9.3	153.22	150.3	26.8	0.9	−0.3	1.9634	124.0
December	31.6	−5.6	n.a.	1.2391	65.3	21.7	8.8	7.8	153.57	150.7	26.7	0.0	−2.5	1.9581	125.3
January 1993	30.9	−6.3	n.a.	1.2132	66.4	22.9	8.8	7.3	151.67	151.3	25.4	1.3	−2.7	1.9592	125.3
February	31.2	−6.7	n.a.	1.1839	66.7	23.9	10.3	9.3	142.87	159.2	26.9	0.7	−1.9	1.9437	125.8
March	33.0	−8.9	n.a.	1.1789	66.2	25.5	10.6	13.8	138.61	164.4			−0.2	1.9399	125.7
April	31.4	−8.6	n.a.	1.2214	64.3	24.6	9.9	9.6	137.17	167.8				1.9483	123.6
May			n.a.	1.2161	63.9	23.5	10.1	9.1	134.15	171.0				1.9548	124.1

Fig. 14.2 International economic indicators table

Although economic statistics from outside the UK are reported on a less systematic basis than the UK figures, a broad range of figures is published throughout the year.

For the world, the most regular and reliable statistics are collated by the IMF in its monthly publication *International Financial Statistics*.

Another useful source of statistical information is the OECD, in particular its annual country reports and the biannual *Economic Outlook*.

For countries outside the OECD, especially in Latin America, Africa and Asia, the most detailed economic coverage, in addition to IMF statistics, is often the FT's special survey of the country, published once a year.

On Mondays the FT includes a table of world economic indicators comparing key variables for the UK, US, Japan, Germany, France and Italy (see Figure 14.2).

INDEX